DAVID HIRSON

La Bête
and
Wrong Mountain

Grove Press
New York

Library of Congress Cataloging-in-Publication Data

Hirson, David.
    La bête ; and, Wrong mountain: two plays / by David Hirson.
        p. cm.
    ISBN 0-8021-3821-7
    1. Street entertainers—Drama.   2. Drama—Authorship—Drama.   3. Theater—Drama.
4. Actors—Drama.   5. Poets—Drama.   I. Title: Bête ; and, Wrong mountain.   II. Hirson,
David. Wrong mountain.   III. Title: Wrong mountain.   IV. Title.

PS3558.I698 B47 2001
812'.54—dc21   2001033090

Grove Press
841 Broadway
New York, NY 10003

01 02 03 04   10 9 8 7 6 5 4 3 2 1

CONTENTS

PREFACE

By bringing together two plays in a single volume, an author, whether he chooses to or not, inevitably invites comparisons between them. Viewed as such, *La Bête* and *Wrong Mountain* represent—to my eye, at least—a paradoxical coupling. On the surface, the plays could not seem more stylistically distinct. Indeed, based on form (heroic couplets v. prose) and milieu (seventeenth-century France v. contemporary America), they appear unrelated to the point of occupying entirely different universes. What's more, *La Bête* defines itself almost exclusively in terms of language, observing the Aristotelian unities of time, place, and action with an ardor that verges on the compulsive. *Wrong Mountain,* while no less verbal, employs a visual vocabulary that is to some degree cinematic, underscoring, commenting upon, or serving as counterpoint to events that occur, in very un-Aristotelian fashion, in several different locations, and over the period of a year.

Yet, for all the manifest ways in which these plays contrast stylistically, the overriding impression, curiously, is one of intense kinship. *La Bête,* after all, is hardly the seventeenth-century French verse play, or the translation of one, that it appears, at first glance, to be; nor, though it contains elements of both, is it wholly pastiche or homage, and to summarize it as such rings suspiciously untrue. It is, in fact, an undeniably American, undeniably contemporary piece of writing that happens to be set in a neoclassical frame. The exigencies of form have less to do with their Molièrian antecedents than with the idea of form itself, which is one of the primary themes of the play.

This sort of "postmodern" self-consciousness applies equally to *Wrong Mountain,* which, in formal terms, is just as strict, if not more so, than *La Bête,* and is therefore something other than the naturalistic American drama that its contemporary setting might lead one to suppose. Dense with imagery, and featuring characters who, in many instances, speak with a fluency that approximates the verve and musicality of rhyming couplets, the play has a nonnaturalistic feel that allies it more closely to the artifice of verse-writing than to the representational aspect of prose.

In neither case, however, do I mean to say that the worlds created by these plays aren't real. If anything, theirs is a heightened reality, taking place in what might be useful to imagine as a parallel universe more vivid than our own, but recognizably human, and rooted in truth. They are worlds where (for those who enter into them willingly) wildly disparate elements seem comfortably to coexist—where, for example, dialectic that aspires to an almost Shavian rigor finds itself at home with low burlesque, and fully rounded, flesh-and-blood characters commingle not incongruously with broadly brush-stroked figures of comic relief. Wordplay is interlarded with slapstick, and life-and-death arguments attempt (successfully, one hopes) to retain their gravity despite the sometimes absurd, even cartoonish, contexts in which they are situated. Both plays, in other words, create their *own* reality, bearing a resemblance to each other in their particular eccentricities of style.

Further similarities may be glimpsed in terms of theme. Both plays are, to varying degrees, concerned with theatre, and each contains a cultural critique in which the role of art, and the artist, in society is examined. Elomire, the playwright-hero of *La Bête*, bristles with aesthetic indignation when forced by his patron, Prince Conti, to consider accepting a vulgar street performer, Valere, into the ranks of his highly cultivated acting troupe. Valere's crowd-pleasing sensibility, the Prince contends, might help to reinvigorate Elomire's work, which, in his opinion, has grown oppressively cerebral and confounding. The street performer, however, is an insufferably voluble, narcissistic boor whom Elomire unyieldingly opposes. Despite the entreaties for moderation by his second-in-command, Bejart, who fears that defying the Prince might jeopardize the troupe's security at Court, Elomire manages to curb his intransigence only long enough to propose a compatibility test, of sorts. He challenges Valere to present one of his plays with the troupe, convinced that the street performer's narcissism will expose him as an unsuitable ensemble player.

The strategy backfires, however, when the company of actors, wearied by what they perceive to be the increasingly didactic nature of Elomire's work, appears to revel in the hijinks of Valere's play, extolling it as the kind of "entertainment" that might even have "popular appeal." As the troupe delights in Valere, so does Valere delight in the troupe. Noting this, and affronted by Elomire's self-righteousness, the Prince offers the street performer a place at Court. Elomire, unwilling to bend his artistic principles, renounces his patronage and reembarks upon a hand-to-mouth existence, calling on his troupe to join him. They refuse. Usurped, and alone with his ideals, Elomire wanders into self-exile, "starting on the journey once again."

Wrong Mountain tells the acidly satirical tale of Henry Dennett, a highly intellectual but obscure American poet in late middle age whose identity is founded on his disdain for a world that has failed to acknowledge him. During a fantastically dysfunctional Christmas dinner with his family, Dennett sets out to prove to his ex-wife's fiancé, an infuriatingly successful playwright, the ease with which a poet of his magnitude could achieve recognition in a form as vulgar (because, in his view, popular) as so-called "serious" contemporary theatre. Dennett, a teacher of modest means, bets a hundred thousand dollars that he can knock off a play, and get it produced, within six months.

Fast-forward to a regional Shakespeare Festival, where the poet finds himself plunged into a New Playwrights Competition, surrounded by fawning thespians and an over-the-top artistic director, Maurice Montesor. The play that Dennett has written, and for which he barely manages to conceal his contempt, is subjected by Maurice & Company to a comically enthusiastic (and, for the

author, unendurable) "development process." A fateful argument
ensues in which Dennett's view of himself as an infinitely superior
artist, stooping to write for the theatre merely to prove a point, is
unwittingly toppled by one of his young competitors, Clifford Pike.
"An artist is an artist regardless of the form," the young man innocently suggests.

Cliff's words, which Dennett ultimately absorbs as lustily as
he does the local spring water (to magically intoxicating effect),
induces in the poet an epiphany—a "volte-face"—whereby he
comes to respect his play, the actors working on it, and the world
around him as never before. His family arrives to find him virtually unrecognizable: he has the beatific mien of a man who has
been "born again." His tranquillity is punctured, however, when
he senses that his play is in danger of losing the competition to
Cliff's.

Ultimately Dennett prevails, but his support erodes soon after,
and desperately seeking approval from anyone who will give it,
he confronts the image of his former self in his son, Adam, who
denounces his play as the work of a hack. Completely alienated,
Dennett clings to his trophy as though to a piece of wreckage,
drowning what remains of his newfound identity in a toast to
success with the magically charged spring water.

It is left to Maurice Montesor, the festival director—whose
career, while never achieving any sort of pinnacle, has nonetheless nourished him entirely—to point Dennett in the direction
of a *truly* successful life, one in which identity is based neither on
the world's approval nor in reaction against it. Maurice's is the
life of a man who knows himself, something that Henry Dennett
has never even begun to do. As the curtain falls, Dennett stands
alone before a forbidding universe, trying to decrypt the words
of a poem that he himself has written. Is it the end of his life, or
the beginning? Is he about to fall, or to soar?

La Bête and *Wrong Mountain* conclude with a strikingly similar
image: that of a man alone onstage, suddenly bereft, who seeks, in

a moment of lyrical contemplation, to come to terms with the catastrophe that has just befallen him. Elomire's speech in quatrains, however, differs dramatically in tone from Dennett's two-stanza finale. The former, in which a hard, yet joyful life of principled resistance to the status quo is pitted against the "grim survival" of compromised autonomy, resonates with a kind of idealism that one normally associates with a youthful (or purely artistic) temperament. That is why, in my original stage notes, I remained deliberately vague about Elomire's age. His parting words—especially "We're measured by the *choices* that we make"—have a desirably different flavor depending on whether the man uttering them is closer to the beginning or the end of his life. The *spirit* of the words, in any event, is undoubtedly youthful: optimistic, free of bitterness, and looking eagerly forward, as though the trauma of abandonment has only emboldened the character in his sense of purpose.

Dennett, on the other hand, is a man who finds himself suddenly without a compass, completely lost and flooded with doubt, holding fast to the edge of a precipice as he prepares, perhaps, to open his eyes for the very first time:

> As though awakened
> In a teeming vault
> Of legendless
> And unfamiliar stars,
> The words that faintly shone
> Like avatars
> Of secret gods
> You labored to exalt

Having toiled, with an ascetic's devotion, to celebrate a divinity that has rewarded him with nothing but the most grueling tests of faith, Dennett begins to wonder, at an alarmingly advanced age, whether he has ever examined himself frankly enough to know if such faith was justified—if, in other words, he has committed his life to expressing his own truth, or someone else's. Words, his instruments of expression, now seem to reconfigure like celestial bodies in a cosmos where self-knowledge is, at least, possible:

> In patterns of
> Reconstellated light
> Emerge at last
> Like questions left unasked:
> Each one a face
> Hung luminously masked
> Between two distant
> Mountains in the night.

Will Dennett, after wiping the dew from his eyes, dare to ask the questions that might lead him to an understanding of his true place in the world? The image that begins and ends the play—that of an opaque moon glowing between two mountains—addresses the issue with an ambiguity that is sphinxlike. Dennett's face, afflicted with a disease that causes the mouth, nose, eyes, and ears to atrophy, transforms, in the play's final gesture, into the face of the moon (directly inverting the opening tableau, in which the moon transforms into Dennett's face). If, in its lunar featurelessness, Dennett's identity has been erased to a blank, could it not also be a blank upon which a new, perhaps more authentic identity is waiting to be revealed? Two mountains rise in the distance. In order to climb the right (and, presumably, to avoid climbing the wrong) one, Dennett will have to discover who he actually is. But how, the play asks, and to what extent, is such self-knowledge attainable, not just for Dennett, but for any of us?

This question, of course, is existential in nature, and *Wrong Mountain,* though it is set into motion by an aesthetic crisis, is fundamentally an existential play. What is a good life? What is success? How is it possible to inhabit the world truthfully? What is identity? Dennett's bewilderment at the end of the play contrasts sharply with his certainty at the beginning. It is a certainty that, in its intensity, resembles Elomire's—so much so that it is almost as if the youthful, hotheaded spirit who strode into self-exile in 1654 had reappeared in the present, separated from his former self by a chasm of time, older, uncompromising as ever, but now grown bitter from years of neglect. Where *La Bête* concludes with a man making a decisive choice, *Wrong Mountain* opens with a man whose choice was made long ago, and who has lived, often agonizingly, with the consequences.

Agony, for Dennett, seems, in fact, all-consuming. The piercing howl that begins the play suggests that his suffering is of a far more toxic variety than that which the committed artistic life advocated by Elomire might be expected to produce, and it is here that the consanguinity between characters may (or may not) cease to obtain. Dennett is not simply beset by vocational hardship; something is clearly eating him alive at the core. Indeed, he is diagnosed, in the opening scene, with a forty-pound worm gnawing away at his intestines: contemptiosuarumcupiditatumfilaria ("contempt for one's own desires"). This would suggest a man who is deeply at odds with himself, but Dennett, when we first encounter him, projects an air of such swaggering confidence in his artistic identity that he appears invulnerable. Not even his lack of public recognition seems to shake him. On the contrary, he seems inflated, rather than diminished, by his obscurity, as if rejection by the swinish masses should in itself be regarded as one of the hallmarks of exceptional talent.

It is not, however, that Dennett disdains popular culture. "Crap," as he calls it, is at least honest in its ambition to entertain, and is, therefore, never less than honorable, even when aimed at the lowest common denominator. His real scorn is reserved for the "sanctimonious kitsch" that is taken seriously in the "middle-class" world of American theatre, "pornography," he says, "that's embraced as high art by an audience of suburban morons dim-witted enough to think that by going to a play they're having some sort of 'cultural experience.'"* That Dennett, a poet, should focus his rage on theatre has more than a little to do, one assumes, with the fact that his ex-wife has taken up with a lionized (and financially successful) Broadway playwright, Guy Halperin. But sexual jealousy alone cannot sufficiently explain why an artist so apparently self-contained would agree to waste months of his life proving his mastery in a form that he considers pornographic. His willingness to enter into a wager with Guy, therefore, implies a deeper longing, perhaps for exactly the kind of acclaim that he professes to deplore. Contemptiosuarumcupiditatumfilaria: might it be that Dennett's identity is less secure than it originally seemed?

Such questions recur with the insistence of a leitmotif. Why, for example, is the author of a volume entitled "Shabbat" sharing *Christmas dinner* with his family? Though it is reasonable to infer that Claire, Dennett's former wife, belongs to a Protestant sect, her co-opting of Yiddish phrases like "a year from *Shavuoth*" and her parodic snapping of a Nazi salute during one of her ex-husband's more militant tirades simply add confusion to the mix. Dennett's relationship to his Judaism, not atypically for a man of his generation who has married outside the faith, contains intimations of ambivalence. (In an earlier draft of the play, Dennett acknowledges, when accused of concealing his roots, that the family name was originally "Densky or Dunkel or something," but adds, defensively, "It was changed by my *grandfather* . . . when he came through Ellis Island.") Because the text of *Wrong Mountain* presents, rather than explains, the

---

*Dennett's attacks on so-called middle-class values take their cue from the Introduction to Strindberg's *Miss Julie,* which he cites at Christmas dinner: "The theatre has long seemed to be a *Biblia Pauperum,* with the dramatist a lay preacher hawking contemporary ideas in popular form, popular enough for the middle classes to be able to grasp what the minority is arguing about. . . ."

ofttimes ambiguous dynamics of the Dennett household, the full task of sorting out oddities and potential inconsistencies is left to the audience. (The uncommented-upon interracial marriage between Dennett's daughter, Jessica, and a "kilt-clad" black man whom we later learn is a cross-dresser is a perfect case in point.)*

This fosters an atmosphere of imaginative inference in which who's who and what's what seem disturbingly up for grabs. And it is made more ambiguous by the jarring sense of Dennett's dislocation. Not only is he a Jew among Christians, and an artist, as he says, among "bean-counters"; having lost his "father's house" to Claire in the divorce, Dennett is not even at home under his own roof. It is little wonder, then, that Cheyenne, Jessica's daughter, continually mistakes Guy for her grandfather. Or that Anne, an aspiring poet in a bookshop, wrongly attributes to Dennett a quotation from W. H. Auden's "The Well of Narcissus": "Every man carries with him through life a mirror, as unique and impossible to get rid of as his shadow. But the properties of our own particular mirror are not so important as we sometimes think. We shall be judged, not by the kind of mirror found on us, but by the use we have made of it, by our riposte to our reflection."

The misattribution of the Auden quotation represents an intricate layering of many of the metaphors used in *Wrong Mountain* to express the idea of an identity in flux. It prefigures the tropes of "faces," "mirrors," and "water" that coalesce, towards the end of the play, in the image of Dennett, like a latter-day Narcissus, gazing at his reflection in the magical Lithia Fountain. And it is made ironic, not only by the fact of literary misattribution—mistaken identity, that is, with a quotation *about* identity—

---

*A significant amount of biographical data in the original draft of *Wrong Mountain* was cut in favor of consolidating Dennett's family, without sacrificing individual identities, into a less naturalistic, more mythic, Greek chorus–like unit.

but because the words are Auden's, Dennett's alleged mentor and the judge who short-listed him in the Yale Series of Younger Poets Competition thirty-five years earlier. (That Anne, whom Dennett brutally eviscerates for the error, is revealed, in the play's penultimate scene, to have gone on to win the competition for which he was merely short-listed, further compounds an already rich irony.)

But if Dennett's sense of self seems continually under siege, it is, from his perspective, everyone else, and not he, who is in the throes of a terrible identity crisis. Everywhere he looks he sees fraudulence and charlatanry, whether it's the inappropriate, showbiz-besotted physician who treats him for his intestinal parasite ("Are you a *real* doctor?" Dennett nervously inquires) or the façade-laden world of the Shakespeare festival, the kind of place, as Jessica observes, "where they tear down an old barn, build a new barn, and hang a sign on it that says 'Ye Olde Barne.'" Maurice Montesor, the festival's artistic director, strikes Dennett as the very epitome of narcissistic self-delusion. With his improbably tinted hair, faux-British accent, and dubious claims to friendship with Laurence Olivier, it is perhaps fitting that Maurice, a man who is teetering on the brink of senescence, should cast himself in the lead of a main-stage production of *Romeo and Juliet:* "Damn it, Maurice!" he chides himself. "Do it now, this season, before you're too old!" Guy shows a similar inclination to believe only in the most flattering self-image. Responding to Dennett's portrayal of him in a play whose characters correspond humiliatingly to the family—a thicket in itself, one might note, of identity confusion, which begs questions about the relationship between fictional personae and their real-life counterparts—Guy says, despite plenty of evidence to the contrary, "I thought I came off pretty good." Jessica's subsequent comment pithily summarizes the phenomenon that Dennett observes all around him: "I guess people see what they want to see."

If, as "The Well of Narcissus" maintains, "every man carries with him through life a mirror," it is only the very rare individual, according to Dennett, who has the courage to respond honestly to his reflection. Self-delusion, he says, is epidemic, not merely on a personal level, but for the nation as a whole, and nowhere does he believe this is revealed more tellingly than in the relationship between Americans and art, especially where it concerns the expectations of the middle class. It is from this group, he argues, that the audience for theatre is "inevitably, hopelessly" drawn, "an easily bored mob" that has been conditioned, he says, "to expect art to show them not who they are, but to indulge the myth of who they believe themselves to be." A playwright, unless he is prepared for an audience revolt, Dennett contends, must seek the mob's approval by supporting its flattering, sentimental image of itself as a fundamentally "decent, caring, humane people." "And you think," the young playwright Cliff counters, "that we're an indecent, uncaring, inhumane people?" Dennett's reply: "I think we're a lot more complicated than that, don't you?"

Ambiguity, in Dennett's view, is something that an American middle-class audience cannot abide. Any acknowledgment of the contradictions or differences among us must be placed in the context of harmonious resolution; any flaw, no matter how grave or unjust, must carry the promise of redemption. Art, in practical, consumer-oriented America, labors under the functional pressure to reassure, even when it purports to challenge the audience's values: "You don't think people in this country go to the theatre to have their values challenged, do you?" Dennett says. "You're wrong! They go to bask in the flattering image of themselves as people who are *open-minded* enough to have their values challenged, which is just another way of saying that they go the theatre to have their values *confirmed*." Art, in other words, is expected to socialize and, potentially, educate; to supply, as Dennett says, "a siloful of cornball rhetoric" and "culturally affirming lies" intended to endorse a democratic way of life. It aims to console Americans with the notion that, despite underlying tensions, they are a compassionate people who have chosen well, and who are, indeed, climbing the Right Mountain. This ethos is, he implies, an unsurprising one for an immigrant culture that has come to the New World in search of a Happy Ending.

Most vital, however, is that Americans should feel good about themselves. Besides being redemptive and unambiguous, the art that is hailed as "important," Dennett argues, plays into the audience's narcissistic longing "to experience collective guilt as a form of collective absolution—a slam-bam catharsis on the order of 'I feel your pain . . . now where we gonna eat.'" Artists who conspire with the audience to achieve this sort of therapeutic "group-grope," he asserts, are the ones who are rewarded with the greatest success. Those who resist the pressure to appeal to middle-class vanity, on the other hand, run the risk not only of failure, but of being silenced altogether, "buried," he says, with a hint of personal anguish, "under a mountain . . . of jimmy crack corn-corn-corn."

The irony, of course, is that the fierce individualist who has no agenda other than remaining true to his imagination, and is, therefore, the artist most likely to reflect honestly the culture that has produced him, tends to be regarded, according to Dennett, with the most acute suspicion, as being inward-looking, elitist, and undemocratic. For a country that prides itself on celebrating the individual spirit, he argues, America is uniquely hostile to individuality in art. It is considered arrogant and discordant. It threatens to disrupt the carefully maintained cultural illusions that guarantee the smooth running of society, and is better off ignored or, more chillingly, effectively suppressed. "And that's the *real* arrogance," Dennett contends. "Because as long as we lack the humility to look into the mirror and see ourselves for who we really are, instead of insisting that it reflect only what we *want* to

see, we'll never be the Lords and Owners of our Faces, to paraphrase the sonnet . . . we'll never even *begin* to live in truth."

It is no coincidence that the same man who condemns his
society for wearing a "face" that's as insubstantial as a mask should
be forced to endure the decomposition of his own, throughout
the play's second act, into a lunar blank. Nor is it happenstance
that, from the moment he arrives at the Shakespeare Festival,
Henry Dennett listens helplessly as his name mutates—from
"Herman" to "Hubert" to "Norbert"—degenerating, finally, with
the twisted logic of Claire's Nazi salute, into absurdist misnomers
like "Heinrich Himmler" and "Adolf Hitler." Dennett's identity is not simply in flux: it is in the process of unraveling. He
seems unconscious of this, however, firmly convinced that he, as
a poet, is living in, and telling, a truth that artists whose success
depends on the approval of a crowd are not at liberty to do. "A
poem," he says, "can be the uncompromised expression of a
unique temperament. It doesn't have to tart itself up. It doesn't
have to dumb itself down. It doesn't have to be made meaning-
ful or intelligible to a middle-class audience."

As the young playwright Cliff points out, however, Dennett's
sense of superiority may be based on an invidious distinction.
Why, he wonders, should the writing of verse be viewed as in-
trinsically more honorable than the writing of drama? Are readers
of poetry somehow more virtuous than patrons of theatre? Are
they any less susceptible to having their taste flattered? Currying
favor—winning approval—is the objective of a craftsman. An artist, on the other hand, is compelled by his nature to express himself truthfully, regardless of the outcome. Why, Cliff wonders,
should a playwright be any less likely than a poet to possess such
a nature, and what, aside from the risk of repudiation, prevents
him from voicing it? In Cliff's view, such self-censorship isn't
even possible. "Who you are always emerges despite yourself,"
he says, "despite whatever it was you thought you were creating." The idea of an "irreducible . . . unalterable essence" is ech-

oed by Duncan, one of the actors rehearsing Dennett's play.*
Commenting on a character who cross-dresses, he says, "Wearing a blouse doesn't change a man into a woman." Duncan's interpretation amounts to a comic reduction of Cliff's central point: form does not define the artist. On the contrary, a true artist leaves traces of his talent behind, like a fingerprint, in whatever form he chooses to undertake. The result, if his gifts are singular enough, will never be less than interesting. "Fiasco, maybe," Cliff says, "and maybe brilliance, too. But never, never mediocrity."

Cliff's aesthetic position has the effect of turning Dennett's world upside-down. Not only does it decimate the monolithic cathedral of logic that the poet has erected to justify his supercilious self-image, but it exposes him, despite his alleged distaste for what he rather arbitrarily designates as "middle-class" values, as being (in his browbeating preoccupation with them) hopelessly in their thrall. A tireless critic of vanity in others, Dennett seems oblivious to the mother lode of self-delusion in himself. He delights, for example, in ridiculing the elderly Maurice Montesor for taking on the role of Romeo, but sees no parallel to himself when he begins to play the same part, in real life, with Maurice's young daughter, Ariel. Not until she rebuffs a kiss from his "old man lips" is Dennett's romantic self-delusion punctured. "I'm hardly an old man," he says, in a last-gasp effort to deny the truth. "Hardly an old man?" Ariel replies. "When's the last time you took a good look at yourself? Hunh, Romeo?"

Given Dennett's "riposte to his reflection" at three critical junctures in *Wrong Mountain,* the answer to Ariel's question is: probably never. Each time a figurative "mirror" is held up before

---

*Identical titles notwithstanding, Dennett's play *Wrong Mountain,* whose overtly sociopolitical themes are referred to later in a scene with Adam, bears little more than a through-the-looking-glass resemblance to *Wrong Mountain* by David Hirson, despite some implicitly shared concerns with personal and national identity.

his face, Dennett abandons rational argument and resorts to ad hominem attack—even physical violence, as though he were shattering the image of himself instead of honestly confronting it. The first of these episodes takes place at Christmas dinner. Dennett, having rhetorically demanded of Guy whether it's possible that, despite his prizes and acclaim, he may have spent his entire life "climbing the wrong mountain," attempts to strangle his rival when the question is turned back on him. The second occurs after Cliff's Socratic dismantling of the illusions that have sustained Dennett's ego through a lifetime of unacknowledged toil. Though he shoves Cliff to the ground in horror, the residue of the young man's argument lingers irresistibly. If Dennett is the singular artist he believes himself to be, then his play, by Cliff's reasoning, should be something other than the blandly laudable mediocrity he set out to create.

Reassessing his work in this new light, Dennett is, perhaps unsurprisingly, persuaded by his narcissism that, between "fiasco" and "brilliance," his play shows unmistakable evidence of the latter; he wouldn't be capable of writing something unremarkable even if he tried. His talent, he giddily realizes, exists at a far deeper level than he imagined. "The truth of who you are always emerges despite yourself, despite whatever it was you thought you were creating," he exclaims to the actors, purloining Cliff's words without so much as a nod to the author. (Dennett, who is a thieving magpie when it comes to quotation—Auden, Shakespeare, and Nabokov are just a few of the writers he cites proprietarily—seems continually to be cobbling together an aesthetic philosophy, if not a sense of self, out of the musings of others. It is worth noting that, at the conclusion of *Wrong Mountain,* the words that Dennett finally quotes, or at least meditates upon, are, at long last, his own.)

From the remnants of his deconstructed identity, Dennett bases a new, apparently less fragile one on Cliff's thesis. "You helped me to understand something fundamental about myself . . . ," he says to the young playwright. "Something that's profoundly . . . consoling." Suddenly comfortable in his own skin, the former blustering tyrant begins to bask in the appreciation of those around him, accepting their praise as warranted. Even a foretaste of the public success and recognition that has eluded him (conveyed metaphorically in his consumption of Lithia water, with its worm-killing, but potentially face-eroding, properties) frees Dennett to appreciate the talents of others in return. He embraces the actors he previously disdained. He becomes playful. He develops a sense of humor about himself. Where earlier he regarded Ariel as an object of prurient sexual interest, he now contemplates her with affection and longing. And, in a departure from his usual tower-ing immodesty, he is even able to speak self-deprecatingly of his unsung poetic stature: "Well, I'm not Joseph Brodsky, am I?"

Recounting for his family how Maurice, playing Romeo, "began . . . to transform," credibly and bewitchingly, "into another per-son," the rehabilitated Dennett may as well be describing himself. In a complete reversal of character, he presents a gift-wrapped package to Cheyenne, who, for the first time, recognizes Dennett, rather than Guy, as her grandfather. This is ironic, of course, because Dennett's face is in a state of decay. To Adam and Jessica he's a total stranger, less because of his altered appearance than for his irrepressibly (and, to their minds, bizarrely) positive man-ner. They listen in disbelief as he recalls a "group hug" shared with the actors. Accustomed, in their frustrated quest to earn "Daddy's" approval, to parroting him, or quoting his aperçus, Dennett's children—to the same extent that their father cribs the phrases of others—attempt to lure this unfamiliar figure back to "reality" by citing memorable barbs of his own coinage. Not only do they fail, however: they seem excluded from his new benefi-cence. Dennett, in his transformation, seems, at least where Adam and Jessica are concerned, no less narcissistic than before. He is vaguely closed off to them, like a visionary who is in the process of "finding God." It is perhaps because they are mirrors of his former self that, rather than reaching out to his children, he rebukes them for their foundationless identities and stingy hearts. "Well, maybe if the two of you were less insecure about who you are," he says, "you could afford to be more generous towards people who are different from you, and to honor an aesthetic to which you might not necessarily subscribe."

The implication of Dennett's remark is clear: success breeds a sense of security that allows one to be relaxed about—even eager to acknowledge—the success of others. The exemplar of this phenomenon is Guy Halperin. Acutely aware of Dennett's unheralded, lone-wolf status ("howling in the dark," as Claire says mockingly, linking the image of her ex-husband's "moon" face to his "lupine" cries of pain), Guy is prone to apologizing for his immense good fortune with an attitude that might be interpreted as smug self-effacement. "You should be the celebrated one, not I," he says at Christmas dinner, questioning the legitimacy of his fame—and Dennett's anonymity—as, perhaps, only a man so revered has the luxury to do. The more skeptically he wears his mantle of acclaim, the more patronized Dennett feels. "I think we're all guilty," Guy says, "of making pat assumptions about the meaning of success, especially in America. It's a national malaise."

For Dennett, the meaning of success is more than a malaise; it's a source of obsessive, gut-wrenching anxiety, however much he affects Parnassian indifference. Although, at the Shakespeare Festival, he experiences, through successive draughts of Lithia water, a serenity he has never known, the prospect of losing in the New Playwrights Competition provokes in him a dread that exceeds the threat of financial ruin. The hundred thousand dollars seems less consuming to Dennett than his intense desire to *win,* even if the prize is nothing more than the sort of tawdry "figurine" that, in his derisive words, some "talentless ninny" clutches to his or her breast "as if it meant something." When he is named the recipient of the Lila B. Hirschorn Memorial Scepter, however, Dennett does just that, rounding out an iconic scene

xxi

of American victory with a tear-shedding acceptance speech. No longer an also-ran, and with his sense of security cresting, Dennett is able, for the first and only time in the play, to express his love for his family.

His contentment proves to be short-lived. From the moment the trophy is placed in Dennett's hands, the ground begins to shift beneath his feet. Cliff, though he congratulates his competitor for his "brilliant" play, does so, paradoxically, in the course of evading a question about the quality of Dennett's verse. This unanticipated blow to the poet's ego sets the stage for his needy solicitations of the views of those around him, as if supportive public opinion could rescue him from the quicksand of self-doubt. Ariel reassures him that "a critic from one of the big-city papers" was rumored to have seen his play, and "loved it." But when pressed for her own reaction, she demurs, emphasizing, in her enigmatic silence, the pointlessness of depending on the judgment of others, critics included, for a sense of validation. "What difference does *my* opinion make?" she says. "*Yours* is the only opinion that matters. You're the one who has to live with himself." The ground shifts again when it emerges that Dennett's work, which Guy hails as a "masterpiece," has precipitated in his rival a cataclysmic identity crisis. Suffering tremors of personal inauthenticity at the thought that a man who neither shares nor respects his passion for theatre could so cavalierly become "the playwright I've spent my whole life trying to be," Guy feels defrauded of his selfhood. Dennett, for his own part, must come to terms with the disorienting fact that a man whom he has previously condemned as a "pornographer" now exalts him as a paragon. Wouldn't this mean that Dennett is the greatest pornographer of them all?

When Adam addresses this question to his father, it not only causes the ground to shift, but sets off an earthquake. Since Adam—whom Dennett, like God, has created in his own image—perfectly embodies his father's former views, it is as if, in the

confrontation between them, Dennett's pre- and posttrans-
formation identities were meeting in a life-or-death showdown.
Dennett, to his son's initial incredulity, no longer considers his
play to be merely a prank. He takes his victory seriously, refer-
ring to an event he once ridiculed—a "standing ovation"—as
evidence of artistic merit. Adam, who regards the play as exactly the sort of "sanctimonious kitsch" that would have scan-
dalized the Dennett of old, chastises his father for "scrambl[ing]
up those well-worn stairs into the Fool's Tower"—for giving
credence to his mediocre work simply in virtue of having been
acclaimed for it. Dennett retaliates, suggesting that Adam in-
habits a "Fool's Tower" of his own—one, of course, in which
Dennett has dwelt for most of his life—where value is measured
in perverse abnegation of public approval.

Using Dennett's own words, Adam chips away at his father as
though trying to reclaim him; and since, in a very real sense, he
exists only as his father's reflection, his urgent desire to reclaim
him represents an attempt to prevent the disintegration of himself. Dennett, in the immediate aftermath of his triumph, frantically seeks confirmation from anyone he can grab on to. Cliff,
though he praises Dennett's play, blindsides him with an implicit
lack of enthusiasm for his poetry, which amounts to an aesthetic
rejection; Ariel, in refusing to kiss him, rejects him sexually; the
Family, feeling exploited (or, in the case of Guy, annihilated),
abandons him emotionally. Now Adam, his chief defender, turns
on him, accusing his father of having become a person he doesn't
even know—perhaps never knew, given the peculiar authenticity with which he has created the kind of meretricious, politically titillating "issue for our time" play that Dennett inveighed
against at Christmas dinner. Picking up where Guy left off, Adam
suggests that Dennett has accomplished the task so convincingly
that everything that preceded it has been thrown mind-bendingly
into doubt. "In some eerie way," he says, "[the play] was more
distinctively your own than any poem you've ever written in your

life." If, as Cliff suggested, "the truth of who you are always emerges despite yourself," the voice that emerges in Dennett's work is not, according to a devastated Adam, that of an artist, but of a pornographer, a voice that could belong to "anybody . . . or nobody."

Having conceded to his son, as though bargaining to hold on to his prize, that his play is no "masterpiece," and might even be "crap," Dennett, now charged with being a pornographer, lashes out, like a cornered rat, dismissing Adam's criticism by indicting him personally. "You're nobody," he says. "What makes you think I give a shit about your opinion?" "Because," Adam concludes, "my opinion *is* your opinion . . . There is no me! I'm you! You might as well be staring into a mirror." Dennett's "riposte to his reflection"—his third in *Wrong Mountain*—is to strike Adam, denying the void that he and his son are mutually forced to confront. It is as though, by demolishing the image of the person he once was, Dennett were attempting to salvage the remains of the person he has become. Adam, his identity in tatters, is left no choice but to wander quietly into the unknown, hectored off the stage by his raging father.

Dennett's petulance, however, expands Shakespeareanly to encompass the world beyond, especially the society of haughty aesthetes of which he, it should be observed, was a charter member. Thumbing his nose at the "Art Police"—the hypocritical "snobs" and "losers" for whom "success is the ultimate betrayal"— it is as if Dennett, in a final, mad flourish, were dancing on the grave of his former self. Totally alone, and clinging to his trophy, he hoists a scepterful, rather than a cup, of Lithia water, bringing to completion, with a second toast, a journey to a mountaintop that began with his cry of *"NOSTROVIA!"* at the end of Act One. "Here's to ME!" he says, defiantly seeking to shore up, by proclamation, an identity in collapse. "Here's to being somebody . . . somebody who matters . . . and not just some nobody." Planting his flag in a summit that is already caving in beneath his feet, Dennett, taking a definitive, mammoth swig of Lithia water, attempts to convert, by talismanic repetition, symbol into terra firma. "Here's to SUCCESS!" he exclaims. "SUCCESS! SUCCESS! SUCCESS! SUCCESS! SUCCESS!"

Tasting the world's approval at last, Dennett, in a tragically ecstatic climax, finds himself on a slope no less slippery than before. An identity based on public acknowledgment is, it seems, just as insecure as one that prides itself on exclusivity. Each is a "Fool's Tower" of self-delusion in which success depends on the judgment of others. Such judgment, Dennett comes to realize, is painfully arbitrary. Whether his play is "brilliant," as Cliff suggests, or "pornographic," as Adam contends, is, of course, a matter of pure subjectivity, a point that we the audience, for whom the work remains invisible, are urged emphatically to consider. Because our knowledge of Dennett's play is confined to hearsay, the weight (if any) that we assign to opinions about its quality will vary according to character and context. (Cliff's encomium, for example, is likely to have more impact than, say, that of Maurice, who tends to love *everything*.) The fact, however, that the full spectrum of possible responses is represented onstage reliably by one or more characters reminds us that it is not what we think, nor what Cliff, Adam, Guy, Maurice, the actors, nor a critic might think, but what *Dennett* thinks of his play that's important. "*Yours* is the only opinion that matters," as Ariel says to him. "You're the one who has to live with himself."*

Dennett's uncertainty, however, compels him to consult others as though canvassing for votes. Where earlier he mocked democratic principles for their inapplicability to the "autocratic" realm

---

*A version of Dennett's play, and those of the other candidates, existed in the original draft of *Wrong Mountain,* but were cut to preserve a sense of abstraction. Seeing Dennett's play would only tempt us to judge it, when the real issue, as mentioned above, is how Dennett comes to judge his play.

of creative expression, he now appears to seek legitimacy for his work by opening it up to a kind of referendum. This very American and, in Dennett's view, stuntingly inartistic desire to be, in Willy Lomanesque terms, well liked—to be popular, that is, at any cost, even at the expense of truth—reveals the poet, by his own definition, to be, paradoxically, the most American of characters.

With no sense of self to cling to, Dennett, taking intoxicating belts of Lithia water to drown out the destabilizing welter of opinions around him, tumbles, ultimately, into an existential abyss. In the desolation and aftershock of the following dawn, what, he wonders, does he really know about the world? Where, and in whom, does wisdom reside? Suddenly sure of nothing, Dennett happens upon Maurice, a man who, in contrast to his own agitation, seems remarkably at peace with himself. The exchange between them is parabolic. Though he admits to having achieved the summit of no mountain, Maurice possesses a degree of serenity that every other major character in the play is driven futilely to pursue. Each is fiercely dedicated to winning something, whether it's approval, respectability, daddy's love, or even a justifying figurine. They are caught, in other words, on a wheel of suffering and folly from which Maurice alone seems enviably free. Ironically, in a work where misquotation, misattribution, and misnomer are thematically significant, Maurice, who gets things wrong with marksmanlike accuracy, gets things right, one might say, where it matters most. He proves himself, despite his ostensible phoniness, to be perhaps the most genuine character in the play.

Showing Dennett a letter that, as a boy, he received from his idol, Laurence Olivier, Maurice reveals that his boasts of friendship with the Great Man, while not exactly true, are not entirely false, either. Hardly the complete charlatan that Dennett presumed him to be, Maurice, in confessing that he is, after all, a bit of a fraud, evinces an authenticity—a three-dimensionality—that some of the play's less overtly spurious characters, thwarted by the single-mindedness of their yearnings, seem to lack. By gently prodding Dennett to make a similar admission ("You didn't *really* know W. H. Auden, did you?"), Maurice is, in effect, encouraging the poet to acknowledge his fundamental humanity. Each of us, he implies, is a bit of a fraud. We are frail, basically preposterous creatures composed of contradictory, often trivial longings, half-truths, and sustaining illusions, the recognition of which confers a degree of humility that makes self-knowledge possible.

When Maurice affirms that, given dashed dreams of Olivier-caliber success, his life "didn't work out," what impresses us, instead, is the profound way in which it *did*. His dedication and generosity to those he loves, and his passion for what he believes, mark him, in a sense, as the most "successful" character in the play. Although, as he says, "You don't always end up becoming the person you thought you were going to be," the person that Maurice has become, we realize, is the rarest of men: someone who, accepting the inevitable disappointments of life, is able to be joyfully and ineluctably himself. His willingness to avow, at his entrance and exit, that he's a complete "buffoon" is powerful evidence, in itself, of how assuredly he's not; indeed, he seems, without being sentimental, the wisest and most graceful, finally, of any character in *Wrong Mountain*.

When, nudged by Maurice, Dennett admits, more to himself than anyone else, the truth—or, rather, semitruth—of his relationship with Auden, it provides occasion for communion between two men who appeared originally to be each other's antithesis. Citing a few lines from Alexander Pope, Maurice reminds Dennett (and us) that to see oneself as absurd—to become humbly conscious of one's own human foibles—is merely a first step in the long journey towards self-knowledge. It is just the beginning, he suggests, of a mountain climb that leads to an unending series of peaks, the scaling of which, if one has the courage, continues for the rest of one's life:

The eternal snows appear already past,
And the first clouds and mountains seem the last:
But those attained, we tremble to survey
The growing labours of the lengthened way;
The increasing prospect tires our wandering eyes,
Hills peep o'er hills, and Alps on Alps arise!

Whatever altitude Maurice may have attained, the mountain he has chosen to climb—as his surname, *Montesor,* implies—is an integral expression of his identity.* Living in truth, he is the "Lord and Owner of his Face" in a way that Dennett, with his deteriorating features, is so evidently not. It was Dennett, of course, who disparaged his culture for lacking "the humility to look into the mirror and see ourselves for who we really are, instead of insisting that it reflect only what we want to see." Now, dimly perceiving Maurice's words as oracular, Dennett, humble for the first time, gathers the courage to confront, unprompted, his own reflection in the symbolic water of the Lithia Fountain.

His "riposte" to what he observes, initially at least, is a kind of forestalling. Fancying himself newly acquired of wisdom, he returns to the bookshop of scene iii, offering a facile apology to the young woman whom he eviscerated a year earlier.† When she spits in his face, it becomes clear that, rather than breaking his fall, his bungled attempt at making amends merely precipitates a more vertiginous plunge. Wisdom, it appears, if it is to be acquired at all, cannot be acquired so easily.

---

*A useful comparison may be drawn to other characters who participate in this sort of Dickensian naming, such as *Clifford Pike,* for example, or Winifred *Hill.*

†Dennett's return to the bookshop, cut in New York for technical reasons, is restored in this edition. For further comment, see footnote on p. 299.

Landing back in the doctor's office where the play began, Dennett, having been denied a quick-fix redemption, casts about desperately for answers. Anybody, he realizes, may, like Maurice, be an oracle. Perhaps everybody is. Where once he saw only fraudulence and stupidity, Dennett is suddenly hyperalert to a world filled with potential soothsayers. Utterances that seemed arbitrary return to haunt him like fragments of a puzzle that he now struggles anxiously to piece together. His entire experience assumes the texture of a fablelike journey in which each encounter, had he listened closely enough, might have supplied critical bits of information. The gatekeeper (or guide) to such a journey is, in a sense, Dennett's physician, who ushers him into and out of the play. Combining aspects of both prophet and lunatic, the doctor, not unlike Lear's Fool, raises fundamental questions about meaning and meaninglessness, and the razor-thin, if not indistinguishable, boundary that separates them. Are the riddles and aphorisms couched within his shtick nothing more than miracle cures peddled by a vaudeville quack? Or are they, in their gnomic allusiveness and tantalizing ambiguity, keys proffered by a sage to decipher life's most vexing conundrums? "We can never know, any of us," Dennett says, reeling with confusion, "whether or not we've spent our entire lives climbing the wrong mountain." "Maybe there's no such thing as a wrong mountain," the doctor replies, positing the notion of a completely rational universe in which everything happens for a purpose. "Then again," he adds, standing the proposition nihilistically on its head, "maybe they're all the wrong mountain."

Contained within the promise of perfect order is the possibility of absolute chaos. Dennett's odyssey is as likely to have been an entirely random, feckless meandering as a "journey" pregnant with significance. Plenum and void, god and godlessness, sense and nonsense seem equally plausible descriptions of reality—unless, of course, there is some kind of essential, anchoring truth to which one can refer like a lodestar. If such truth exists—and there is no guarantee that it does—it can be arrived at only through a process of self-discovery, as Dennett belatedly apprehends. That process, the doctor implies, may be harrowing. "And are you experiencing any discomfort right now?" he asks, repeating at the end of the play a question that no longer points, as it did at the beginning, strictly to the howling agony of Dennett's internal conflict, but to the existential terror of man's confronting his identity in the mirror of a potentially unknowable universe.

Thus do the final moments of *Wrong Mountain* proliferate not with answers, but a series of questions that Dennett strives earnestly to ponder. Is he a poet or a pornographer? Is his play magnificent or execrable? Is he somebody or nobody? "What if a man achieved the greatest triumph of his life," he asks, "for something that he viewed with absolute contempt?" Such questions will remain purely academic, the doctor reminds him, until Dennett knows himself well enough to judge. Relying on the external world for answers dooms one to a perilous relativity. The Right Mountain, after all, is different for every person, and no mountain, unless one abdicates to the authority of family, culture, or a particular faith, is inherently more worth scaling than another. Each of us alone must determine how to live and what to think and who to love, a course that, given the constancy of change and the threat of error, entails perils all its own. The alternative, however, is to risk waking up, like Dennett, to the possibility of having wasted one's life by never having possessed it. As Duncan asks, when discussing Dennett's play: "Is it better to live according to a noble ideal of yourself, however false or misguided, or to courageously and honestly face who you actually are?" This question, of course, has both personal and national resonance, and *Wrong Mountain* offers no definitive resolution.

Instead, the play leaves Dennett, a man who, at the start, seemed obdurately certain of everything, in a directionless swirl of interrogatives. When the doctor asks him which way he is headed,

Dennett acknowledges that he's "not sure." "Well," his physician urges him, with Delphic obliquity, "that's a start." Could admitting that one is lost be a precondition to finding one's way? In losing his face, might Dennett be on the verge of truly owning it? In perceiving himself as nobody, is he setting the stage for becoming somebody at last? Quoting for a second time an epitaph first heard at Christmas dinner, but omitting, as though in a cliff-hanger, its three critical, final words, Dennett humbles himself before the universe, appealing for help: "Betwixt the stirrup and the ground," he says, "Mercy I asked. . . ." But will mercy, ultimately, be found? Is there hope for Dennett, or for any of us? Will the heavens take pity on him? As the wind that began the play kicks up once more in gusts that suggest fullness and emptiness simultaneously, a vault of night sky flecked with "unfamiliar" stars appears in the firmament above Dennett's head. The stars are unfamiliar not because they are new necessarily, but because, like the words of his poem, they present themselves to Dennett in a way that he has perhaps never truly seen, or understood, them before. As Eliot writes in "Four Quartets":

> We shall not cease from exploration
> And the end of all our exploring
> Will to be arrive where we started
> And know the place for the first time.

And so, as Dennett, against the backdrop of two mountains and a moon into which his face regresses, haltingly sifts his own words for clues, the play, which is swept in by the wind, is blown away like a scrap of paper as the wind crescendos again, overwhelming the theatre. *Wrong Mountain* is elemental. It begins and ends with the wind and the moon and the mountains and is suffused with images of water and corn. It reminds us, in the way that this story of human folly and longing is framed, of a natural world that predates man, and that will continue long after man is gone.

Where *Wrong Mountain* is elemental, *La Bête* is hermetic, claustrophobically sealed off against the world, both scenically and linguistically, in a way that produces a high-gloss surface unreality. The central dilemma posed within its artificial atmosphere, however, is anything but unreal, one of many contradictions that ripples disorientatingly throughout the text. It's possible, of course, to view the conflict between Elomire and Valere as a straightforward narrative of art debased by the vulgarity of artistic pretension. But *La Bête*, like *Wrong Mountain*, is so freighted with ambiguity that the play seems to exist on multiple levels, inviting, perhaps, a subtler scrutiny.

In schematic terms, Elomire is presented as a protypical hero, Valere a classic grotesque, their divergent features exaggerated almost to the point of caricature. Dramatic convention directs us to sympathize with the beleaguered Elomire, who, from the outset, is mercilessly steamrolled by the garrulous interloper, most notably in a twenty-two-minute, six-hundred-line monologue that is a panegyric to his own genius. Valere's monologue provides ample grist for Elomire's subsequent critique of language that aims to obfuscate rather than reveal, privileging style over substance and commentary about art over the experience of art itself. But Elomire's personal style is itself an issue. However attractive (or self-evident) the ideas expressed in his diatribes against mediocrity might seem, they are espoused with a self-righteousness that is likely to strike some as less than embraceable. This ambiguity plays out not only in the context of the drama—in Elomire's relationship with the Prince, for example, or to his Troupe—but in the audience's relationship to the character, as well.

The same is true of Valere, but with the ambiguity reversed. Though chockablock with inanity and, at times, callousness, his "logorrheic spasms" have about them an appealing recklessness that compares favorably with Elomire's buttoned-up, missionary rectitude. Valere is, in theatrical terms, precisely what Elomire is not: a shameless entertainer. That he says monstrous or idiotic things seems secondary to the bull-in-a-china-shop sense of fun that his manner evokes. It's exactly the kind of victory of style over substance that Elomire rails against, and it sets up an interesting tension. Our sympathies, which are sorely tested by the putative artist-hero, are titillated, with the relish of a guilty pleasure, by the so-called beast, or fool.

This, of course, mirrors precisely the events that transpire onstage. The members of Elomire's Troupe, though initially appalled by Valere's vulgarity, gradually warm to the abject silliness of the street performer's geek-show attraction *The Parable of Two Boys from Cadiz,* in which they are conscripted to perform. A welcome antidote, they maintain, to the straitjacketing didacticism of Elomire's recent tracts, *The Parable* seems to refresh the Troupe with its accessibility and liveliness. A few questions loom, however. How much of the actors' enthusiasm, one wonders, is a result of Valere's successful flattering of their egos? And to what extent does their reluctance to give up a comfortable existence at Court ultimately inform their decision to abandon their leader? Does their willingness to be seduced by Valere have to do strictly with the pleasure that they experience in performing his *Parable?* Or is it also a reaction against the increasingly "ponderous" themes that, in their view, have come to plague Elomire's work, themes such as "the bloated state of language and its ethical dimension," which, according to Marquise-Therese, "tend to bore instead of entertain." Has Elomire, his Troupe worries, lost touch with the sense of playfulness that is an essential part of theatre? Has he, in his dry intellectualism, come to resist the idea that theatre, after all, *is* play?

Prince Conti's motives are similarly abstruse. At face value, his plan to introduce Valere into the Troupe appears to be a purely aesthetic gesture. It's an attempt, he says, to energize Elomire's work, which, he complains, has bogged down into tendentious impenetrability. Does he truly believe, however, that the addition of a boorish street clown to such a super-refined company will constitute the most fitting or efficacious remedy? The answer depends on whether his exaltations of Valere's talent are to be accepted unironically. Only a simpleton, of course, could regard the *Parable* as a "masterpiece," which is how Prince Conti glowingly describes it. But if the Prince were merely a simpleton, why would he have installed a playwright of Elomire's stature at his Court in the first place, and what would account for the complex relationship that apparently exists between them?★ Power—not aesthetics alone—seems to play a role here.

To what degree, one might ask, is the Prince's fanaticism for Valere genuine, and how much of it is an expression of sadism towards his most prized possession, the arrogant artist whom he suspects he cannot control? Elomire's hauteur, though appearing praiseworthy to Prince Conti at times, seems also to enrage him, perhaps because hauteur is a princely quality, and there is room for only one Prince. The clash between them, therefore, may not amount simply to the witless commission of an aesthetic faux-pas by an aristocratic pinhead; it may, in fact, represent a patron's calculated assertion of authority over an artist whom he has respected, indulged, and, ultimately, grown wary, or even resentful, of. Now, by way of reminding his courtiers of his power (and also, one imagines, to amuse himself), he proceeds to torture both Elomire *and* Valere, as though tugging whimsically on marionette strings.

This raises an interesting question. What responsibility, if any, does Elomire owe to his patron? Artistically, one might say, his foremost responsibility is to himself. As an artist whose work has a specific social dimension, however, Elomire's responsibility might extend, as well, to the company of actors that he manages. Their livelihood and morale depend on him. What's more, he has been blessed with a patron who is so "uncompromising," Elomire says, in his support of "me, my thoughts, my troupe,

★Elomire is renowned throughout the provinces, according to the Prince, as "rival to the genius of Corneille."

my art," that, when asked by such a benevolent Medici to compromise, he might, were he less doctrinaire, consider it his responsibility to seek common ground. Never, however, does the idea of compromise enter seriously into Elomire's mind. His artistic prerogative to remain true to his principles takes precedence over everyone and everything, including the Troupe that relies on him and the sensibilities of the monarch who underwrites him.

So eager is he to assert that prerogative, in fact, that he is given to fits of undiplomatic overstatement on occasions when well enough may have been more wisely left alone. The most dramatic example of this occurs at the conclusion of *The Parable*. Prince Conti avows, earnestly or not, to have detected, upon a second hearing of Valere's tale, parallels to contemporary France that initially escaped his notice, and which lend the work an air of not-so-oblique social commentary. "*The Parable of Two Boys from Cadiz,*" he insists, "Critiques, therefore, at least implicitly/ The foibles of our *own* society." Portraying the debased culture to which those foibles give rise—a realm "where mediocrity is bound to thrive/ While excellence must struggle to survive."—is hardly likely to flatter one of the sovereigns who presides over it, as Prince Conti's increasingly peevish reaction seems to indicate. "Vain fools control the world, *that's* what you're saying!/ Because of them our standards are decaying," he remarks, witheringly, to the author.

Having, perhaps, inadvertently offended a Prince, Valere begins to vamp desperately, as though trying to stave off potential banishment or, worse, execution. But if either were to be his fate, we will never know. Elomire, unable to hold his silver tongue, unwittingly preempts Valere's downward spiral with an impeccably reasoned but unsolicited tirade against the street performer's bombast that comes dangerously close to being bombastic itself.*

*This notion is reinforced by Dorine when she responds to Elomire's speech-ending declaration of "For us the less that's said the better" with the doubly intended monosyllable "TRUE!"

Is Elomire guilty of a kind of overkill that tips the balance, finally, in Valere's favor? Had he not lectured the Prince at such a critical turn, might the matter have been decided differently? Given the arguably poor timing of Elomire's rhetorical intervention, the reliability of Prince Conti's claim that he was delighted to discover in Valere's play a message "that made it more/ Intriguingly disturbing than before" seems, at the very least, open to debate. Is it truly aesthetics that spurs the Prince, in the end, to offer Valere a place at Court, or a desire to punish Elomire's insubordination? Could both, perhaps, be true? On this point *La Bête* remains forever, and ineluctably, ambiguous.

What *is* clear is that Elomire's artistic principles intersect with the lives of his Troupe and patron to form a nexus of potential social and political responsibilities. The extent to which we sympathize with his single-minded adherence to those principles, therefore, varies partly according to our differing expectations about what an artist's social and political responsibilities might be. Depending on one's perspective, Elomire may appear, in his hard-line intransigence, a figure of heroically laudable passion or an extremist who is every bit as vain and megalomaniacal as Valere. Could it be to Elomire, rather than Valere, that "The Beast" (or "Fool") of the play's title actually refers? This seems to be the question raised by Prince Conti when, in bitter farewell to his Court playwright, he says, "One really has to wonder: who's the fool?" The same question, of course, might be asked of the Prince himself. Shades of vanity and megalomania operate in the dispositions of all three central players—the "artist," the "poseur," and the "potentate"—leaving it up to us to determine to which of them, or how many other characters onstage, the term "La Bête" may legitimately apply.

Nor are we, ourselves, immune. Because the play mirrors our reactions to it, "Who's the fool?" is a question that spills beyond the footlights into the lap of any audience member who is willing to confront it. And, since its milieu is the world of theatre, the play inevitably asks the question of itself. Is *La Bête* the work of an artist or a poseur? Does it represent a standard of excellence, or is it a contribution to the very cultural decline that it seems to bemoan? Is it more likely to have come from the pen of Elomire or Valere? If from Elomire, how is one to account for the play's buoyant silliness, its shtick-filled cadenzas and antic comic monologues (including one that, outrageously, takes up most of the first act) that would seem more akin to Valere's taste.* And if from Valere, how is one to make sense of the play's more sober ambitions, its concern, for example, with "the bloated state of language and its ethical dimension," the very theme that Marquise-Therese cites as having come to weigh so ponderously on Elomire's work. Whose aesthetic, after all, is reflected in *La Bête*?

Apparently, there are elements of both, implying a theatrical ideal in which art and entertainment are inseparably linked. Still, the play maintains about itself an almost schizophrenic skepticism, as though it were viewing its elements separately, and self-mockingly, through the alternating eyes of its two central combatants. This produces a chronic sense of disorientation that calls upon us to examine not only our own relationship to the play, but the play's relationship to itself. Is *La Bête* more infatuated with its eloquence or appalled by its glibness? Is it more bent on saying something or on gleefully pulling the rug out from under whatever it seems to want to say? It's a rich irony, indeed, that a first act that's given over almost entirely to a jubilant celebration of form over content—in Valere's cascading couplets—is glowered upon, in the second act, through a ringing denunciation of a world that celebrates form over content, with specific reference

---

*It's equally difficult to imagine, for example, the vaudeville and slapstick of *Wrong Mountain* as having flowed from the pen of Henry Dennett.

to couplets. Thus does the play's form itself become an ambiguous subject of the play. As Elomire remarks of Valere's *Parable,* "'I do my play in rhyme,' he says with bluff/ As though refined expression were enough/ To pardon an impoverishment of thought."

Whether *La Bête*'s true spirit lies closer to self-satisfaction or self-bemusement, self-love or self-loathing, depends, again, on our perspective—on how drawn or repelled we are by the central characters, and the degree to which the play's ambivalence towards them, and itself, sits comfortably with us. That ambivalence reaches its most dizzying complexity, perhaps, in the character of Valere. He is, after all, the irrepressibly scene-stealing, scenery-chewing star attraction, regardless of the danger he is alleged to represent. The play belongs to him (or, rather, is taken over by him) in a way that it never quite belongs to Elomire. For those who don't shut down immediately to his gargantuan narcissism, he offers the irresistible pleasure of a thrill ride, inducing ecstasy and nausea at hairpin turns.

But who *is* he? Can we ever really even begin to know? "My lord, this is a strictly *one-man show,*" he says, discouraging the participation of others in his *Parable,* "Where I play every part, speak every line." Insisting on being everybody, Valere, in effect, ends up being nobody, filling, in art as in life, the void of his bottomless ego with whatever identity will most effectively serve to promote him. His relationship to the truth is as provisional as Elomire's is adamantine. Nowhere does this sense of contingency collapse into a more disorienting black hole than in the presentation of the *Parable,* a play within the play that turns out to be a reductio ad absurdum of the play. *La Bête*'s themes are satirized into their most cretinously simplistic components, with Valere casting himself in Elomire's role as the pure artist defending his culture against the seemingly inevitable incursion of mediocrity. But isn't the *Parable,* Elomire asks, an example of the very mediocrity that it purports to defend against? (A question, again, that *La Bête* inevitably asks of itself.) "To mourn decaying values in a play," he says, "Which only reinforces the decay/ Devalues the idea that it expresses!"

Ideas are further devalued, Elomire contends, when Valere offers a commentary on his own work. Not content to let the play speak for itself, he makes grandiose claims for it, compounding falsity upon falsity. This devalues not only ideas but language itself, Elomire insists, removing words so far from reality that they merely provide "an excuse to babble on." "On words *themselves* do such false words reflect," he says; "Indeed, instead of having an effect/ They yield more *words*—they yield *interpretations!*" Language, he argues, becomes so unmoored from truth that meaning can be found only in surfaces. "And when the honest word is stripped of sense," he says, "Its form assumes unnatural consequence." This is precisely what makes Valere so unknowable, and, to Elomire, threatening. He is incessantly cloaked in a tornado of stylishly if fatuously turned "verbobos"—his own "word," he boasts, "for 'words'"—making it impossible, finally, to determine whether he is guileless or manipulative. He is, simply, a "gaping hole," as Elomire says, opaque because language conceals him, and dangerous because language is all an artist has to defend against him. So the question is joined. Does Valere represent a "lethal trend," as Elomire asserts, because of the threat to aesthetics posed by his linguistic obfuscations, or is it simply that his aesthetics happen to conflict with Elomire's? After having been thus tortured, language is unlikely to supply an uncomplicated answer.

"I shall not tolerate another word," declares Elomire in the opening line of a play that seems to regard with suspicion its own articulateness, and loquacity, from first word to last. Only at the crucial moment when he pleads with his Troupe to remain loyal does Elomire's otherwise unerring command of language desert him, along with the members of his company: "To ask you . . . to give up this life for one/ Whose hardships we had only just begun/ By mercy to forget . . . no . . . WORDS . . ." he splutters, ". . . will do." Once abandoned, however, he again takes refuge in language, this time in quatrains whose mood of elegiac formality suggests distance, even isolation, from the torrent of heroic couplets that has preceded them. And they conclude, innocently perhaps, with what is almost a rallying cry:

> Against great odds one gamely perseveres
> For nature gives advantage to a fool:
> His mindless laughter ringing in your ears,
> His thoughtless cruelties seeming doubly cruel;
>
> His power stems from emptiness and scorn—
> Debasing the ideals of common men;
> But those debased ideals can be reborn . . .
> By starting on the journey once again.

Were the play to end here, one might be left with a lingering sense of an unalloyed endorsement of Elomire's idealism. But this, of course, is not how the play ends. It ends with Dorine, who, according to the stage directions, "blows a kiss to Elomire; her eyes welling with tears, she turns to face the audience in silence as the curtain falls." What, one wonders, do Dorine's tears signify? Are they expressed poignantly for an artist-hero who, against overwhelming odds, sets out to defy the brutal cynicism of a corrupt world? Or do they suggest compassion for a not-quite-whole man who is committing himself to a life of terrible and perhaps unrelenting loneliness with nothing but the courage of his potentially wrongheaded convictions to sustain him? Could there not be a myriad of other possible interpretations? Dorine's tears, at last, may be noteworthy less for what they signify than for what they intimate—the realm of the ineffable, that which is not (or can never be) spoken—just as she herself, the exemplar of monosyllabic resistance to *La Bête*'s swelling tide of polysyllables, provides not a "final word" to this most verbal of plays, but a mysterious coda of absolute, and, ultimately, indecipherable silence.

If *Wrong Mountain* is an existential play set into motion by an aesthetic crisis, *La Bête* is an aesthetic play set into motion by an existential crisis, each deploying its many contradictions in an architecture that supports contradiction. Where, however, *Wrong Mountain* is constructed in three dimensions, its core themes of identity, success, and judgment counterpoised ironically from one scene to the next, *La Bête* is linear and involuted, like a snake swallowing its own tail to the brink of self-extinction. Though, perhaps, confusing, neither play is, I hope, conceptually confused: elusive, perhaps, without being muddled. And while each undoubtedly has serious intentions, grounded in the faith that an audience is willing to withstand high degrees of potentially disturbing ambiguity, both are also wild comedies that are designed to be enjoyed at the level of pure boulevard entertainment, which may explain, in part, their Broadway pedigrees. They do not, in other words, occupy different universes at all, nor do they even make for a paradoxical coupling. They are, in a profound sense, companion pieces.

★

The original Broadway productions of *La Bête* and *Wrong Mountain* provoked a furor that has become an indelible part of their history and legacy. Not only because of the strangeness of the material, but because of the audacious—some might say *surreal*—nature of their appearance on Broadway, the plays are remembered in New York not simply as pieces of theatre, but as gladiatorial "events" that inspired controversy of spectacular intemperance. This fact alone may constitute the most compelling reason for uniting them in a single volume.

What is it about these plays that generated—and continues to generate—such a peculiar amount of electricity and, at times, heat? Part of the answer, at least, has to do with the anomalous circumstances of their debuts, and the state of the commercial theatre in America at the end of the twentieth century. When *La Bête* opened in February 1991, it had the high-profile distinction of being one of the last of what was rapidly becoming a dying breed: a new American play produced directly on Broadway.★ That it was, in the words of *The New York Times,* a "nervy, wildly distinctive" work "written with a hard-to-fathom audacity" by a first-time playwright helped to "polarize" critics "to the degree where the cliché is applicable: you either loved it or you hated it." That the author was "then just 32 years old," the *Times* went on to say, reflecting on the play's premiere a decade later, "only enhanced the conflicting views that his gifts were either prodigious or prodigal."

La Bête ignited a fiery public debate that has never been forgotten. Scorned by some critics, it was praised lavishly by others, several of whom launched passionate counterattacks against the play's detractors, an extraordinary gesture in the normally complacent world of New York theatre. In an even more extraordinary gesture, a group of twenty-eight luminaries including Jerome Robbins, Katharine Hepburn, Joanne Woodward, Harold Prince, Liv Ullmann, Kevin Kline, David Henry Hwang, Peter Shaffer, and Jules Feiffer banded together to write a letter of protest to *The New York Times* (whose critics had dismissed the play) urging readers to judge this "amazing evening in the theatre" for them-

---

★In theatre parlance, this refers to a method, standard in previous generations but now rendered virtually defunct by the increasingly prohibitive risks to investors, by which a new play is optioned by commercial producers, booked into a Broadway house, rehearsed for four to six weeks, warmed up out of town in a place like Boston, New Haven, or San Francisco for a month, and then brought straight into New York City.

selves.* Members of the audience were equally bewildered by the denunciations leveled at the play. One letter to *The New York Times* said, "Reading the reviews of David Hirson's new play *La Bête* was like watching someone shoot down an exotic bird that has magically appeared among a flock of sparrows."

When asked, in a 1996 interview, to comment on the impact that professional theatre criticism has had on his work, Edward Albee dryly replied, "From most critics I learn how long my play will run. That's about it." Any dramatist who has been privileged enough to receive the attention of the press would undoubtedly concede the truth of Albee's remark. It bespeaks the perennially uneasy relationship between artist and critic that exists regardless of the discipline—whether one writes or paints or composes. Albee, whose career is a virtual object lesson in the vicissitudes of critical assessment, declares uncompromisingly (and without bitterness) that the reaction to his work is a matter of interest, but not necessarily import, since it inevitably reflects the fashion of the times: "So you're in and out of fashion. I'm back in fashion again for a while now. But I imagine that three or four years from now I'll be out again. And in another fifteen years I'll be back. If you write to try to stay in fashion, if you write to be the critics' darling, you become an employee."

On the basis of their eccentricity alone, neither *La Bête* nor *Wrong Mountain* put the author in any danger of being considered the critics' darling. *Wrong Mountain,* whose production history is no less singular than *La Bête*'s, was viewed as another wildly unconventional, rarefied piece of writing. Like its predecessor, it had the high-profile distinction of being produced directly on Broadway, the first new American play, as it was preposterously touted, of the

---

*The *Times* chose not to publish the letter; it eventually appeared in *TheaterWeek* (March 4–10, 1991).

millennium. And, as the second play by a writer whose maiden effort was so hotly disputed, it was at least as much of a lightning rod as the first, if not more of one. Passionate exponents and rabid detractors expressed themselves with equal fervor, creating once again an atmosphere of stormy, sometimes rancorous critical debate. This is as it should be. It is part of what makes theatre exciting: it is, as Albee says, the measure of how effective a dramatist has been in getting the audience to think as they leave the theatre, instead of immediately focusing on "where we parked the car."

Rancorous debate, however, hardly bodes well for the fate of a commercial play, at least not in an age when soaring ticket prices cause potential theatregoers to pause in the face of a negative review, particularly one from a major newspaper. But to what extent should the commercial fate of a play be of concern artistically? One might argue that it's blessing enough simply to get a hearing for one's work, let alone the incomparable exposure afforded by a first-rate Broadway production. Gratitude is what's called for, regardless of whether the work is well or poorly received, or whether it runs for one night or one year. The length of its survival, especially in the status quo environment of commercial theatre, is obviously irrelevant, at least from an artistic point of view.

From the point of view of one's colleagues, on the other hand, as well as that of the audience, it is, I have come to learn, quite another matter. The remarkable campaign waged to save *La Bête* suggested deep concern within the theatre community—concern bordering on alarm. Valiant efforts notwithstanding, the play closed after only three weeks, its final performance in New York attended by a virtual Who's Who of American Theatre. That it went on to receive a shelfload of prizes at the end of the season and won, for the London production in 1992, Britain's Laurence Olivier Award was cold comfort for those who saw in its quick demise worrying implications for the future of the American theatre, and the role that Broadway seems gradually to have abandoned in maintaining it as a vital cultural force.

Nine years later, the alarm expressed by audiences and colleagues at the negative reaction to, and short life of, *La Bête* had evolved into something more like despair. When *La Bête* opened at the Eugene O'Neill Theatre in February 1991, it was one of only a handful of new American plays running on Broadway. When *Wrong Mountain* opened at the same theatre, in January 2000, it was the *only* new American play running on Broadway. In less than a decade, Times Square had been transformed by corporate interests into a vast entertainment complex that had effectively wiped out the ideal of a mainstream theatre that could also claim to be artistically ambitious.

But is such an ideal worth maintaining? Writing about *La Bête* in 1991, one critic said, "If such a work cannot impress Broadway, then what hope is there for Broadway? There is of course an American theatre without Broadway, but there is no apparatus for proclaiming the arrival of important new work at a regional theatre; no medium through which such energy can radiate. And that is why the continued existence of commercial Broadway is essential to an artistic American theatre."

With these sentiments in mind, I initiated, eight days after *Wrong Mountain* opened on Broadway to reviews that were as polarized as *La Bête*'s, a series of talkbacks that I pledged to continue after each performance for the run of the play. Having been besieged, as I was nine years earlier, by colleagues and audience members who were dismayed by the turbulence of the critical response, I felt that an open discussion of the play and the sharply divided reaction to it might prove illuminating.

Astonishingly, not dozens but hundreds of people, forgoing dinner reservations and train schedules, remained in their seats at ten-fifteen each evening—close to seven hundred on the first Saturday night. Aside from asking many lively, penetrating questions about the play itself, talkback audiences were eager to explore why *Wrong Mountain* (and *La Bête*) managed to hit such a raw nerve with some critics while exciting such rare delight in others. Particular concern was expressed about the spirit of the negative criticism. As one letter to *The New York Times* put it, "One wondered at the violence of the attack."

Talkback audiences offered a recurring hypothesis. Neither *La Bête* nor *Wrong Mountain,* it was pointed out, conforms to any recognizable genre. They are, in stylistic terms, "exotic birds," species that tend to be met, traditionally, with either euphoria or intolerance—"the kind of show," *The New Yorker* wrote of *La Bête* in January 2000, "you'd expect to dazzle some critics, infuriate others. *Wrong Mountain,*" it concluded, "has all the markings of an equally, if not more, confounding work. . . ."★

Unfortunately, controversy of this sort, while hardly undesirable artistically, virtually guarantees a short life in the commercial theatre. Except in the case of big-budget musicals, British imports, and star-driven revivals, anything less than unqualified approbation from the mainstream press tends to be regarded, understandably, as off-putting by theatregoers paying exorbitant Broadway prices. A new play in the commercial theatre, in other words, can no longer afford to evoke genuine controversy, when genuine controversy is exactly what's needed to breathe life into the commercial theatre. It requires a kind of Good Housekeeping Seal of Approval to survive. Over time, this alienates audiences with a greater sense of adventure. Eventually—as many people in the talkbacks informed me—they stop going to the theatre altogether.

As costs have continued to escalate, matters have grown worse. Theatre (both on and off Broadway) has become increasingly conservative, more and more dependent on the imprimatur of professional commentators. Few, if any, new American plays are produced directly on Broadway these days. They are developed

★*The New York Times,* writing about *La Bête* in 1991, said, "To say this is not the usual fare on Broadway is self-evident. This is not the usual fare anywhere."

through what has become a farm system of regional theatres or are first produced off-Broadway in the hope of gaining the sort of critical support that can make a move to Broadway possible. This is safer, but is it good for the theatre? Doesn't it discourage innovation and risk-taking, and abdicate, to the press, the decision about which plays a Broadway audience will ultimately be allowed to see? Could the fact that the producers of *La Bête* and *Wrong Mountain* bucked this trend, the talkback audiences wondered, have been viewed by some critics as an act of hubris that needed to be punished?

Wrong Mountain closed, like *La Bête,* in less than a month. From a playwright's perspective, this is not necessarily a bad thing. If *La Bête* is any example, damning criticism and a short run on Broadway can, if posterity judges the work favorably, confer upon it a cachet, even a stature, that more conventionally well-received pieces seldom attain. Though it is still too early to tell with *Wrong Mountain, La Bête*'s turbulent history has, in the context of the play's rich afterlife, already come to be regarded as a fascinating footnote that, rather than detracting from the play's luster, actually adds to it. As *The New York Times* wrote in January 2000, "*La Bête* closed after 24 performances and 15 previews, marking it in Broadway lore as a cause célèbre casualty of critical perception and theatre economics." Or, as *Playbill* reported it even more succinctly, "In the nine years since it closed on Broadway . . . *La Bête* has risen to the level of legendary production."

For my colleagues in the theatre, however, *Wrong Mountain*'s early closing had chilling implications, even more so than *La Bête*'s. As voices of American playwrights become increasingly marginalized, the rare, hopeful sign of powerful Broadway producers putting their weight behind a dangerous new American drama quickly gave way to the depressing spectacle of a critical response that in too many instances descended to the level of personal vilification. It remains to be seen whether this event will aggravate an already unhealthy state of affairs by discouraging commercial producers from taking risks on dangerous new plays in the future.

Nothing seemed more troubling to talkback audiences, finally, than the personal bullying that they felt was evident in so many of the critical assaults on my plays. But where pieces like *La Bête* and *Wrong Mountain* are concerned, I proposed, this manner of attack, though depressing, is, to some extent, to be expected, and not simply because of the plays' stylistic unfamiliarity. A significant feature of both works, after all, is their satire, and no satire that receives an immediate embrace, especially from the mainstream press, can be thought to be accomplishing its primary objective, which is to draw blood. The more effective the satire, the more vituperative the response, and where better to rain down recriminatory blows than on the head of the satirist himself? It's only natural for those who feel wounded by an author's work to hurl invectives at the author. Not only my plays, therefore, but I, as a person, am regularly described by unsympathetic critics as arrogant, self-congratulatory, pretentious, and—to their utmost distaste—a show-off with words! The obnoxious prig they describe is a creature whom, I sometimes shudder to think, I am condemned to spend twenty-four hours a day with for the rest of my life!

In reality, of course, I am far less colorful, a person who is haunted, as he labors at the profoundly difficult, often agonizing task of writing, by the same sense of inadequacy and fraudulence that seems to be shared by every artist I have ever known and respected. No critic, I am sure, has entertained greater doubts about my work, nor treated it more harshly, than I myself. Those who regard me as arrogant are responding, I imagine, to the self-assurance with which my plays are written, and if self-assurance were the measure of arrogance then theirs is a view to which I would heartily subscribe. What they fail to consider, perhaps, is that I arrive at self-assurance only after wading through endless mires of insecurity and self-doubt. A play, for me, is the concatenation of months, even years (one and a half in the case of *La*

Bête, two and a half for *Wrong Mountain*) of moments, fleetingly grasped, when I am able to trick myself, it sometimes feels, into believing that I have talent, and can find the courage to express it on paper. As a distillation of such hard-fought-for moments, the plays represent both me and something other than myself; they are artifacts that both encompass and, one hopes, transcend the drudgery of artistic aspiration. If the outcome strikes some as the work of a show off, it seems to me that one has no business writing for the theatre unless one has something to show off. A writer's presumption that his gifts are worthy of the attention of otherwise occupied people is, no doubt, a supreme arrogance, but it's an arrogance that depends on the crushing humility of constantly confronting the insufficiency of one's own talent, and of striving to send forth into the world the best that one has to offer.

There is the matter, too, of autobiography. Any satire that is deliberately confrontational, as both *La Bête* and *Wrong Mountain* most assuredly are, is bound to set off a foxhunt to locate where the voice of the author truly lies, especially among those who feel satirized. Since neither play exists strictly as satire, however, the quest to identify such a voice inevitably proves fruitless, an irritant that merely stokes the urge to manufacture a pernicious and didactic straw man upon whom to heap indignation. A fair reading of either of my plays reveals no figure so unambiguous. Neither Elomire in *La Bête* nor Henry Dennett in *Wrong Mountain,* the characters most frequently seized upon as mouthpieces for the author, is anything other than a deeply flawed human being whose militant rhetoric is hardly crafted to command an uncomplicated allegiance! The fact that they engender so much anxious speculation about their relationship to the author, however, suggests that their words contain enough truth to carry a satirical bite. Do I agree with what they say? If I knew the answer to that question, there would have been no reason to write the plays. My impulse as a dramatist is not to advance a thesis but, from a position of perpetual doubt, to set characters and ideas in conflict and let the chips fall where they may. No one character expresses my views; rather, there is a small part of me in every character, even those, I suppose, in whose monstrousness I would shrink to recognize myself. Nor is there an idea in either of my plays, as far as I know, that is permitted to remain unchallenged, that isn't turned inside-out and put through the wringer a dozen times over in the course of the evening. These are not works in which an omnipotent author stands aloof from the satire. On the contrary, given the way each seeming "thesis" is continually undercut, the ultimate object of satire is neither audience nor critics but the author himself. By exposing, in lurid contradiction, what I suspect to be the best and worst in me, I am inviting members of the audience to recognize the best and worst in themselves, and to contemplate their own contradictions. These are not plays that have a "message." They are not vehicles for ideas that we are encouraged to applaud or deplore. To reduce them to simple autobiographical equations misses, I think, the point.

There have been, and probably always will be, audience members who, like some critics, experience uncontrollable anger in the face of my work. Verbal assaults and booing are not unknown to me, and, after the third preview of *La Bête,* I endured a baptism-by-fire when a seemingly calm theatregoer, having identified me as the playwright, punched me full-throttle in the face and fled, inexplicably, into the night. As I regained consciousness, my back in the snow and my mouth bleeding, I vowed never again to acknowledge being the author of the play without first ascertaining whether or not the person asking had enjoyed it!

Against such outrage, however, I have received a level of support from theatregoers that few playwrights are ever privileged to know. I have been especially fortunate to count among those supporters a prodigious number of artists, many of whom—figures, to me, of unimaginable accomplishment—have risked their reputations to take a public stand, or contacted me personally, to

1

voice their abiding faith in my work, and to exhort me to press forward undaunted. As *The New York Times* wrote in January 2000, "Whether or not audiences and critics embrace Mr. Hirson's intellectual gymnastics . . . *Wrong Mountain,* as did *La Bête,* clearly speaks to—and for—his theatre colleagues."

It is with certain members of the press, however, that these works have always created a special tension, perhaps for no other reason than the fact of having to write about them. Both plays are so relentlessly self-reflective that commentators, finding themselves entangled in a wilderness of mirrors, inevitably run the risk, simply by rendering judgment, of making themselves appear foolish, an especially nettlesome phenomenon, one imagines, for the faint of heart or thin of skin. As the *Village Voice* wrote of *La Bête,* "[The play] seems to be designed as a trap for critics: Since the subject of David Hirson's comedy is people's varying views of art, any opinion you express has been anticipated onstage, and puts you in danger of becoming just another clown in the comedy."

No one is in greater danger of appearing foolish, however, than the author himself, and nowhere is this made more apparent than in the Preface to this volume. Have I not, in offering commentaries on my own work, committed precisely the indiscretion that Elomire finds so loathsome in Valere, and at a length that even Valere might find excessive? And isn't my skepticism about a writer's exegesis of his own work—as though it should count for *anything!*—what motivates me, in Elomire-like fashion, to endow it with a shape, and a rigor, that might, at least, make it appear less unseemly? Have I not, like Guy Halperin in *Wrong Mountain,* pronounced grandly on the future of Broadway and the fate of the American theatre? And isn't there, in the cant of my words, a whiff of Henry Dennett's overweening desire for recognition, however much I, at a relatively young age, have enjoyed a hearing for my work that he, late in life, has been so frustratingly denied? Is it not possible to see Cliff's diffident self-possession, Prince Conti's mercurialness, and Dorine's reticence—the strong implication of what's *not* being said—in each page of this Preface and throughout both of the plays? These works, as I said, represent both me and something other than myself. They reflect the dual impulse to be known and to remain hidden, to be all of my characters and, ultimately, to be none of them. In writing these sentences I mark myself, I suppose, as not just another "clown in the comedy," but, it would seem, as the biggest clown of all. And that, perhaps, *is* the point. As Maurice says, in both hail and farewell, "I told you . . . I'm a complete buffoon."

La Bête and *Wrong Mountain* have brought me great joy, and I'm thankful to have them in my life. They have also exposed me to acts of generosity and unkindness so extreme in both directions that I often wonder what conclusion, if any, to draw from the experience. During the final talkback in New York, a young man asked me if I didn't feel, based on the intense, not always pleasant response to my work, that I might, perhaps, be climbing the wrong mountain. I said then, as I do now, that I would never have written either of these plays if I knew the answer to that question.

David Hirson
New York City
Winter 2000–2001

ACKNOWLEDGMENTS

Many friends, acquaintances, and loved ones have contributed, in ways of which some of them are probably unaware, to the writing and production of these plays. For their help in the creation and birth of *La Bête,* I wish to thank Orest Bedrij, Bob Borod, Scott and Sarah Bryce, Cicero and Bird "B," Jean Desaulniers, Barnold Elliott, Tyler Gatchell, Michael Gendler, Jane Gottlieb, Matthew Guerreiro, Martyn Hayes, Chris Hirson, Alan Hollinghurst, Jill Hooley, Richard Hudson, Siri Huntoon, Mick Imlah, Nicholas Jenkins, the Jujamcyns (Rocco Landesman, Paul Libin, and Jack Viertel), Michael Klein, Stewart and Lee Klein, Marta Korduba, David Kuhn, Ron Leibman, Alice Miskimin, Ann Ostrow, Kate Ostrow, Andrew Paulson, Max Scheider, Dori Shedlin, Meg Simon, Jessica Teich, Joshua Tonkel, and Andrew Lloyd Webber.

Many of the above, and several others, were instrumental in bringing *Wrong Mountain* to life, or in keeping me sane during the process. They are: Angelo Bellfatto, Jay Binder, Jack Bowdan, Pages Horse Brittson, Adrian Bryan-Browne, James Busby, Giles Cadle, Marguerite Camaiore, Louise Clark, Philip Clark, Heather Cousens, Les Dickert, Billie Eubanks, Edwin Eubanks, Ariel Fernando, Cary Fuller, Gary Gersh, Jim Harker, Deborah Harwood, Carla and Ted Hawryluk, John Michael Higgins, Kevin and Jody Hirson, George Lane, Fred Martell, Spencer Neyland, Angela Nosari, Pippa Pearthree, Nina Tovish, and Maggie Welsh.

I owe a special debt of gratitude to Jennifer Tipton, whose honesty and clear-sightedness were invaluable assets to me on both of these productions.

My dear friends Frank Farance and Margaret Salinger have been unstintingly generous with their love, understanding, and wise counsel. I cannot thank them enough. Johann Carlo's penetrating mind benefited me greatly in the writing of *Wrong Mountain*. She is forever in my heart.

Someone once described these plays as "messages in a bottle where the message reads, 'If you like this, get in touch.'" I'm grateful to the many who have, in letters of such eloquence that they've often been a marvel to behold. Of those, the one I received from the poet and translator of Molière's plays, Richard Wilbur, is among my most treasured, and I thank him for it.

John Ashbery's attendance at a performance of *Wrong Mountain,* and his meeting with members of the company backstage afterwards, thrilled everyone, and I wish to record my gratitude to him here.

Angelo Bellfatto's patience, artistry, and intellect have profited me enormously in the writing of the Preface to this volume. Other indispensable conversations were had with Frank Farance, Peter Clark, Ilana Levine, Jim Stoeri, and my mother and father. Eric Price and the people at Grove Press have worked painstakingly to make these plays look so handsome on the page. My thanks to them all.

I am deeply grateful to my stepparents, Stephen Elliott and Jean Hirson, for their love and support.

The actors who originated the roles in *La Bête* and *Wrong Mountain* were more than collaborators. They were fearless crusaders whose sensitivity and protectiveness towards me personally, and whose fierce intelligence about the work, have left me forever in their debt. Of their many extraordinary feats of valor, none is more remarkable than Tom McGowan's mind-boggling high-wire act a decade ago, the memory of which, for those present for it, time has done nothing to diminish. To Tom, Michael Cumpsty, Jimmy Greene, Johann Carlo, Dylan Baker, Pat Kilgarriff, Michael Higgins, Holly Felton, Bill Mesnik, Suzie Plakson, Eric Swanson, Cheryl Gaysunas, Ellen Kohrman, Michael McCormick, Michael James Reed, Ron Rifkin, Danny Davis, Beth Dixon, Annie Dudek, Tom Riis Farrell, Reg Flowers, Jody Gelb, Danny Jenkins, Ilana Levine, Bruce Norris, Mary

Schmidtberger, and Michael Winters: I love you dearly. Thank you for your immense courage in bringing my plays to life!

Without a producer, a playwright's words are consigned to molder in a drawer, never, perhaps, to be heard. For the two plays that I have written, I have been blessed to find producers who gave them not only a hearing, but a launch that was more magnificent and public than any writer could hope for in his wildest dreams. That they did so on Broadway, incurring a level of risk that many of their less intrepid or idealistic colleagues would regard as pure folly, is a measure not only of their love for the plays, but of a conviction that not to produce them in this fashion would have betrayed their original love for the theatre. It's probably consistent, therefore, that, without abandoning their practical hats, none of them ever treated my work, or me, with anything less than respect bordering on tenderness. Ed Strong, Sherman Warner, Robert Strickstein, Carey Perloff, but especially Stuart Ostrow, Michael David, and Lauren Mitchell: thank you for everything. You deserve not only my love and gratitude, which you will have always, but a sense of honor that I hope these plays have brought you, and will continue to bring you, for the rest of our lives and into the unforeseeable future.

In the production of any new play, no decision is more crucial than the choice of a director. Richard Jones, to whom I have entrusted both of my plays, approached them with an intelligence and imagination so unique that he opened up creative avenues that were entirely new to me. That he has become, in the process, a valued and beloved friend, means that ours has been not simply a stimulating collaboration, but a providential one. Like anyone who has had the good fortune to work with him in the past, I look forward to working with him again in the future. Richard: my love and thanks always.

Peter Clark has been significant in my life in many ways, but none more inspiring than in the profound understanding, deep empathy, constant encouragement, and sharp insight that, as a musician, singer, and scholar, he has so selflessly imparted to brighten some of the darkest hours in a creative process that is, for me, frequently tormenting. Peter, I love you. Nobody said I wasn't crazy, least of all you!

My mother and father have stood behind and beside me, stalwart but not unworried, through every step of the writing of these plays and their subsequent productions. Unwavering in their support, perpetually available, and never obtrusive with their advice, they have given me no reason to do anything other than my best, though it pains them, I know, to watch me suffer when I feel that I am falling short. Theirs is a gift that I can never adequately repay. I must leave it to the Dedications of my plays to express to them, and the five aforementioned, not only my love, but eternal gratitude for the faith without which I'm not sure I could have completed, or even begun, these two most incredible journeys. Stuart, Michael, Lauren, Richard, Peter, but especially Mom and Dad: thank you for believing in me.

LA BÊTE

for

MY PARENTS

and for

STUART OSTROW

La Bête was originally produced on the Broadway stage by Stuart Ostrow and Andrew Lloyd Webber at the Eugene O'Neill Theatre on February 10, 1991. It was directed by Richard Jones; the set and costume designs were by Richard Hudson; the lighting design was by Jennifer Tipton; the sound design was by Peter Fitzgerald; and the production stage manager was Bob Borod. The cast was as follows:

ELOMIRE	Michael Cumpsty
BEJART	James Greene
VALERE	Tom McGowan
DORINE	Johann Carlo
PRINCE CONTI	Dylan Baker
MADELEINE BEJART	Patricia Kilgarriff
DE BRIE	John Michael Higgins
CATHERINE DE BRIE	Holly Felton
RENE DU PARC	William Mesnik
MARQUISE-THERESE DU PARC	Suzie Plakson
SERVANTS	Eric Swanson, Cheryl Gaysunas, Ellen Kohrman, Michael McCormick

In New York, *La Bête* won the John Gassner Award of the Outer Critics Circle, the New York Newsday/Oppenheimer Award, the Marton Prize of the Dramatists Guild, the special Best Play citation in *Best Plays 1990–91,* as well as nominations for five Tony Awards and six Drama Desk Awards, including Best Play 1991.

In London (where Alan Cumming was featured as Valere, Jeremy Northam as Elomire, and Timothy Walker as Prince Conti), *La Bête* won the 1992 Laurence Olivier Award for Comedy of the Year.

CHARACTERS

Members of the Troupe:

ELOMIRE, leader of the Troupe
BEJART, his second-in-command
MADELEINE BEJART, Bejart's sister
DE BRIE
CATHERINE DE BRIE, De Brie's wife
RENE DU PARC
MARQUISE-THERESE DU PARC, Du Parc's wife

VALERE, a troubadour
PRINCE CONTI, patron of the Troupe
DORINE, a serving maid

SERVANTS

TIME

1654

PLACE

Prince Conti's estate in Pezenas
Languedoc, France

Note: This play is meant to be performed in an absurdly high-comic style, at lightning speed and with rhymes and iambs respected. The costumes are seventeenth-century bouffe.

Lines spoken simultaneously are indicated by brackets. Where two different conversations are taking place simultaneously they are bracketed and set side by side in two columns.

La Bête is presented in two acts; the action is continuous.

ACT ONE

Before the curtain rises, Dorine appears. She surveys the audience and is gone.

The antechamber of the dining room in the actors' cottage: a blazing white environment furnished with a gilt chair and table. Busts of Greek and Roman orators line the cornice. Enter Elomire, storming into the room, followed by Bejart.

ELOMIRE
I shall not tolerate another word.

BEJART
But Elomire . . .

ELOMIRE
Enough, I said . . .

BEJART
I heard!

ELOMIRE
THAT COCKATRICE . . . !

BEJART
Shhhhhhh!

ELOMIRE (*Whispering, but viva voce.*)
Do it! Throw him out!!

BEJART
Good Lord! You whisper . . .

ELOMIRE
. . . louder than I shout?

So I've been told. Well, good! It's for the better.
(*Booming.*)
LET'S HOPE WE'RE OVERHEARD DOWN TO THE
    LETTER . . . !

BEJART

You carry on as if we had a choice!

ELOMIRE

We do!

BEJART

No!

ELOMIRE

Bejart, listen to my voice:
Our patronage, you say, requires that we
Add one more player to our company;
The rationale for this escapes me quite . . .
(*Bejart begins to protest, but Elomire anticipates.*)
BUT . . . knowing that the Court is always right,
I'm willing to oblige without dispute.
However, on one point I'm resolute:
A rash selection simply isn't wise,
(*Pointing to the other room.*)
And *that* bombastic ninny I despise!
Naught could induce me, save a Holy Writ,
To share the stage with that dull hypocrite!
(*Bejart extracts a document from his sleeve.*)
What's that?

BEJART

A writ.

ELOMIRE

You mock me.

BEJART

Au contraire:
(*Elomire, gasping, snatches the document from Bejart's hand and buries his nose in it.*)
The Prince, it seems, *adores* Monsieur Valere;
And though you say he cannot be abided,
Apparently the matter's been decided . . . !

ELOMIRE (*Slumping into a chair, groaning.*)
O GOD!! I'M GOING TO DIE!!

BEJART

Well, even so . . .

ELOMIRE
BUT I *DETEST* VALERE . . . !!

BEJART

We know, we *know:*
Repeatedly you've made that understood!
Withal, the fact remains, our livelihood
Depends upon a Court decree, and since
Valere's thought so amusing by the Prince,
Not only are we bound to cast him . . . WORSE!

Bejart points to a specific clause in the document; Elomire reads, incredulously.

ELOMIRE
"The troupe—might—even—stage his—comic verse"!?
I'm breaking out in hives! This is obscene!
What verse? That doggerel that, in between
Great gulps of *my* Bordeaux, he dared recite?—
In love with his own voice, the *parasite!*
"Self-cherishing" is much too mild a phrase
To give a sense of the coquettish ways

9

He forms a sentence, flirting like a girl:
The tiny cough that says,
(*With a tiny cough.*)
                              "I've dropped a pearl,"
The eyelids all a-flutter, and the sniff
While striking poses with his handkerchief!
For all of that, he never speaks . . . he *spits!*
I almost drowned in that man's affricates!
AND HE COMPARES HIMSELF TO SCARAMOUCHE!!
O, really he's just so grotesquely *louche*
On all accounts I'd say. Don't you agree?

BEJART (*Hedging.*)
Well, what about his generosity
In showing admiration for your plays . . . ?

ELOMIRE
I'd much prefer his censure to his praise!
Beware of men who laud you to the skies:
It is *themselves* they mean to lionize!
Valere finds what he thinks I'd like to hear,
Then spouts some panegyric that will steer
The conversation back to his *renown!*
(*Imitating Valere.*)
"But have you seen my own, *The Dying Clown?*"
(*Ridiculing it.*)
The Dying Clown!

BEJART
                              I saw it!

ELOMIRE (*Surprised.*)
                              Really? Where?

BEJART

A year ago in Brussels, at a fair.

ELOMIRE

Well, was it good?

BEJART

              I don't remember now;
(*But he gradually begins to remember.*)
  It was a pantomime . . . he had a . . .
(*Squinting in disbelief at the memory.*)
                 . . . cow . . .
Dressed up as Anne of Austria!

ELOMIRE (*Keening.*)
             O PLEASE!!
(*Slumping to his knees.*)
  Look here, Bejart: I'm getting on my knees
  To beg the Lord that we be spared this hell:
  "Dear God, we pray . . ."
(*To Bejart.*)
            . . . get on your knees as well!
(*Bejart ignores him.*)
  "DEAR GOD, WE PRAY . . ."
(*Clutching the pocket of Bejart's coat and pulling him down to his knees.*)
             . . . I *mean* it, man, get *down!*
  "DEAR GOD, WE PRAY YOU LOOK UPON THIS
    TOWN
  WHERE SEVEN HUMBLE ACTORS MAKE THEIR
    HOME
  THANKS TO PRINCE CONTI, BY WHOSE GRACE
    WE ROAM
  THE COUNTRYSIDE ITINERANT NO MORE . . ."

BEJART
Amen.

ELOMIRE
      Amen? What did you say that for?

BEJART
I thought you'd finished.

ELOMIRE
               No.

BEJART (*Fed up with the histrionics.*)
               May we get up!?

ELOMIRE
"DEAR GOD . . ."

BEJART
        I'm standing . . .

ELOMIRE (*Reaching out and restraining Bejart.*)
       ". . . FROM THY BRIMMING CUP
OF MERCY LET US DRINK . . ."

BEJART (*Trying to stand.*)
             Let go!

ELOMIRE
                  STAY THERE!

BEJART
O, stop it, Elomire! Since when is prayer
A genuine expression of your creed . . . ?

ELOMIRE
When all else fails, goddammit!

BEJART
          Damn indeed.

ELOMIRE

    All right, then: tell me, what do you propose
    Aside from *"Pity that's the way it goes"?*
    How very helpful, what a good solution;
    I do applaud your stunning contribution . . .

BEJART

    We simply have no choice!

ELOMIRE

                          Depressing beast.

BEJART

    At least I'm honest . . .

ELOMIRE

                       At the *very* least!
    Such honesty makes liars of us all:
    Just *kneeling* next to you makes me feel small!
    Forgive my lack of rectitude, but I,
    Immorally, must falsely hope, or die;
    Because the merest thought that this *Valere*
    Should be forever tangled in my hair
    Is so repellent, so abjectly grim,
    That, forced to choose between an hour with him
    And hanging by my thumbs in Zanzibar . . .

BEJART

    Now don't you think you're taking this too far . . . ?

ELOMIRE

    . . . or writhing in a scalding tub of lye . . .

BEJART

    What would it hurt to give the man a try . . . ?

ELOMIRE

    . . . or rotting in a ditch consumed by lice . . .

BEJART
In time, I'm sure we'll find he's very nice . . .

ELOMIRE
. . . or racked with plague, bubonic glands protruding . . .

Enter Valere.

VALERE
GENTLEMEN! I hope I'm not intruding . . .

ELOMIRE (*Through clenched teeth.*)
That *voice!* Mon *Dieu!*

VALERE (*Seeing Elomire kneeling.*)
Good Lord! You're deep in prayer . . .

BEJART
No, no. Come in. Come in, Monsieur Valere.

ELOMIRE (*Rolling his eyes at Bejart.*)
Come *in* . . . ?

VALERE
Well Heaven Bless Us! *NOW* I see:
It was a sudden burst of piety
That took you from the table, am I right?
(*Bejart opens his mouth to speak.*)
I'm so relieved! I thought, perhaps, your flight
Was caused by something *I* had said or done . . .
(*Elomire opens his mouth to speak.*)
No, don't explain. GOD BLESS US EVERY ONE!
I, too, am *very* pious, *most* devout:
I cross myself . . . twelve times (or thereabout)
Before I take my morning tea each day!

At lunch I'm up to forty; and I'd say
By nightfall it's . . . a staggering amount;
But what a foolish waste of time to count!
(*Sniffs and extends handkerchief.*)
DEVOTION COMES TO NOTHING IF WE COME
TO SUMMARIZE DEVOTION IN A SUM.
(*A slight cough, eyelids flutter, and a self-loving bow.*)
A tiny play on words . . . doth please you not?
I swear I made it up right on the spot!
I don't know *how* I do it, I just . . . do.
These epigrams they . . . come to me as dew
Collects upon a budding daffodil . . .
A curse? A blessing? Call it what you will,
It's mine to bear this "genius of the word"—
DID I SAY "GENIUS"?: I think it's absurd
When people call you that, don't you agree?
To us it comes like breath: so naturally.
It seems like sorcery to those below!
I cite that telling phrase from Cicero:
"DE BONUM EST" . . . "DIS BONUM EST" . . .
    O, shit . . .
Well, anyway, you get the gist of it.
I *do* love Latin. Does it show? It's *true!*
I'm something of a scholar in it, too.
I've read them all (yes, even *I'm* impressed)
From Cicero to . . .
(*Nervous gulp.*)
                    . . . you know . . . all the rest . . .
Whom I could quote in full without abatement:
But I digress . . .

ELOMIRE (*Under his breath.*)
            O, what an understatement.

15

VALERE

> That meal! You must have gone to great expense!
> How cruel of me to keep you in suspense!
> *DID* I enjoy it? *WAS* the meal a hit?

(*A long pause.*)

> He turns them slowly, slowly on the spit.

(*Thinking he has tortured them, he expounds jubilantly.*)

> Be at your ease, my friends! I thought the meal
> Was excellent . . . if not . . . you know . . . "ideal."
> The vinaigrette: a touch acidic, no?
> And I prefer less runny *haricots;*

(*Singing this line.*)

> More butter in the velouté next time;
> And who, for heaven's sake, told you that lime
> Could substitute for lemon in soufflé . . . ?
> These tiny points aside, please let me pay
> My compliments to all your company,
> So generous in breaking bread with me
> (Albeit bread that was a wee bit stale);
> But I don't want to nitpick. Did I fail
> To mention what a charming group they *are?*
> Marquise-Therese! *She's* going to be a *star!*
> No, no . . . I'm *sure* of it! I *know* these things!
> So

(*Cupping his hands over imaginary breasts.*)

> "gifted," and I'm told she even sings!
> As for the others, well they tend to be
> A little too . . .

(*With a theatrical flourish.*)

> . . . "theatrical" for me . . .
> But, *darling,* otherwise, words can't *describe*
> My deep affection for your little tribe
> With whom, I do amuse myself to think,
> I shall be privileged to eat and drink

(As we have done this evening) every night!
That is, of course, assuming it's all right.
Am I mistaken? Stop me if I am . . .
But it seemed obvious to this old ham
That we had an immediate rapport!
Well-educated people I adore!
It's such a joy to know there's no confusion
When I, whose speech is peppered with allusion,
Refer to facts which few but scholars know:
Arcane, pedantic things like . . .
(*Nervous gulp.*)

                              . . . Cicero . . .
And . . . other larnèd oddments of that kind
(*Indicating himself.*)
(Which, to the truly cultivated mind,
Are common knowledge more than erudition . . .)
But I digress!
(*Slapping his own wrist.*)
                    O, damn me to perdition!
(*To himself.*)
"SHUT UP! SHUT UP! GIVE SOMEONE *ELSE* A
    CHANCE!"
(*He covers his mouth with his hands for a beat; then, unable to
contain himself for more than a second, he plows on.*)
I've had that said to me all over France . . .
All over Europe, if the truth be told:
To babble on completely uncontrolled
Is such a dreadful, *dreadful, DREADFUL* vice!
Me, I keep my sentences concise
And to the point . . . (well, nine times out of ten):
Yes, humanly, I falter now and then
And when I do, naïve enthusiasm
Incites a sort of logorrheic spasm:
A flood! I mean I don't come up for air!

And even though such episodes are rare
I babble on . . . you can't *imagine* how . . .
(My God! I'm almost doing it right now!)
NO, NO! I'M ONLY JOKING! NOT TO FEAR!
In fact, I'm far *more* guilty, so I hear,
Of smugly showing that "My lips are sealed . . ."
When *I'm* the leading expert in the field!
Of haughtily refusing to debate
When I could easily pontificate!
Instead, I turn away with icy mien
And look . . . intimidatingly serene:
As if—you know—the wisdom of the ages
Were silently inscribed upon the pages
Of some majestic tablet in my mind.
But I lay claim to nothing of the kind!
It's others who surround me with this lore;
Myself, I know I'm just a troubadour
With very few accomplishments to boast . . .
But, then, I'm more self-critical than most.
You think me *too* self-critical?! Alack,
Ten thousand *more* have launched the same attack!
(*Weighing the gem.*)
    That's awfully good: ". . . have launched the same attack!"
    "Ten thousand *more* have launched the same attack!"
(*With an oratorical flourish.*)
    "YOU THINK ME TOO SELF-CRITICAL?! ALACK,
    TEN THOUSAND *MORE* HAVE LAUNCHED THE
        SAME ATTACK!"
(*The gem is priceless! Thunderstruck.*)
    That's *VERY* close to genius, don't you think?
    If only . . .
(*Searching the room with his eyes.*)
            . . .YES! You *HAVE* a quill and ink!

(*Rushes to them.*)
　　I *would* be very grateful . . . may I please?
　　No time me to lose when lightning strikes the trees!
　　What did I say again? How did it go?
(*As he thinks, a rolling hand gesture to Elomire and Bejart.*)
　　(Keep talking . . . I'm still listening, you know:
　　This won't take me a second.) Yes, that's right!
(*Scribbling it down.*)
　　"Ten thousand more . . ." O, what a pure delight!
　　One must act quickly on one's inspirations
　　That they're preserved for future generations;
　　Behaving otherwise, it seems to me,
　　Ignores the grave responsibility
　　Imposed on us (for it's not ours to choose)
　　By . . . what?
(*Forms inverted commas with fingers.*)
　　　　　　　　. . . "the lyric gift" . . . "the tragic muse" . . .
　　I translate rudely from the words in Greek;
　　But any tongue sounds coarse when used to speak
　　Of something so ineffable and high.
　　Believe me, greater scriveners than I . . .
　　(All right, not "greater," "different": is that fair?)
　　Have racked their brains and torn out all their hair
　　In vain pursuit of some linguistic sign
　　By which mankind might utter the divine.
　　But what?—"afflatus"? "talent"?—"they're too crude,
　　And I'm a stickler for exactitude
　　Who chafes at clumsy, earthbound turns of phrase.
　　True eloquence rings out like godly praise:
　　There's no mistaking it, it just takes wing.
　　And, frankly, my own phrase, "THE WONDROUS *THING*,"
　　Seems loftiest . . . more lofty than the Greek!
　　O, HOW DISGRACEFUL! SLAP ME ON THE CHEEK!

WHAT HUBRIS! WHAT VULGARITY! WHAT NERVE!
NO, SLAP ME! SLAP ME! THAT'S WHAT I DESERVE!
What gall that *I,* the commonest of sods,
Presume to speak more finely than the gods!
Of *course* it may be true, that's not the *point!*
What's ugly is my choosing to anoint
Myself instead of giving you the chance.
No doubt you both must look at me askance
For such a gross, conceited indiscretion:
I pray it won't affect your good impression.
I'm so relieved to get *that* off my chest!
Now that we've put that nagging point to rest
I shall return to my initial theme,
Which is, in short, in fact, to wit, I deem
By way of introduction, SILENCE ALL:
(*A pause; then, with fatuous self-ridicule:*)
I HAVEN'T GOT A CLUE! BLANK AS A WALL!
NO, *REALLY.* I'M QUITE SENILE! IT'S NO JOKE!
MY HEAD IS LIKE AN EGG WITHOUT A YOLK!
AND DON'T THINK THIS IS JUST A WAY OF
     STALLING . . .
MY MIND HAS *BUCKLED*—ISN'T THAT
     APPALLING!?
THERE'S NOTHING BUT A SPACE BETWEEN MY
     EARS!
(*Change of tone.*)
One time I had amnesia in Algiers,
Where everyone is *black* who isn't *white!*
(But that's another tale . . .
(*With a wink.*)
                                    . . . some other night.)
Suffice to say I lost a whole December . . .
Or was it August? . . . Whoops, I don't remember!

You see how absentminded I can get!?
(*Acting both parts.*)
"WHEN DID YOU HAVE AMNESIA?" "I FORGET!"
(*He laughs, thrilled.*)
   Is that not comic genius? I must use it!
   I'd better write it down before I lose it!
   What did I say . . . again . . . about forgetting . . . ?
   O, CHRIST! I've just FORGOTTEN! How UPSETTING!
(*Shaking his fist at the sky.*)
   COME BACK! COME BACK, YOU TANTALIZING GEM!
   YOU TEASE! YOU BITCH! YOU FICKLE APOTHEGM!
   I GAVE YOU LIFE, AND NOW YOU FLY FROM ME!!
(*Apologetically.*)
   This happens with annoying frequency.
   It leads me to exclaim and caterwaul!
   Well! Now you've *really* seen me, *warts and all.*
(*Sudden, remembering.*)
   ALGERIAN AMNESIA!
(*Disappointed.*)
                     . . . no, that's wrong;
   O, never mind. More gems will come along;
   They always do. Now *where* was I? . . . Ah, yes:
   You've seen me in a state of stark undress,
   My warts exposed, my manner slightly odd:
   Well, what would you prefer? Some cheap façade
   Of blemishless perfection? Not from ME!
(*With a dismissive flick of the wrist.*)
   GO ELSEWHERE, YE WHO SEEK DISHONESTY;
   MY LIFE IS TRUTH, AND TRUTH MY GREATEST
      PASSION!
(*Dawning, a revelation.*)
   Good heavens, both of you are looking . . . ashen!
   I've been *too* honest, haven't I? But *when*?

WHY CAN'T I LEARN RESTRAINT LIKE OTHER
    MEN
INSTEAD OF SPILLING EVERYTHING AT ONCE?
(*Realizing.*)
    THE VINAIGRETTE! OF COURSE! I'M SUCH A
        DUNCE!
    HOW COULD I? Please accept my deep regret!
(*Putting on his best face.*)
    Look, I . . . *enjoy* . . . acidic . . . vinaigrette . . .
    It really makes me . . .
(*Exploding.*)
                        . . . GAG!!! . . . O!!! THERE, YOU SEE!
    I CANNOT LIE! *DAMN* MY INTEGRITY!
    I want to spare your feelings, yes I do;
    But that means saying things that aren't true,
    And of my meagre talents, that's not one.
    You see, I find that dwelling in the sun
    Of honest criticism brings more joy
    Than rotting in the darkness of some coy
    And sycophantic coterie of slaves.
    God! Eloquence comes over me in waves!
    Did you hear *that* one? We *all* raised our brows . . .
    Permit me . . . just the . . . tiniest of bows.
(*He bows.*)
    I thank you very much, you're far too kind;
    As Cicero has famously opined,
    "To hear one's peers applaud" . . . no! That's not it!
    You know the one . . . the *famous* one . . .
(*Exasperated.*)
                                    . . . O, shit!
    THE . . . ONE ABOUT . . . THE NOBLEMEN . . .
        COMPETING . . .
(*After a desperate pause.*)

Well, it's so famous it's not worth repeating.
The point is, when a man whom I revere
As highly as the famous ELOMIRE
(*Bows to him.*)
Should greet my stabs at wit with such approval,
I faint . . .
(*He slumps into a chair.*)
        . . . go fetch a cart for my removal!
It's true. No, absolutely, I'm not acting:
The lights grow dim, my pupils are contracting,
My knees go wobbly and my knuckles white,
I'm fading out. Good night, sweet world, good night . . .
(*Pause.*)
I'm totally unconscious now, I swear.
CAN ANYBODY HEAR ME? ARE YOU THERE?
Perhaps you think I'm being too dramatic;
But, really, I just droop when I'm ecstatic.
(*Snaps wide awake.*)
What *causes* that? Do either of you know?
A mystic in Gibraltar said I'm low
In some peculiar energy which lies
(For Leos, Capricorns, and Geminis)
Astride the cusp of Saturn's largest moon.
Well, *fine*. But does that tell me *why* I swoon?
Of course it doesn't! What a lot of bunk!
Believe in that stuff and you're really sunk!
Thank God our age has banished superstitions!
(Except for things like sprites and premonitions
Which I think almost certainly are true;
And voodoo dolls and fetishism, too,
Seem eminently credible to me—
And tarot cards and numerology
And cabalistic rituals and such . . .)

But that *astrology!* Now there's a *crutch*
That's used by *fools* with *half* a brain, or *none* . . .
(*Slaps his forehead, and is struck by a vision.*)
   WELL, SPEAK OF VISIONS! SOFT! I'M HAVING ONE!
(*He describes the vision, eyes half-closed.*)
   We're standing in a public square in Ghent
   (I think it's Ghent. It looks like Ghent.
(*"Let's just say it's Ghent."*)

                                        It's *Ghent.*)
   A scarlet banner reads: "A Great Event:
   AUGUSTE VALERE and ELOMIRE Present
   Their Brilliant Spectacle Hailed All Through France . . ."
   (And then the title:) "ROMAN . . . ," no, "ROMANCE
   OF . . .
(*Trying to make it out.*)
         . . . SOMETHING . . . SOMETHING . . ." Then:
            "The Town of Ghent."
(*Impatiently, triumphant.*)
   (I . . . *told* you it was Ghent.) Then there's a tent
   Around which throngs the very cream of Flanders!
(*Pauses to savor it.*)
   A rousing vision (though it almost panders—
   By promising *such* glory—to my dream
   That like two cloths sewn neatly at the seam
   Our talents might, someday, this world enfold).
   A fancy, merely? Or a truth foretold?
   Won't someone say *which* of the two he thinks it?
   No, no. Don't answer: that would only jinx it,
   And fate's a cranky governess gone gray
   (I coined that phrase in Zürich, by the way,
   When I was EIGHT YEARS OLD! YES, ONLY *EIGHT!*
   Precocious? *Try* PHENOMENAL! *Try* GREAT!
   The envy I provoked just knew no ends.

(*Rubbing his hands together.*)
   Imagine how despised I was by friends!
   My tutor fell in love with me, of course;
   He thought my every word a *tour-de-force!*
   I pitied him for doting on me so,
   But, then, I *was* a . . . *strapping* lad, you know . . .
   Don't look at me as if I led him on!
(*With increasing vehemence, obviously reliving some past tribunal.*)
   You'd blame a *child* before you'd blame a *don!!??*
   I ONLY DID WHAT I WAS TOLD TO DO!!
(*Full abreaction.*)
   LIES! I NEVER JUMPED HIM! THAT'S NOT TRUE!
(*Quickly regaining himself.*)
   Good heavens! Suddenly it all came back!
   So sorry . . . seems I wandered off the track . . .)
   Um . . . FATE! . . . that's right . . . a governess gone gray:
   She guides our every movement, and I'd say
   Her stewardship goes well beyond the grave;
   But if all things are fated, why be brave . . . ?
   Or noble? Or industrious? Or fair?
(*Schoolmasterish pause—"Do I see hands?"*)
   Is that all you can do? Just blankly stare?
   Don't tell me this has *never* crossed your mind!
   If not, you've waltzed through life completely blind!
   Such questions are essential, don't you see?
   A solid grounding in philosophy
   Is vital to a proper education!
   It never entered my imagination
   That you could lack this bare necessity . . .
   (The things I just *assume!* Well, foolish me!)
   At risk of sounding pompous or uncouth,
   I'd like to list some volumes from my youth
   Which might flesh out the . . .

(Expressing this as if it were the perfect metaphor, unconscious of the contradiction.)

                      . . . bald spots in your learning.
They've made *my* brain more subtle and discerning,
Those great Moroccan-bound and gold-tooled classics,
Which we—the prefects—in our flowing cassocks
Had tucked beneath our arms . . .

(Bringing fingers to nose.)

                      . . . I smell them, still!
Indulge me for a moment, if you will.
I recommend you read . . . no, I insist . . .
An author whom, *remarkably,* you've missed
Since he's the cornerstone of ancient thought
(And—if he's not already—*should* be taught
To every child in every French lycée:)
His name, of course, is . . . wait, it *starts* with "A" . . .
A *very* famous name, don't help me out;
I *know* it's "A"; it's "A" without a doubt.
It starts with "A." It's "A."

(Slight pause.)

                    Or *maybe* "D."

(Banishing the ambiguity.)

No, "A." It's "A." I'm sure it's "A."

(Another ambiguity.)

                    Or "P."
It *could* be "P."

(Slight pause.)

          Or "M."

(Now he's got it!)

                IT'S "M"! IT'S *"M"!!*

(Crestfallen.)

O, never mind. It could be all of them.
Well, this is terrible; I'm just appalled.

My God! He wrote the famous . . . WHAT'S-IT-CALLED,
COME ON! Don't leave me hanging on a limb!
You're acting like you've never heard of him,
And *everybody* has. He's world-renowned!
His writings turned philosophy around
By altering the then-prevailing view—
That what is real is really falsely true—
To what is true is really falsely real . . .
(*A perplexed squint; then, resuming:*)
    Well, *either* way, it's BRILLIANT! Don't you feel?
And I'm not saying I don't see the *holes;*
Still, it's a stunning glimpse into our souls
No matter *how* you slice it, Q.E.D.
(He won a prize for it . . . deservedly.)
But who remembers prizes? It's the *FAME!*
The names of brilliant men like . . . what's-his-name . . .
Can never be forgotten: *that's* the PRIZE!
Such men live on when everybody dies!
They *laugh* at famine, pestilence, and drought:
And isn't that what life is all about?
(*Deep breath, as a signal of summation.*)
    In any case, we've really talked a streak!
Aren't you exhausted? Me? I'm feeling WEAK!!
We've hardly met, and yet you're like my brother
(*Playfully sparring.*)
    The way we banter and play off each other.
We've chatted, chortled, changed our points of view,
We've laughed a little, cried a little, too,
We've had some hills, some valleys and plateaus,
We've traded secrets, quipped in cryptic prose,
We've dropped our guards, we've learned to give a damn!
We've proudly cried, "Yes! This is who I am!"
We've said it all, and then . . . found more to say;

In short, we've, quote, "just talked the night away."
And surely that's a sign, at least to me,
That this—our partnership—was *meant* to be!
For though we're strangers (in a narrow sense),
In several ways more striking and intense—
Our gift for words, our love of the sublime—
We've known each other since the dawn of time!
(*Weighing the gem.*)
    O, *very* pretty: ". . . since the dawn of time!"
(*With an oratorical flourish.*)
    "WE'VE KNOWN EACH OTHER SINCE THE
    DAWN OF TIME!"
(*Concluding, slapping hands together.*)
    Well, good! That's all I really planned to *say,*
    Except to thank you for a fine soirée
(*Treading on eggshells, as if he's saying it for the first time.*)
    Spoiled only by acidic vinaigrette,
(*Hearing a bell.*)
    But then I've said that . . . more than once, I'll bet!
    My head is in the clouds: pay no attention!
    It's off in some ethereal dimension
    Where worldly thoughts not instantly deleted
    Are roundly and mechanically repeated
    As if to pacify the earth below.
    How galling it must be for you to know
    That even as we speak, within my mind
    I might be off in some place more refined—
    That even though I'm present by convention,
    You may not really have my full attention . . .
    I don't mean *you specifically,* dear friend!
    Good heavens! Would I dare to condescend
    To someone as illustrious as you!?
    I mean, of course, the *common* people who
    Would stoop to kiss my hem they so adore me:

Forgive them, Lord! They know not how they bore me
With idle chatter of their simple ways!
I'm sorry, but my eyes begin to glaze
And it's a chore to keep myself awake
When someone's telling me about a rake
Or if his soil will yield a healthy grape.
I smile and nod, but silently escape
To knowledgeable regions in my dome
More crowded than a Roman hippodrome!
I have, for instance (and it's not a fluke)
Verbatim recall of the Pentateuch!
Incredible? It's *true!* Just watch and see:
From Genesis to Deuteronomy
I now recite the Scriptures, LEARNED BY HEART!!:
"IN THE BEGINNING . . ."
(*Squinting, trying to remember more.*)
                                          . . . yes, well that's the start;
(*Moving right along.*)
     It goes on just like that till Moses dies.
     A superhuman task to memorize?
     Not really. It's so *good,* it rather *stuck* . . .
(*To himself.*)
     But I digress! SHUT UP, YOU STUPID CLUCK,
     AND LET *THESE* GENTLE PEOPLE TALK A MITE!
(*Dramatically extending handkerchief.*)
     Look, gag me with this handkerchief, all right?
     I know that sounds extreme, and I'm a stranger,
     But trust me: you are in the gravest danger!
     For my digressions (left unchecked) can reach
     The vast proportions of a major speech;
     And you have no *idea* how close I am
     To just that sort of frantic dithyramb!
     So why not spare yourselves a living hell
     And gag me!

(He touches the handkerchief to his mouth, snapping it away long enough to finish the line; he continues to do so, the handkerchief hovering.)

GAG ME! TIE ME UP, AS WELL!
RESTRAIN ME! DISCIPLINE ME! HOLD ME BACK!
HUMILIATE ME! GIVE THE WHIP A CRACK!
DISGRACE ME: MAKE ME BARK AND WEAR A DRESS
AND LICK THE FILTHY FLOOR WHEN I DIGRESS!
But in the meantime, gagged I *should* remain:
It's better that way, no? It's such a sane
And healthy way to curb my domination.
I find it a *complete* abomination
(No matter how distinguished one might be)
When every word is "ME ME ME ME ME."
ME, I'm far too interested in others;
And frankly, friends, were I to have my "druthers"
I'd utter not a peep for weeks untold,
Preferring to . . . absorb the manifold
Of human speech: the "babel" of the masses.
Just stop and *listen* to the lower classes!
You'll have an education when you're done
That rivals twenty years at the Sorbonne!
For in their mindless grunts, the bourgeoisie
Express what I call "wise stupidity."
But no one listens anymore, I fear,
And when I die, so too will disappear
That subtle art, whose practice now grows faint.
And I'm not saying I'm some stained-glass saint
Who *always* listens. Always? No, indeed!
My God! I'm human! Cut me and I bleed!
It's simply that, as far as mortals go,
I'm sensitive (and some say too much so)
To any nuance in a conversation

30

Which *might, PERHAPS,* suggest my domination.
Thus, in mid-sentence often I just cease . . .
(Despite the countless times I've held my peace
When, in the end, I might as well have chattered
Since only *I* said anything that mattered!
I know that sounds repulsive, but it's true.)
The point is, this is something that I do
Against all logic; so don't be distraught
If, in the middle of a brilliant thought,
I stop like this . . .
(*Freezes; continues.*)
                    . . . depriving you of more;
Or if, commanding reverence from the floor
For awesome skills debating pro *or* con,
I simply stop like this . . .
(*Freezes; continues.*)
                    . . . and don't go on!
A trifle strange, *n'est-ce pas?* But, if you please,
Ask any of my many devotees:
They'll tell you that this quirk (at first appearing)
In time becomes . . .
(*Freezes; continues.*)
                    . . . incredibly endearing!
(*Guffaw of self-delight.*)
To *me* it seems *obnoxious,* heaven knows;
But most say it's a charming trait that grows
More sweet with each encounter! TELL ME WHY!
I just don't see it . . . but: then who am I?
At any rate, THE GAG! OF COURSE! Let me:
Observe with what profound simplicity
It does the job. I think you'll be surprised.
VOILÀ!

(*He stuffs the gag into his mouth, then continues, half-audibly.*)
        Now isn't this more civilized!
I'm silenced and I think we're *all* relieved!
We've nipped me in the bud, and thus retrieved
The limelight for our precious Elomire.
Speak on, my friend! This player longs to hear
If in posterity you'll deign to share
Your splendid name with one AUGUSTE VALERE!
Please answer lest I talk you both to death:
(*Removes the gag.*)
  I wait on your reply with bated breath.

*Valere stuffs the gag back into his mouth, assumes a theatrical pose,
and: blackout. Lights come up quickly. Silence. A moment passes.
Elomire and Bejart circle the frozen Valere, reaching out to touch him
and jerking their fingers back. Finally, Elomire faces him directly.*

BEJART
                        Do you think he's ill?

ELOMIRE
  O, yes.

BEJART
      Then we should . . .

ELOMIRE
               No, Bejart! Be still!
Let's use this brief caesura while we can!
MONSIEUR VALERE: You seem to be a man
In love with words, a *true* aficionado . . .

VALERE
  I'm *that* transparent!?

ELOMIRE
            Yes . . .

VALERE

But it's bravado!
Don't let my gift—"the silver tongue"—deceive you;
I'm *really* foolish . . .

BEJART

Yes, we both believe you. ⌉

ELOMIRE

Yes, we both believe you. ⌋

VALERE (*Bowing.*)
You're gentle . . .

ELOMIRE

Nonetheless it's very clear
That language is a thing which you hold dear . . .

VALERE
Too mild! Too mild! It's, more than dear to me!
I liken syntax to morality—
Its laws inviolate in such a way
That damned is he who dares to disobey!
Diction, like aesthetics, is more free:
It's where we show our creativity
By choosing metaphors and ways of speech—
I'd say "the shell-crushed strand"; you'd say "the beach."
Semantics is like . . . (hang on . . . let me see . . .
I've *used* aesthetics and morality . . .)
Semantics is like . . . SWIMMING! . . . (no, that's bad!
O, DAMMIT! DAMMIT! DAMN, I thought I had
A brilliant speech developing! *DOMMAGE!*)
Well . . . back to our exciting persiflage . . .
(*Deep inhale, eyes cross.*)
Where were we . . . ?

33

ELOMIRE

Language.

VALERE

Gasp! My greatest passion!

ELOMIRE

But . . .

VALERE

Please no buts! It *can't* go out of fashion!
Verbobos are as ancient as the birds!

ELOMIRE

Verbobos?

VALERE

Yes.

ELOMIRE

What's that?

VALERE

My word for "words."

ELOMIRE

Your word for "words"?

VALERE

Correct.

ELOMIRE

Why?

VALERE

"Words" sounds dreary;
"VERBOBOS." I prefer it. It's more . . . cheery!
"VERBOBOS"! Say it! COME ON, *EVERYONE!*

34

BEJART
Verbobos.

ELOMIRE (*Wheeling on Bejart.*)
Shut up.

VALERE

THERE! YOU SEE!? IT'S FUN!!

ELOMIRE
You make up words?

VALERE

Why, yes. Is it a crime?

ELOMIRE
You can't just do that . . .

VALERE

Do it *all the time!*
For instance . . .
(*Searching the room with his eyes.*)
. . . "CHAIR": now there's a pallid noun!
Well, I refuse to say it sitting down!
"FRANCESCA" is the word I use instead;
Or "TABLE": there's a word that's good as dead!
One might say "escritoire" but that's too frilly,
And "desklike thing" sounds just a little silly,
So I say *"CARABOOMBA"* . . . which, you see,
Endows the "TABLE" with nobility.
(*Valere, demonstrating, takes the quill and scrawls the words on the wall, as if writing on a blackboard; Elomire and Bejart stare in shock and disbelief.*)
"FRANCESCA CARABOOMBA": most expressive!
It really is amazingly impressive
How clearly the *verbobos* I invent
Outshine (and do not *simply* supplement)

35

The ancient phonemes of our mother tongue.
But that's a "*flecund*" point which you must "*drung*" . . .

ELOMIRE
Monsieur Valere: I *hate* to interrupt . . .

VALERE
I know the feeling . . .

ELOMIRE
But I'll be abrupt,
And speak to you directly if I can:
You know as well as I that you're a man
Whose talents and abilities would be
Much better served in some . . . fraternity . . .

BEJART
A guild, perhaps . . .

ELOMIRE
Precisely! In some GUILD,
Where you would feel more happy and fulfilled
Than you could ever feel by staying here . . .

Valere's attention has wandered to Bejart's humpback, which he notices for the first time.

VALERE (*To Bejart.*)
Is that a humpback?

BEJART
Yes.

VALERE
O, DEAR DEAR DEAR!
How *deeply* nauseating! How *unsightly!*
There's just no way of putting this politely!
(*Speaking loudly to Bejart as if he were deaf.*)

YOU MAKE ME ILL; I'M SURE YOU
   UNDERSTAND!
(*Examining the hump.*)
   Perhaps if I could . . . touch it with my hand—
   You know—for luck . . .
(*As Valere reaches out to touch the hump, Bejart pulls away in
disgust.*)
                         . . . all right then, BE that way!
   MY GOD! We're all so *sensitive* today!

ELOMIRE
   DID YOU JUST HEAR ME?

VALERE
                        HOW WAS *I* TO KNOW!??
   At dinner, hunched above his escargots
   He seemed ill-mannered merely, not contorted;
   But clearly my impression was distorted . . .

BEJART
   How dare you!

VALERE
            No, I think it's *good!* I *DO!*
(*Trying to envision a potential hump on the other side.*)
   Too bad there can't be even *more* of you!
   I'm thrown, that's all; but isn't that expected?
   I've seen you act, but never once detected
   Until this moment, standing in this room,
   That you were . . . *ripped untimely from the womb!*
   Now *why* is that?

BEJART
            I don't know *what* to say . . .

VALERE (*Wheeling on Elomire; a revelation.*)
   YOU WRITE A HUMPBACK INTO EVERY PLAY!

ELOMIRE

Monsieur Valere . . . !

VALERE

                Of course! That's it! It's *true!*
(*Turning to Bejart.*)
    The reason that I'd never noticed you
    Were cruelly maimed is that you play the roles
    Of humpbacked beggars, philistines, and trolls
    Which Elomire specifically designed
    With your misshapen body in his mind!

BEJART

You're MAD . . . !

VALERE

          You mean I'm RIGHT . . . !

BEJART

                     I mean you're MAD . . . !

VALERE

You mean I'm *RIGHT!!*

BEJART

          You're *MAD!!*

VALERE

               I'm *RIGHT!!*

ELOMIRE

                   I'VE HAD
ENOUGH! ENOUGH! ENOUGH OF THIS . . . !

VALERE

                    ME TOO!
(*Pause.*)
    Enough of what, exactly, though . . . ?

ELOMIRE

                        . . . of YOU!!

VALERE

I'm sorry?

ELOMIRE

        YOU! AND LET THERE BE NO DOUBT!

VALERE

I hear you, darling, you don't have to shout . . .

ELOMIRE

O, yes I do! And let me tell you why:
I've listened to you speak . . . no, "speechify"
For what seems like a century in hell:
Enough, I think, to know you all too well—
Or well enough to wish I didn't know you . . . !

VALERE

You lost me there . . .

ELOMIRE

                O, yes? Then let me show you
In very *basic* language if I may . . .

BEJART

Don't be a fool . . .

ELOMIRE

          I'M GOING TO HAVE MY SAY!

BEJART

THE WRIT!

ELOMIRE

      I KNOW!

BEJART

WELL, IF YOU KNOW, DESIST!!

VALERE

(Good heavens! Is there something that I missed?)

BEJART

OUR HANDS ARE TIED!!

ELOMIRE

NOT MINE!! NOT
ANYMORE!!

BEJART

THEN PICK HIM UP AND THROW HIM OUT THE
DOOR!!

ELOMIRE

I PLAN TO!!

BEJART

IF THAT'S SO WE'RE FINISHED HERE!!
Prince Conti's writ is absolutely clear,
And I, for one, am not, like you, prepared
To risk what we've achieved . . .

ELOMIRE

Because you're *scared!*

BEJART

Because I'm *CAUTIOUS!*

ELOMIRE

God! That's even WORSE!

VALERE

(It's like a drama—only not in verse . . .)

BEJART

What shame is there in safety? What disgrace?
In middle age are you prepared to face
What we, the decade past, have struggled through?
And I'm not thinking just of me and you—
Marquise-Therese . . .

VALERE

(Now there's a "gifted" wench!)

BEJART

. . . De Brie, and Catherine, whom you would wrench
Away from all the comforts of this "home"—
Again to sleep in haylofts and to roam
From burg to parish living hand-to-mouth!
Remember how they booed us in the south?

VALERE

(The *south?* The *SOUTH?* Why, in the *SOUTH* they *cheer*
me!)

BEJART

I just don't think it's worth it, do you hear me?

VALERE

(And I don't mean applause, I mean *OVATIONS . . .!*)

BEJART

Why jeopardize this best of situations
For lack of patience? Life is compromise!
We learn to live with that which we despise
In cases where the benefits outweigh
Whatever penance we are forced to pay.
Forbearance is a virtue . . .

ELOMIRE

In a *saint!*

But men who would endure without complaint
An insult to preserve some meagre gain
Deserve not only pity but disdain.

VALERE

(I side with *him!*)

BEJART

                That's very well to *say,*
But who on earth can ever live that way?
We're hypocritical, by definition . . .

VALERE

(I think he's swaying me to *his* position . . .)

BEJART

We're all more guilty than we'd dare admit
Of daily bending principles to fit
Ignoble appetites, which I contend
Is nobler than deciding *not* to bend
One's principles despite the likelihood
That they may finally do more harm than good.

VALERE

(Well, that's what *I* would say . . .)

ELOMIRE

                         I disagree!
To suffer for one's principles, to me
Seems nobler than to prosper from their lack.

VALERE

(That's true. Good point . . .)

BEJART

                    It's not so white and black!
I'm arguing for something in between . . .

VALERE

(He's right, you know . . .)

ELOMIRE

By which, of course, you mean
You advocate a plan that when applied
Insures that everyone's dissatisfied.

VALERE

(O, that's *so* true. I'm on *your* side again!)

ELOMIRE

Our lives are governed by such *foolish* men!
And we're to blame because, misguidedly,
We hold to the belief that it would be
More difficult to keep a fool at bay
Than simply just to . . . let him have his way.
At first this seems a harmless compromise,
But hot air has the tendency to rise
Until it finally overwhelms your life!
That's when a fool will *really* twist the knife—
When he gets power! And he always does!
Then grit your teeth and swallow hard because
He'll mock you every day with your mistake
Of underestimating what a snake
A fool can be if given half a chance!
He'll treat you like the footman at a dance
And revel, with Mephistophelean glee,
In how his presence shall, eternally,
Evoke, with sharp refrains of ridicule,
The cutting truth that *you've* been made the fool!!
But wait—you're really *more* the fool than he,
Because no simple fool could ever be
So foolish to neglect the simple rule
That only fools will tolerate a fool!

43

Tonight was just a warning—DID YOU HEAR HIM!!??
And sitting silently because we fear him
Is no solution in the grander scheme.
He won't just disappear like some bad dream:
We're going to have to face this matter squarely!

BEJART
I really think you're acting most unfairly!

ELOMIRE
Unfairly? How?

BEJART
     I'm *so* embarrassed!

ELOMIRE
          Why?
Because of *me?*

BEJART
     You know as well as I!

ELOMIRE
You mean because I'm showing him our hand?
I promise you, he doesn't understand.
They never do! The foolish aren't that wise!

BEJART (*He pivots to Valere.*)
Monsieur Valere: I must apologize
For this disgraceful spectacle . . .

ELOMIRE
       . . . *disgrace!?*

BEJART
AND DAMAGING!

ELOMIRE
     But how is that the case?

44

I promise you our words went unattended!
Valere, I ask you: have you been offended
By anything I've said?

VALERE

                    Me? Heavens, no!
I'm on *your* side in this, I *told* you so!
(*Half taking Elomire aside, speaking in a stage whisper.*)
    (You're such a better speaker than *that* chap!
(*Indicating Bejart's humpback with a wink.*)
    But then . . . of course . . . he's got a handicap.)
    No, why on earth should I have felt abused!!??
    I'm *flattered* by that "M"-word that you used!
    "MERISTORELEAN" was it . . . ?

ELOMIRE (*To Bejart.*)

                              There, you see?

VALERE

    I'm touched you'd think it might apply to *me!*
    "He's so MERISTO—" what? . . .

ELOMIRE

                    Mephistophelean.

VALERE

    MERISTORELEAN! YES! MERISTORELEAN!
    "He's so *MERISTORELEAN!*" . . .

ELOMIRE (*To Bejart.*)

                              There, you see?
    Completely blinded by his vanity.

Cross-talk as Valere poses, trying on the word "Meristorelean," and Elomire continues to lecture to Bejart. We should hear Elomire clearly, Valere as background.

ELOMIRE

And I assure you that it
wouldn't matter
If I just served it to
him on a platter!
The bluntest terms
would float beyond
his ken;
I'm telling you: I *know*
these kind of men!
You don't believe me?
Watch! I'll demon-
strate:
Monsieur Valere: permit
me to restate . . .

VALERE

He's so MERISTORELEAN
when he walks!
He's so MERISTORELEAN
when he talks!
He's so MERISTORELEAN
when he prays!
I envy his MERISTORELEAN
ways!
MERISTORELEAN! *So*
MERISTORELEAN!
MERISTORELEAN! *So*
MERISTORELEAN! . . .

ELOMIRE

MONSIEUR VALERE! I need your full attention!
I wonder: might I have the chance to mention
In more specific terms (if that's all right)
My own impressions of our chat tonight?

VALERE

O, *be* specific! YES! *Please* do! I'm *rapt!*

ELOMIRE

Well, good . . . !

BEJART (*To Elomire.*)

You know, you really should be slapped!

VALERE

But let me sit in this

VALERE

FRANCESCA.

46

ELOMIRE

FRANCESCA.

VALERE

Wait!
O, good idea! Now I can concentrate!

He looks ostentatiously riveted.

ELOMIRE

I'm glad you're concentrating. Listen closely:
You've said a lot tonight and said it grossly.
In fact . . . I've been appalled by every word!
I find your views on life and art absurd,
And yet one hardly notices above
The mountain of your towering self-love!
Your ignorance is even more colossal—
Your brain is like some prehistoric fossil:
It must have died ten thousand years ago!
But on and on and on and on you go
As if you were the fount of human learning!
And selfishly, contemptuously spurning
The moves that others make to interject,
You act as if you're one of "the elect"
Whom God appoints like Jesus Christ our Savior!
It really is contemptible behavior
Whose only saving grace (if one there be)
Is in the unintended comedy
Arising from your weightiest pronouncements!
You seem to feel you have to make announcements
Instead of speaking in a normal tone;
But by your orotund and overblown
And hectoringly pompous presentation,
You simply magnify the desolation,
The vast aridity within your soul!

47

In short, I think you're just a gaping hole—
A talentless, obnoxious pile of goo!
I don't want anything to do with you!
I can't imagine anyone who would!
And if it makes me better understood
To summarize in thirty words or less,
I'd say you have the power to depress
With every single syllable you speak,
With every monologue that takes a week,
And every self-adoring witticism! . . .

VALERE

Well, do you mean this as a *criticism?*

ELOMIRE (*Throws up his hands; to Bejart.*)
I rest my case.

VALERE

              And when you say "depress"
Do you mean *bad* "depress" or *good* "depress"?
And "overblown's" defined exactly *how?*

ELOMIRE

There, Bejart? Do you believe me *now?*

VALERE

Would it be overreaching to request
That you write down, so that I might digest
At greater length, and also at my leisure,
The comments you just made, which I shall treasure!

BEJART

I'm flabbergasted! I don't understand!
I've never heard a more perverse demand!
Why would you want them written down?

VALERE

To read them.

BEJART

Well, yes. Of course. But why?

VALERE

I'm going to need them.

BEJART

But *why?*

VALERE

Because I'm anxious to *improve!*
Is that so strange, my wanting to remove
The flaws from my persona? Surely not!
I loathe a blemish! I despise a spot!
Perfection is the goal towards which I strive
(For me, that's what it means to be alive)
And, hence, I'm grateful for a shrewd critique:
It keeps my talent honest, so to speak!
We of the theatre share that common view—
The criticisms of the things we do
Inspire our interest, not our hurt or rage:
We know it's part of "being on the stage"
To have oneself assessed at every turn,
And thus we show a willingness to learn
From judgments which might wound another man.
I much prefer to any drooling fan
A critic who will SLICE me into parts!
GOD *LOVE* THE CRITICS! *BLESS* THEIR PICKY
    HEARTS!
Precisely, and in no uncertain terms,
They halve the apple, showing us our worms.
(*Staggering slightly.*)
(My God, that was a *brilliant* illustration!)

49

(Regaining himself.)
    Don't get me wrong: to hear some dissertation
    On all one's failings gives a twinge, of course:
    It smarts when someone knocks you off your horse—
    That's true for anybody, I should think!
    But climbing on again in half a wink
    And knowing that you're better for the spill
    Instructs us that it's love and not ill will
    That motivates a critical assault.
    You've *honored* me tonight by finding fault!
    Which doesn't mean I don't feel vaguely crushed . . .
    I do! I'm *bruised!* But who would not have blushed
    To hear himself discussed so centrally?
    "My God," I thought, "are they denouncing *me,*
    These men of such *distinction* and *renown!?*
    How thrilling *I'm* the one they're tearing down!!
    What joy that Elomire, whom people say
    Is destined to become the next Corneille,
    Should slander *me* in such a public forum!"
    And, by the way, it isn't just decorum
    Which prompts me to express my awe of you;
    Your plays, I think, show genius, and a few
    (Like *Mandarin*) I've seen five times or more.
    Now there's a play that really made me roar!
    I haven't laughed so hard in years and years!

ELOMIRE
    It was a tragedy.

VALERE
                But through my *tears*
    The laughter seemed more painful . . . (O MY GOD!
    WELL, OPEN MOUTH, INSERT THY FOOT, YOU
    CLOD!

COULD THAT HAVE BEEN MORE AWKWARD?
SURELY NOT!
(*Fanning himself.*)
I'M SO EMBARRASSED! WHEW! MY FACE IS HOT!)
Forgive me, Elomire. What can I say?
I'm sure it was a very solemn play.
But why, then, did *I* find it such a hoot?
The crippled peasant boy who played the flute:
Hysterical! I mean I was delirious!
I must have nodded off when it got serious!
Are you quite sure it was a tragedy?

Bejart intervenes sternly, extending his hand to Valere.

BEJART
It's time to say good night, it seems to me.

ELOMIRE
No no, Bejart: It's time to say good-*bye!*

BEJART
That's not an option!

ELOMIRE
Why?

BEJART
I've *told* you why!

Enter Dorine, the serving maid. She speaks in a high-pitched falsetto.

ELOMIRE
Then . . .

DORINE
BLUE!

BEJART
Hello?

ELOMIRE

Who's there?

VALERE

Your maid.

ELOMIRE

Ah, yes!

Come in, Dorine.
(*She descends the step.*)

Be careful with your dress.

DORINE

BLUE!

ELOMIRE

Good girl. Now what's the matter, dear?

DORINE

BLUE!

ELOMIRE

Yes, blue; blue *what?*

DORINE

BLUE!!

ELOMIRE

"Blue" is clear;

Blue what, though!?

DORINE

BLUE!!

ELOMIRE

Blue *what!?* Blue *what!?*
(*He sighs deeply, as if overwhelmed by the tedium of having to go through something which he has endured many times before; rolling his eyes.*)

$$\text{Blue . . . SKIES?}$$

(*Dorine shakes her head no.*)
   Blue . . . MOON?
(*Dorine shakes her head no.*)
      Blue . . . CHEESE?

Dorine shakes her head no.

VALERE (*To Bejart.*)

$$\text{What's going on!?}$$

ELOMIRE

$$\text{Blue . . . EYES?}$$

Dorine shakes her head no.

VALERE (*To Bejart.*)
   Is this some sort of guessing game she plays?

BEJART
   No, no. It's just an adolescent phase . . .

ELOMIRE
   Blue . . . *WHAT*, DORINE!? This drives me up the wall!!

He pinches the bridge of his nose and continues to search his mind in irritation.

VALERE (*To Bejart.*)
   What sort of phase?

BEJART

$$\text{She never speaks at all}$$
   Except in monosyllables like . . .

DORINE

$$\text{BLUE!!}$$

BEJART

. . . or words which rhyme to that effect like "two"
Or "do" or "shoe": don't ask me to explain;
These adolescent phases are insane!

VALERE

She only speaks in words which rhyme with "do"?

BEJART

That's right.

VALERE (*Gravely.*)

What are our children coming to?
(*Back to Bejart.*)
How long has this been going on?

BEJART

For weeks!

VALERE

But can you understand her when she speaks?

BEJART

Well, yes and no: it takes some time, you see.

Dorine indicates her left wrist as if playing a game of charades.

ELOMIRE

Blue . . . what? Blue what? Blue WRIST!?

BEJART

Eventually
She gets her point across . . .

ELOMIRE

Blue WRIST!? Blue . . .

Dorine slashes her left wrist with her right hand.

54

DORINE (*Emphatically.*)

                                        BLUE!!

VALERE
  Now what's she doing?

BEJART
                        Giving us a clue.

Dorine is slashing at her wrist emphatically.

ELOMIRE
  You're slashing at your wrist.
  (*Dorine nods vigorously.*)
                        Blue SLASH?
  (*Dorine shakes her head no, impatiently trying to get someone to say*
  "blood.")
                                        Blue . . . CUT!?
  (*Dorine continues her miming.*)
  O, I don't know, Dorine! Blue WHAT!? Blue WHAT!?

Dorine mimes an act of hara-kiri, at the end of which her internal
organs figuratively spill out onto the floor.

VALERE
  Blue blood.

Dorine snaps her fingers and points to Valere, giving an "On the
nose: he got it!"

ELOMIRE
                        Blue *blood?*
  (*She nods vigorously, still pointing at Valere, jumping up and down.*)
                        That's it? You mean he's right?

More of the same from Dorine; Valere throws up his arms victoriously,
as if acknowledging the adulation of a large crowd.

VALERE
Well! This is turning out to be my night!
I wasn't even trying and I won
(Which makes the victory that much more fun!!).

ELOMIRE
But what does "blue blood" signify?

BEJART
                                        To me
It would imply the aristocracy . . .

ELOMIRE
Or royalty, perhaps . . .

Dorine points excitedly.

BEJART
                    Ah, yes! That's true!

Dorine is pointing, nodding; "royalty" is correct! Cross-talk as Valere presses on in his own direction.

ELOMIRE
That's *it,* Dorine? That's what you meant by BLUE??⌉

DORINE
                                        BLUE!!

VALERE
The answer came to me out of the   BLUE!! ⌋

VALERE
I realize now I should have warned you, though,
That I'm an ace as far as word games go . . .

ELOMIRE (*Nailing it down.*)
So "royalty," Dorine, would be correct?

Dorine nods vigorously.

VALERE
One Easter, while performing near Utrecht

VALERE
(A dreary, dreary backwash of a town) . . .

ELOMIRE (*To Bejart.*)
It's "royalty": at least we've nailed *that* down . . .

BEJART
But what's significant about the crown?

VALERE
. . . I fell into a local Flemish game . . .

ELOMIRE
Indeed, Dorine!

VALERE
. . . "BAMBOOZLE" was its name . . .

ELOMIRE
Just why is "royalty" so apropos?

VALERE
. . . Whose rules—MY GOD!—I didn't even know . . .

BEJART
Speak up, my girl!

VALERE
. . . But somehow I kept winning!

DORINE
NEW!

BEJART
New WHAT?

ELOMIRE

New *WHAT?*

DORINE

NEW!

ELOMIRE

New . . . BEGINNING!?

Shaking her head no, Dorine cradles an imaginary baby in her arms; and Valere responds to Elomire as if "BEGINNING" referred to the story that he has been telling.

VALERE

BEGINNING? . . . *Yes:* I'd never played before!

ELOMIRE (*Responding to Dorine's pantomime.*)
New . . . BORN??

Dorine shakes her head no.

VALERE

That's why, when tallying the score,

VALERE	**BEJART**
I gasped and turned a thousand shades of red To find the victor's garland on my head . . .	New CHILD?? New INFANT? What else could it be??
	ELOMIRE
	Dorine, you're really irritating me!!

ELOMIRE (*Continuing; to Bejart.*)
She tries my patience!

VALERE

. . . *And* I won a prize . . . !!

ELOMIRE
I'm fed up with these single-word replies!!

VALERE
. . . A silver goblet . . . !!

DORINE (*Still cradling an imaginary baby.*)
NEW!!

ELOMIRE
Enough, Dorine!!
Now act your age and tell me what you mean!!

BEJART
New BABY, maybe?

Dorine shakes her head no.

VALERE
. . . no no no, it's *pewter* . . .

ELOMIRE
If she goes on like this I'm going to shoot her!

BEJART
New BIRTH?

Dorine shakes her head no.

VALERE
. . . or . . .

BEJART
New ARRIVAL?

Dorine excitedly nods, jumps up and down, and gives the "On the nose" signal.

VALERE
. . . is it copper . . . ?

BEJART

ARRIVAL?? New *ARRIVAL??*

Dorine is nodding vigorously.

ELOMIRE

                              Can't we stop her?

VALERE

. . . Or is it brass . . . ?

BEJART

                    No need to, Elomire:
The answer's "new ARRIVAL," did you hear?

VALERE

. . . In any case, I keep it on display . . .

ELOMIRE

That's *it*, Dorine? That's what you meant to say?

Dorine nods vigorously.

VALERE

. . . and clutch it to my breast when I'm in bed . . .

Bejart is squinting, trying to piece it together.

BEJART

Dorine, repeat the first word that you said!

VALERE

. . . which isn't . . .

DORINE

          BLUE!

BEJART

                Which means

VALERE

. . . because I'm proud . . .

BEJART

That royalty is

DORINE

NEW!

VALERE

. . . it's that I vowed
To guard that chalice with my life and limb!

BEJART (*A solution dawning.*)

My God! Of course! It must refer to him!

ELOMIRE

My God of course it must refer to *whom?*

VALERE

. . . One time I had it stolen from my room . . .

BEJART

PRINCE CONTI'S HERE!

ELOMIRE

PRINCE *CONTI?*

DORINE

TRUE!!

VALERE

. . . In shock . . .

ELOMIRE

But why?

BEJART

Because

VALERE

          . . . I checked behind the clock . . .

BEJART (*Emphasizing the words as if to say, "It's obvious."*)
A *new ARRIVAL!* Blue for *ROYALTY!*

VALERE
  . . . And lo! . . .

ELOMIRE

       Good heavens!

DORINE

             TRUE!!

ELOMIRE

                 You're right!

VALERE

                      . . . I see
My trophy wedged against the wall! . . .

ELOMIRE

                  DORINE!
PRINCE CONTI'S HERE RIGHT NOW? *THAT'S*
WHAT YOU MEAN!?

Dorine nods vigorously.

VALERE
  . . . It must have slipped . . .

ELOMIRE

            WELL, SEND HIM IN!

VALERE

                    . . . My cup
Had, therefore, *not* been stolen . . .

ELOMIRE

HURRY UP!

VALERE

And I was *so* relieved at simply knowing
That it was mine again . . .
(*Seeing Dorine leaving*)

WAIT! WHERE'S SHE GOING?

(*She turns around.*)
Before you leave . . . one question please, Dorine:
How old are you, dear?

DORINE

TWO!

BEJART (*Translating.*)

She's seventeen.

ELOMIRE

NOW RUN ALONG!

Exit Dorine.

VALERE

Then why did she say "two"?

BEJART

I thought I just explained that quirk to you.

VALERE

Ah, yes! Indeed! The adolescent phase!
I must admit, I felt my eyebrows raise
When she said two years old! I was astounded!
I thought, "My God! Just 'two,' and so well . . .
(*Cupping his hands over his chest like breasts.*)

. . . rounded!"

ELOMIRE (*To Bejart, reproving.*)
You didn't tell me he was coming here!

BEJART

Because I didn't know it, Elomire:
They handed me this writ, that's all I knew!

VALERE

Who's coming here?

BEJART

Prince Conti.

VALERE

Is that true??

(*Bejart nods.*)
Good Lord! Am I presentable? MY TEETH!!—
(*Opening his mouth.*)
Do they look crooked? Is there dirt beneath
(*Holding out his hands.*)
My fingernails? My doublet—does it smell?
I've shown that I take criticism well,
So *please* be brutal, *heap* me with abuse!
Assume that I'm exceedingly obtuse . . .

ELOMIRE

(O, what a leap of the imagination!)

Servants and Dorine rush in and begin to prepare the room for Prince Conti's entrance.

BEJART (*To Elomire.*)
It's not the time to force a confrontation!
The Prince might hear us . . .

ELOMIRE

Which would be ideal!
Well, after all, he did arrange this meal
Intending (so you led me to believe
Before you plucked that writ out of your sleeve)

To introduce us to a candidate
Whom we'd be trusted to evaluate;
Not someone whom, despite what we might say,
Would be imposed upon us anyway!
The very thought that we're not *worth* consulting
Should strike you as sufficiently insulting
To tell the Prince, as I will, face-to-face,
Exactly how we feel about this case.

Bejart, on the verge of protesting, is interrupted by a booming organ chord signaling the entrance of Prince Conti; Valere, seeing the Prince's shadow before anyone else, exclaims—or rather howls—the piercing hosanna 'MY LIEGE!!" as the curtain falls.

ACT TWO

*The action continues. As the curtain rises, Valere is dropping
to his knees before the Prince.*

VALERE (*Shrieking.*)
  MY LIEGE!! MY SOVEREIGN!! IS IT TRULY THOU??

ELOMIRE (*Bows head.*)
  Good day, Your Grace.

BEJART (*Bows head.*)
                              My lord.

VALERE (*Virtually prostrating himself in the salaam position.*)
                              Then let me bow
  So *deeply* that, by bowing any more,
  I'd be completely prostrate on the floor.

PRINCE
  Good day to you . . .

VALERE
                              For could I but descend
  A fraction lower than you see me bend,
  A fraction lower I would bend indeed!

PRINCE
  My thanks.

VALERE
                              So *low* . . .

PRINCE
                              But really: there's no need!

VALERE
. . . that "low" would seem . . . comparatively high!

ELOMIRE (*To Valere.*)
Get up, for heaven's sake.

VALERE
                              And yet I shy
When basking in thy autocratic glow
From using such a lowly word as "low."

BEJART (*Echoing Elomire.*)
Stand up, Valere.

VALERE
                    STAND UP!? THAT'S SACRILEGE!!
Already it's too great a privilege
To be facedown in close proximity
To one of such divine divinity!

PRINCE
I'm overwhelmed. I'm truly overcome . . .

VALERE (*Indicating the numbing effect that the salaam position has on his legs and genuflecting wildly.*)
Admittedly my legs are getting numb,
But in my other bones, down to the marrow,
I feel thy presence *deeply,* noble pharaoh!
"In mine is thine, for thine and mine entwine" . . .
(*Eyes pop.*)
My God! That was a *lapidary* line!
I'm speaking poetry out of the
(*With a wink to Dorine.*)
                              blue:
A poetry, my King, inspired by you!

PRINCE
I'm hardly King . . .

VALERE (*Feigning incredulity.*)
                    Art thou not King of France!?
Thou *shouldst* be King!! Thou *shouldst* be King of France!!

PRINCE
I'm grateful for your paeans, but I fear
That I have interrupted something here . . .

VALERE
Impossible, my sultan!

ELOMIRE
                    Not at all.
In fact—why were you waiting in the hall?
You should have come in straightaway, my lord.

PRINCE
O, no. I think that would have been untoward.
Besides, I've been here longer than you know!
When I arrived a half an hour ago
Your troupe, assembled in the dining room,
Described how suddenly (and I assume
How anxiously) Bejart, Valere, and you
Dashed off to have a private interview.
I urged them thus, as far as I was able,
To please remain discreetly at the table,
So you'd be free to form a pure reaction
Unvexed by any ripples of distraction.
And yet I broke the rule myself, you see?
Bedeviled by my curiosity
I simply couldn't keep from interfering:
I'm much too eager at the thought of hearing
Exactly how your *tête-à-tête* concluded.

68

And I don't mean to leave Bejart excluded!
He's part of this as well, let's not forget;
So shall I say your *"tête-à-tête-à-tête."*

VALERE

A *"TÊTE-À-TÊTE-À-TÊTE"*!! MY LORD, YOU'RE
   BRILLIANT!!
There's not a wit more nimble or resilient
Than that which you possess! Not now or ever!
A *"tête-à-tête-à-tête"*:
(*Laughing and applauding.*)
                              O, *very* clever!
Bravo, my Sovereign! Daunting is the ease
With which you weave linguistic tapestries!
Astounding is your skill at verbal play:
Each sentence seems an intricate ballet
Where pronouns leap, and gerunds pirouette!
That phrase, again . . . ?

PRINCE

                    A *tête-à-tête-à-tête* . . .

VALERE

A *TÊTE-À-TÊTE-À-TÊTE*! IT'S *TOO* DELICIOUS!
My lord, thou art so . . .
(*Searching his mind for the perfect word.*)
              . . . what? . . . so . . .
(*Positively blurting it out.*)
                    . . . LOVALITIOUS!! . . .
A word I've just created on the fly!
For "LOVALITIOUS" seems to typify
(As common metaphors would fail to do)
The deep-down . . . *LOVALITIOUSNESS* of you.
Yet were I bound by ordinary speech,
Thy every phrase I'd liken to a peach

Which thou hast coaxed (no mortal can say how)
To ripeness on the philologic bough;
Yes, like a shepherd to linguistic herds,
Thou hast—in short, my liege—a way with words.

PRINCE

You honor me too much with this reply!

VALERE

IMPOSSIBLE, O MONARCH OF THE SKY!

PRINCE

But eloquence is *your* domain, not mine!

VALERE

I've never heard more wisdom in *one* line!
Was everybody listening to that?
I take off my imaginary hat
To thee, my lord; I click my heels as well—
For how else could this tongue-tied actor tell
A wizard of the *logos* (*comme vous-même*)
How totally he cherishes each gem
Thou effortlessly cast upon our ears . . .

PRINCE

That talent, though, is yours and Elomire's:
Because of it I wanted you to meet!
Alone, your plays, though great, seemed incomplete,
And, therefore, I was driven to know whether
I could, by bringing both of you together,
Create a whole out of your separate arts
Which might surpass the sum of all its parts.

VALERE

Breathe not my name with that of Elomire:
I'm bound to earth, he skirts the stratosphere
(As playwright *and* as actor, brilliant, clearly—

Where I am but a brilliant actor, merely.)
My couplets tend to lack the common touch,
A vulgar knack I envy overmuch
In masters like our darling Elomire . . .

ELOMIRE
Don't call me "darling"! Ever!

VALERE
                                        Sorry, dear . . .
Well! *That* was rather on the snippy side!
I seemed to have misjudged your sense of pride!
Still quaking at my quibbles even yet?
Don't crucify yourself on vinaigrette—
I didn't mean to stir up such ado!
To punish me for being frank with you
Seems—I don't know—a wee bit juvenile.
"A MAN SHOULD TAKE HIS LICKINGS WITH A
    SMILE."

PRINCE
I know that line . . .

VALERE
                        But can you pin it down?

PRINCE (*Gasping.*)
Of course . . . !

VALERE
                    That's right.

PRINCE
                            Your play . . . !

VALERE
                                    The Dying Clown!

PRINCE

THE DYING CLOWN! I *LOVED* THAT!

VALERE

                                        Most agree.

That you remember it surprises me.

PRINCE

Remember it? I wept throughout Act Two!
It's where you showed that clowns have feelings, too—
How mirth with sorrow in each soul competes . . .

VALERE

I leave such chitchat to the exegetes.
I'm useless as a critic—I *create!*
An artist's at a loss to explicate
His raw ideas; to him, they're heaven-sent.
"That clowns have feelings" . . . *is* that what I meant?
Perhaps. And if I did . . .
(*Small giggle at the realization.*)
                              . . . it's rather *good.*

Guffaw of self-delight.

PRINCE (*To Elomire.*)
Have you not seen it?

ELOMIRE

                    No.

PRINCE

                              O, then you *should.*

BEJART
I saw it.

72

VALERE (*Grovelingly acknowledging the remark as if Bejart had just said, "It was a work of genius."*)
Thank you. *Thank* you.

PRINCE

Really, where?

BEJART

A year ago in Brussels at a fair.

VALERE

O *NO!!* NOT *BRUSSELS!!* I WAS OFF THAT NIGHT!!
I had a chest cold and—to be polite—
Let's call it "something wrong beneath my waist"!
You saw me *then?* O God! I feel disgraced!

PRINCE

Well, why don't you make up for it right now?

VALERE

Make up for it, my Sovereign? Tell me how!

PRINCE

By doing just a tidbit from the play.

VALERE

O, no no no, my lord! O, nay nay nay!

PRINCE

But *please* . . .

VALERE

O *nein!* O *nicht!* O *niente!*

PRINCE

Why?

VALERE

I can't, Your Grace.

PRINCE

Why not?

VALERE

Because I'm shy.
And out of context it would be . . .

PRINCE

O boo!
I'm asking for a simple line or two!

VALERE

Without the cow . . . they wouldn't understand . . .

PRINCE

This isn't a request, it's a command.

VALERE

Command, you say? Well, since I'm at your beck,
I'll smooth the hackles rising on my neck
And grant, unwillingly, a brief recital
Of Baba's tearful farewell to his title
As *"clune extraordinaire"* du *"Cirque Soleil":*
This is the final couplet of the play.
(*Sniffs and extends handkerchief.*)
"CAST DOWN MY POLKA-DOTTED PANTALOONS,
MY RUBBER LIPS, MY COLORFUL BALLOONS" . . .
And then I blow my nose and kiss the pigeon . . .
(*Kisses cupped hands and releases imaginary pigeon.*)
Well, anyway, that's just a tiny smidgen
From something that took decades to perfect.

The Prince looks to Elomire and Bejart, who are clearly unimpressed.

PRINCE (*Slightly embarrassed.*)
You'll understand I mean no disrespect
By telling you, Valere, that, while delightful,

74

The Dying Clown seems somewhat less insightful
(And Baba's death less poignantly sublime)
When one observes the scene a second time.

VALERE (*Swept by a wave of panic, he blurts out:*)
But that was my *INTENTION!!*

PRINCE (*Genuinely.*)
                              Was it!?

VALERE (*Clearly relieved and encouraged.*)
                              YESSSSSSS!!
How gratifying, lord, that you should guess!
Departing from theatrical tradition,
The play is so designed that each rendition
Deliberately lessens our esteem
Until, oppressed by every blotch and scam,
We're stunned by the respect that first we had
For something which is so supremely bad.

PRINCE
You mean the play's *intended* to go *stale!?*

VALERE
To be successful, lord, the play must fail.

PRINCE
But that's *ingenious!*

VALERE
                    Sire, I do my best.

And he staggers away, slightly wounded.

PRINCE
Why, Elomire: you must be so impressed!
Imagine planting in a play's construction
The seeds which guarantee its self-destruction!

75

The concept seems both daring and nouveau!
Could you have thought of it? Be honest.

ELOMIRE (*He's onto something; his mind is racing ahead.*)
                                        No.

PRINCE
Voilà! This news exceeds my expectations!
I'm dazzled by dramatic innovations!

ELOMIRE
Still, won't you show, Valere, how you excel
At forms much more conventional as well?

PRINCE (*To Elomire, excited.*)
Another play?

ELOMIRE (*Matter-of-fact.*)
                    I'd *love* to see him in it.

PRINCE (*To Valere, "I told you so."*)
Did you hear *that?*

BEJART (*To Elomire, perplexed.*)
                    Excuse me . . .

VALERE (*Suspicious.*)
                                        Wait a minute . . .

ELOMIRE (*To Bejart, sotto voce.*)
Have faith, my friend.

PRINCE (*Enjoying his prescience about the Elomire-Valere team.*)
                    I *knew* that this would work!

ELOMIRE (*To Valere.*)
GO ON!

VALERE (*Nervous.*)
                    No no.

PRINCE (*To Valere.*)
                    YOU MUST!

BEJART (*To Elomire, sotto voce.*)
                              Are you berserk . . . ?

ELOMIRE (*To Bejart, sotto voce and final.*)
Just trust me.

PRINCE (*To Valere.*)
                    Now!

VALERE (*Trapped.*)
                    Well . . . could'st thou be specific?

PRINCE
O, do that thing you do that's so terrific . . .
The . . . what's-it-called . . . come on . . . you know the play!

VALERE
Might Lordship fling a *tiny* clue my way?

PRINCE
The one that stands out like a shining star . . . !

VALERE
That *could* mean my entire repertoire!

PRINCE
 No, no. I mean your masterpiece, Valere.

VALERE
Which *one?*

PRINCE
                    You did it in the public square
Six weeks ago . . .

VALERE
                    You don't mean *Death by Cheese!*

PRINCE
No, that's not it.

VALERE

The Life of Damocles?

PRINCE
Another one . . .

VALERE (*Snapping his fingers, thinking he's got it.*)
The Bishop's Macaroon!!

PRINCE
Another . . .

VALERE

Well, there's *Goddess from the Moon* . . .
(*Prince squints as if that may be it. Valere supplies more detail.*)
Where I get all dressed up as Aphrodite . . . ?

PRINCE (*Waves it off.*)
No, it's the one where you *don't* wear a nightie.

VALERE (*Realizing.*)
O, *now* I think I know which one it is . . .
(*Sniffs and extends handkerchief.*)
The Parable of Two Boys from Cadiz!

PRINCE

*MY GOD! THAT'S IT! YOU'RE RIGHT! THAT'S
WHAT IT IS!!*
THE PARABLE OF TWO BOYS FROM CADIZ!!

VALERE
But lord, I can't . . .

ELOMIRE

Why not?

VALERE

                                          O, please don't ask.
To do it *well* is such a grueling task:
It takes the most amazing concentration!

ELOMIRE

Then we'll allow for lack of preparation.

VALERE

I'd need my juggling balls and my prosthesis . . .

PRINCE

Why can't you just suggest them through mimesis?

VALERE (*With his eyes on Elomire.*)
You've missed the point, my lord, if I may dare.
My props are in my gunnysack out there—
It's not for want of them that I resist;
It's more that I'm a staunch perfectionist
Who, bristling at the slightest compromise,
Won't utter *"faute de mieux"* until he dies!
How quaint that sounds in this corrupted age
When half-baked twaddle dominates our stage,
But lower standards make me feel *degraded*.
I thus refuse (and cannot be persuaded)
To vulgarize a work which at the core
Demands a day of preparation—MORE!—
A week, perhaps, if I'm to get it right.
Hence I cannot fulfill your wish tonight!

PRINCE

Then I'm afraid you're finished here, Valere.

VALERE

I'll need about three minutes to prepare.

He bows kissing his fingertips, making a backwards exit.

PRINCE

Ah! Wonderful! I'm glad you've changed your mind!
Bejart and Elomire, I think you'll find
The Parable of Two Boys from Cadiz
Is everything that I have said it is!

ELOMIRE

I long for it to start . . .

PRINCE

                    In fact, Bejart,
Go fetch the others—you know where they are—
I want the troupe to see this!

BEJART

                            Very well.
(*Pointedly, to Elomire.*)
I'm sure if Elomire decides to tell
Your Lordship of the words we shared alone,
He'll honor my opinion as his own.

Glancing at Elomire, he bows and exits. Dorine exits.

PRINCE

I'm sure he will.
(*To Elomire.*)
                    Now what was *that* about?

ELOMIRE

O, never mind, my lord. I highly doubt
Such trivia would interest you at all.

PRINCE (*Excitedly.*)
Then what about Valere? Did he enthrall
The company at dinner? Was he witty?
Did he recite that syncopated ditty
About the gnome whose trousers scrape the floor . . . ?

ELOMIRE (*Nodding, pained.*)
He did indeed, my lord, and *so* much more.
(*As if to say, "What planet does he come from?"*)
Where did you *find* him?

PRINCE

                              In the public square!
Can you *imagine?* In the open air—
A talent of *that* magnitude . . . !

ELOMIRE

                              It's frightening.

PRINCE
When I first saw him I was struck by lightning!
A voice inside of me cried out, "NOW HERE,
NOW HERE'S A MAN WHO *MUST* MEET ELOMIRE!
A COMMON STREET CLOWN, TRUE, BUT WHAT
    A GIFT!
AND CERTAINLY THE TROUPE COULD USE A
    LIFT!"

ELOMIRE
A lift? What sort of lift?

PRINCE

                    A . . . "perking-up."
(*Pause.*)
For several weeks now I've been working up
The courage to reprove you, Elomire,
For faults caused (unavoidably, I fear)
By too much time unchallenged—by *stagnation!*
The troupe seems listless, in my estimation:
Not daring as it was a year ago!
Remember how you strove, with every show,
To break *some* rule, to shatter *some* convention?

What happened to the talent for invention
That earned you your exalted reputation
In all the provinces throughout the nation
As rival to the genius of Corneille?

ELOMIRE

If you're as disappointed as you say
What's needed to improve the situation?

PRINCE

New blood to stimulate the circulation!
A year at Court has undermined your morals:
You've grown content to rest upon your laurels
As if afflicted by some dread ennui.
Valere will challenge your complacency!
Between two men of talent, competition
Can be a most desirable condition
For it propels them both to greater heights
Until, producing myriad delights
Which, separately, they *never* would have done,
The rivals come to see themselves as "one"—
A team, depending each upon the other!
Tonight you've met your spiritual brother:
A man whose gifts provide (it seems to me)
A rare and welcome opportunity.

ELOMIRE

Perhaps less opportune, my lord, than rare:
I'd welcome anyone *except* Valere!
If that's too blunt, forgive me, but it's true:
I see no purpose in deceiving you . . .

PRINCE (*Completely incredulous.*)
Deceiving me? You mean you didn't *like* him?

ELOMIRE

I mean that not to *strangle* him or *strike* him
Required unbelievable restraint . . .

PRINCE

Good God!

ELOMIRE

WAIT! That's the least of my complaint!

PRINCE

The LEAST?

ELOMIRE

The *LEAST!*

PRINCE

Now don't be cross . . .

ELOMIRE

But lord . . .

PRINCE

I'm not insisting that he be adored,
But only that . . .

ELOMIRE

WE'RE . . . NOT . . . COMMUNICATING . . .

PRINCE

. . . You overlook what you find "irritating"
About Valere . . .

ELOMIRE (*Tensely, pained.*)

But NOTHING would remain!

PRINCE

You're being churlish!

ELOMIRE
                    Lord, would I complain . . .

PRINCE (*Cutting Elomire off, haughtily.*)
    Valere, you either could or could not see,
    Is really something of an oddity . . .

ELOMIRE
    I *could* see that . . .

PRINCE
                    He is, and there are few,
    An *"idiot savant"!*

ELOMIRE
                    That's *partly* true.

PRINCE
    That's *partly* true?

ELOMIRE
                    I mean I *half* agree!

PRINCE
    Explain yourself!

ELOMIRE
                    How pointed can one be?
    I think the man's an idiot

PRINCE (*Completing this phrase as if they were in agreement.*)
                    —savant.

ELOMIRE
    No no, my lord. A chucklehead

PRINCE
                    —savant.

84

ELOMIRE
No no, my lord. Not *"chucklehead savant."*
Just chucklehead. Just idiot

PRINCE
                —savant.

ELOMIRE
The man's a cretin, lord!

PRINCE
                O, no no no!

ELOMIRE
A nincompoop! A boob!

PRINCE
             That isn't so!
You've totally misread him, Elomire . . . !

ELOMIRE
I haven't!

PRINCE
          Quite egregiously, I fear.
In fact, I'm nothing short of stupefied
That you, an artist, trained to look *inside,*
Should base your views on *superficial* flaws.
It's one of life's profound, unwritten laws
That people whom you least expect it of
May harbor, like a hand inside a glove,
Some mystery, some talent left unproved
Because the glove has never been removed!
The baker's wife, for instance: just suppose
A prima ballerina's in her toes!
The butcher: might he not, behind his hams,
Be peerless at unscrambling anagrams?

85

Perhaps the milkman loves Etruscan art;
The barber may know Ptolemy by heart;
The priest might be a stunning acrobat;
Well, one could just go on and on like that . . .
The lesson here is that the naked eye
Is often insufficient to espy
The wealth of *natural* talent left unseen
Unless one probes beneath or checks between.
You haven't really looked at this Valere . . .

ELOMIRE
I have, my lord . . .

PRINCE
                              Not deep enough to bare
The soul of his achievement, which transcends
Theatrical performance and extends
To realms the likes of which you'd never guess:
He taught the King of Sweden to play chess!

ELOMIRE
Who told you that?

PRINCE
                        He told me!

ELOMIRE
                                    O, my *God!*
And you *believed* him?

PRINCE
                        Yes—is that so odd?
(*Irritated and impatient with this argument, he cuts it off.*)
I'd HOPED that you'd have liked him as a man.
Still, you can *work* together . . .

86

ELOMIRE

NO! ⎤

PRINCE

YES . . . ⎦

PRINCE (*Deadly.*)

you can.
By which I mean you will. Or, otherwise—
(*Mounting frustration.*)
If you can't make *one tiny compromise*
Respecting ME—
(*A flash of anger.*)

then get your troupe and go!
(*Petulance.*)
You have no *right* to flout my wishes so!
I CANNOT STAND THIS IN YOU, ELOMIRE!
I've always given you your freedom here
Supporting you like kings when half the time
Your work's too dark or dense or fails to rhyme
Or makes no sense, or takes strange points of view.
This man has gifts that will inspire you!
Now that's what *I* believe—and, in the end
MY say-so is what matters. Why, my friend,
Are you so stubborn?! You've not seen his play.
(*Hapless, uncomprehending.*)
Why is it so IMPORTANT, anyway?
He's just ONE MAN . . .
(*Princely.*)

whose talent pleases me.
(*Stern and final.*)
Now you'll accept him as a courtesy . . .
No less than that which I have shown to you
By setting up this meal . . .

87

ELOMIRE

If that were true

My judgment would be honored, not ignored.

BUT *THIS*—

(*He produces the writ.*)

IS *THIS* A COURTESY, MY LORD?!

I never thought you'd show me such contempt!

I'd fooled myself to think we were exempt

From pressures of this sort since (from the start)

You've honored me, my thoughts, my troupe, my art

In such a rare, uncompromising way,

That naturally we've struggled to repay

Your kindness with new work that's just as rare.

But now you force upon us this . . . VALERE . . .

And tell me I should get my troupe and *go?!*

Have we so *failed* you?

PRINCE (*Moved by this.*)

No. Of course not. No.

It pains me that you say that when it's clear

How deeply I admire you, Elomire.

This troupe has been, for me, a source of pride . . .

ELOMIRE

Then why not, please, let *all* of us decide?!

And why not let this *Parable* of his,

This . . .

PRINCE

Parable of Two Boys from Cadiz

ELOMIRE

Be crucial in determining his fate.

PRINCE

I've *seen* it, though. It's charming.

ELOMIRE
                              Yes, but wait:
Remember when you watched *The Dying Clown*
A *second* time you felt . . .

PRINCE
                       That's true . . .

ELOMIRE
                                   . . . let down.

PRINCE
   But he explained that brilliantly.

ELOMIRE
                           What's more,
He acts *alone,* my lord, not in a corps
Of players like our own, where all take part.
His monologue's a selfish pseudo-art
Which puts the man himself above the group.

PRINCE
   I take your point.

ELOMIRE (*The idea really clicking in.*)
                           Why not . . . allow the troupe
To join him in this *Parable* and see
If he could truly serve the company
Instead of . . .
(*Expansive.*)
                  taking over!

PRINCE
                        I don't know . . .

ELOMIRE
   A joint performance cannot fail to show
How much an asset or a threat he'd be.

PRINCE

A *threat?!* But that's absurd hyperbole!

ELOMIRE (*In sincere pain.*)
He'd RUIN us.

PRINCE (*Intrigued.*)
You *mean* it, Elomire.

ELOMIRE
I couldn't be more serious . . .

PRINCE

O, dear!
(*He walks upstage and thinks about it. Then, with gentle, eerie
sarcasm, bemused by the fraught situation and his power to affect it:*)
You'd think the world itself were at an end!
(*Chortles, rather menacingly.*)
You're funny you're so serious, my friend.
(*Half-smiling.*)
Commitment to your art deserves respect,
(*Fast and beseechingly.*)
But not when it compels you to reject
As "*monstrous*" any change that fails to suit
Your own designs—
(*Incredulous.*)
and *this* seems so minute;
(*Sighing, frustrated but with respect.*)
Still, rigidly you press your point of view.
(*Brief pause. He studies Elomire. Then—shaking his head—
ambiguously, so that his words are simultaneously affectionate and
chilling:*)
Whatever am I going to do with you?
(*The Prince laughs, surprisingly, inappropriately. Then, dead serious,
he gestures for Elomire to come close. A smile creeps back around the*

corners of his lips and he snatches the writ from Elomire's hands, tearing it up and throwing the pieces into the air like confetti.)
All right then. Very well.

ELOMIRE *(Sighs, tremendously relieved.)*
                              Our thanks, my lord!

PRINCE
But let us have a *mutual* accord:
If I review him in this different light
You must be less *insistent* that you're right.
My mind is open—tell me yours is, too.

ELOMIRE *(Under the strain of a bargain.)*
I like to think, my lord, that's always true.

PRINCE *(Satisfied enough.)*
Then this should be great fun, don't you agree?
We'll neither praise nor fault too eagerly . . .

Enter Bejart and his sister Madeleine, followed by De Brie and his wife Catherine, and Du Parc and his wife Marquise-Therese. They are talking amongst themselves, but Bejart overhears the Prince's last sentence.

BEJART
Um . . . finding fault with whom?

PRINCE
                              Ah! Here they arc!

BEJART
With whom? With us?

PRINCE
                    O, heavens no, Bejart!
(Generally)

COME IN! COME IN! WE HAVE A TREAT IN
  STORE!
BUT FIRST I NEED YOUR HELP TO CLEAR THE
  FLOOR—
A SPACE RIGHT OVER THERE, I THINK, WILL
  DO . . .

BEJART
  Is it all right . . .

MADELEINE
  Excuse me, lord . . .

DU PARC
  May I request . . .

MARQUISE-THERESE
  A moment, please . . .

DE BRIE
  I wish to speak . . .

CATHERINE
  Would you allow . . .

PRINCE

                  I CAN'T HEAR *ALL* OF YOU!!

BEJART
  I understand, my lord . . .

MADELEINE
  Then let me quickly say . . .

DU PARC
  He's absolutely right . . .

MARQUISE-THERESE
  It's vital that you know . . .

DE BRIE
Be quiet, everyone . . .

CATHERINE
I simply want to ask . . .

PRINCE

PLEASE! SETTLE DOWN!

BEJART
You heard him! Settle down . . .

MADELEINE
Be quiet, everyone . . .

DU PARC
Of course: but if I may . . .

MARQUISE-THERESE
I would if there were time . . .

DE BRIE
The point I want to make . . .

CATHERINE
He can't hear anything . . .

PRINCE
YOU'RE MAKING SUCH A DIN! YOUR VOICES
DROWN

BEJART
He can't hear anything!

MADELEINE
Just let me talk, all right?

DU PARC
Good gracious! Hold your tongues!

MARQUISE-THERESE
Would everyone shut up!?

DE BRIE
You're stepping on my speech!

CATHERINE
An utter waste of time!

PRINCE
EACH OTHER OUT COMPLETELY! WHAT A
CLAMOR!

MADELEINE
BUT LORD!

DU PARC
BUT LORD!

MARQUISE-THERESE
BUT LORD!

PRINCE
IT'S LIKE A HAMMER
POUNDING ON MY SKULL!!

DE BRIE
BUT LORD!!

PRINCE
BE *STILL!!*
(*Pause, to gather control.*)
Now: one by one.

BEJART
My lord, despite the skill

MADELEINE
My lord, we've had our fill

94

DU PARC
> My lord, Therese is ill

MARQUISE–THERESE
> My lord, I have a chill

DE BRIE
> My lord, while quite a thrill

CATHERINE
> My lord, though it's your will

BEJART
Valere has shown.

MADELEINE
Of him tonight . . .

DU PARC
I'm sad to say . . .

MARQUISE–THERESE
And need to rest . . .

DE BRIE
To see Valere . . .

CATHERINE
That we remain . . .

PRINCE
THIS REALLY IS IMPOSSIBLE!

PRINCE
> BE *QUIET!!*
YOU'RE BABBLING LIKE A RABBLE IN A RIOT . . .

BEJART
Well, if we are . . .

95

MADELEINE
  Whose fault is *that?*

DU PARC
  But that's because . . .

MARQUISE-THERESE
  You're blaming me?

DE BRIE
  I know, I know . . .

CATHERINE
  But, please, my lord . . .

PRINCE

                    I'M TELLING YOU TO STOP!!
(*Pause.*)
  NOW: why don't we just take this from the top.
  Who wants to speak?

BEJART
                    I DO!

MADELEINE
                    I DO!

DU PARC
                         I DO!

MARQUISE-THERESE
                         I DO!

DE BRIE
                              I DO!

CATHERINE
                              I DO!

BEJART
With your permission . . .

MADELEINE
If Lordship pleases . . .

DU PARC
As I was saying . . .

MARQUISE-THERESE
I think it's vital . . .

DE BRIE
My instinct tells me . . .

CATHERINE
It isn't proper . . .

PRINCE
SILENCE! ALL OF YOU!
Bejart. Can you account for this display?

Bejart and Madeleine peel off downstage to the Prince; the other members of the troupe cross up to Elomire and confront him.

BEJART
My lord, the troupe is in a rush to say

MADELEINE (*Jumping in, theatrically enthusiastic.*)
We're grateful

DU PARC (*Confronting Elomire.*)
WE DEMAND AN EXPLANATION.

ELOMIRE (*Insouciant.*)
FOR WHAT?

PRINCE (*Genuinely, to the Bejarts.*)
For what?

97

DE BRIE (*To Elomire.*)

THIS AWKWARD SITUATION!

BEJART (*To the Prince.*)
For having had the chance to meet

MADELEINE (*Jumping in again; expressed with a certain horror.*)
that man.

MARQUISE-THERESE (*As Elomire continues to feign ignorance.*)
DON'T SHRUG AS IF WE'RE CRAZY!

BEJART (*Indicating Madeleine.*)
She's a fan . . .

MADELEINE (*Too eager.*)
Who wouldn't be.

ELOMIRE (*Querulously, to the troupe.*)
YOU ALL SEEM SO EXCITED.

BEJART (*To the Prince.*)
It's late, though . . .

DU PARC (*To Elomire.*)
WE WERE TOLD THAT YOU INVITED
THAT *FOOL* TO DO HIS . . . WHAT?

BEJART (*Continuing, to the Prince.*)
. . . and, as it is,

ELOMIRE
THE PARABLE OF TWO BOYS FROM CADIZ

BEJART
The Parable of Two Boys from Cadiz

BEJART
Could never be unstintingly admired.

ELOMIRE (*To the troupe.*)
I DID SUGGEST IT, YES.

MADELEINE (*Nervously yawning.*)
We're all too tired . . .

DE BRIE (*Extremely displeased, to Elomire.*)
WHAT *ARE* YOU UP TO?

ELOMIRE
TRUST ME.

BEJART (*To the Prince.*)
Yawn yawn yawn!

CATHERINE (*To Elomire.*)
JUST TELL US, *PLEASE!*

Elomire simply holds his hands up reassuringly.

MADELEINE (*To the Prince.*)
Indeed, it's nearly dawn.

MARQUISE-THERESE (*To Elomire.*)
WE *HAVE* TO WATCH THIS? *NOW?!*

Elomire nods confidently.

PRINCE (*To the Bejarts.*)
It's barely eight!

ELOMIRE
NOT MERELY WATCH—YOU'LL ALL PARTICIPATE!

The members of the troupe are stunned, astonishment silencing their confusion for a moment. The Prince, having heard Elomire make this pronouncement, breaks away from the Bejarts and crosses up to Elomire and the troupe.

PRINCE
Yes! Wonderful! Did everybody hear?!

A grand suggestion, thanks to Elomire:
It's *his* idea that you should all . . . "join in."

*The heads of the astonished members of the troupe swivel back to
Elomire.*

ELOMIRE (*Eagerly.*)
There's no time like the present to begin
To test how well our new-formed team will do.
(*Indicating the Prince.*)
Whenever others voice a point of view
That's different from my own, I . . .
(*He bows to the Prince.*)

           think again.
Valere, I realize now, like many men
Has flaws which might disguise great talent . . . MIGHT!
The Prince has seen it—could it be, *he's* right?!
(*Silence; slapping hands together.*)
Well,
(*The Du Parcs turn upstage, plotting; the De Bries, dumbstruck,
hover nervously between cheer and anguish—they are confused, caged
animals.*)
   acting in this
(*Deferential, to the Prince.*)
       "masterpiece" that is
The Parable of Two Boys from Cadiz
Will help us get a feel . . .

DU PARC (*Turns and interjects.*)
        UMMMMMM!

PRINCE
           Yes, Du Parc?

DU PARC
Therese is ill, my lord. Her tongue's gone dark.

PRINCE

Her tongue's gone dark?

DU PARC

                    Yes, very.

PRINCE

                    Let me see.

Marquise-Therese sticks out her tongue.

DU PARC

It's darker than a normal tongue should be . . .

PRINCE

Well, if it is, so what?

ELOMIRE

                    Precisely!

BEJART

                    PLEASE!

Bejart takes Madeleine's hand and they cross to Elomire. Du Parc continues to address the Prince. The three following conversations take place simultaneously. They are synchronized to be of exactly equal length and should be recited in an established rhythm, like a fugue.

DU PARC	**MADELEINE** (*Hissing whisper.*)
The point is that it might be some disease	Would you be quiet! Can't you see that she's
That left untreated could, for all I know	Attempting to convince the Prince to spare
Infect the lot of us . . . !	The troupe from this recital by Valere?

PRINCE

    She's healthy,
though!

DU PARC

  Perhaps! But since we're
  not completely sure
  Prevention is the most
  effective cure!
  She must be put to bed!
  And, as it is,
  The Parable of . . . ?

PRINCE

  . . . *Two Boys from Cadiz* . . .

DU PARC

  Would better be
  performed on some
  occasion
  When we would feel
  less threated by
  contagion.

ELOMIRE

  By feigning illness? What
  can that achieve
  Except, at best, a very
  short reprieve?
  Just tell the truth as I've
  already done . . .

BEJART

  I hope you didn't speak
  for everyone!

ELOMIRE

  Well if I did, would
  there be some
  objection?

MADELEINE

  There would if it
  results in our
  ejection!

DORINE (*Entering, speaking as Du Parc says "Perhaps!"*)
SHOE!

CATHERINE

    I'm sorry?

DE BRIE

      What?

CATHERINE

      Did you say "SHOE"?

DE BRIE
  I didn't, no.

CATHERINE
        Well, if it wasn't you
  Then who just said it . . .

DORINE
        SHOE! . . .

DE BRIE
              Why, it's Dorine!

CATHERINE
  Come in!

DE BRIE (*To Dorine.*)
        Did you say "SHOE"?

CATHERINE
              What could it mean?

DE BRIE
  HELLO! HELLO! HELLO!
  (*His voice emerging from the babble.*)
              HELLO! HELLO!

DE BRIE (*Clapping hands together.*)
  ATTENTION!! HUSH!! Does everybody know
  Dorine is standing here and saying "SHOE"!?

CATHERINE
  Indeed she is . . . !

DU PARC
  She's saying "SHOE" . . . ?

DE BRIE
        BE QUIET, ALL OF YOU!

Come in, Dorine. Be careful with your dress.
(*Dorine descends the step.*)
    You have a little message for us, yes?
(*She nods.*)
    What is it, dear?
(*She opens her mouth to speak but, teasingly, doesn't.*)
                    Just *say* it, please, Dorine!

DORINE
    SHOE!

DE BRIE
        Shoe—WHAT!?

DU PARC
            Shoe—*WHAT!?*

CATHERINE
                            Well, "SHOE" could mean
    Shoe—LACE.

DE BRIE
            Or—STRING!

CATHERINE
                        Or—MAKER!

DE BRIE
                                Are we right?

Dorine shakes her head no.

CATHERINE
    Shoe—HORN?

DU PARC
        Shoe—SIZE?

DE BRIE

Shoe—LENGTH?

DU PARC

Shoe—WIDTH?

CATHERINE

Shoe—

HEIGHT?

Dorine continues to shake her head no.

DU PARC

Or is it "SHOO-SHOO-SHOO, BEGONE! GET OUT!"?

Dorine shakes her head no.

PRINCE (*To Madeleine.*)

Now what the devil is *this* all about?

MADELEINE

Dorine, my lord, is going through a phase.

PRINCE

O, not *again* . . . !

DE BRIE

Is there another phrase

That might make sense of "SHOE"?

MADELEINE

And it's unique:

CATHERINE

Shoe—SOLE?

DU PARC

Shoe—POLISH?

DORINE

SHOE!

MADELEINE

She will not speak
Except in monosyllables that rhyme!

DE BRIE

Shoe—TOE?

PRINCE

At least that's better than the time
She hummed E *flat* incessantly, remember?

DU PARC

Shoe—HEEL?

MADELEINE (*Nodding.*)

Or worse, that fortnight in December
(*Dorine shakes her head "no" impatiently in response to Du Parc,
and then begins to mime exaggerated emotions and perform wild
gesticulations.*)
When all she did from dawn to dusk was whirl!

PRINCE

Just . . . spun around?

Madeleine nods.

CATHERINE

Shoe—LACE?

*Dorine shakes her head no impatiently and becomes even more
exaggerated.*

PRINCE

Peculiar girl!

DE BRIE
No, "LACE" was said already . . .

PRINCE
What's she *doing?*

CATHERINE
Perhaps the word is "ISSUE" or "ESCHEWING" . . .

Dorine shakes her head no and continues to gesture wildly.

MADELEINE
She's acting out a clue . . .

DU PARC
I'VE SEEN ENOUGH!

DU PARC
TO PUT UP WITH THIS ADOLESCENT STUFF

DORINE (*She sings the word.*)
Shoooooooooooooooooooooooooooe!!!

DU PARC
. . . IS MORE THAN I CAN BEAR!
(*Fanning Marquise-Therese in a chair.*)
. . . Therese is *dying!*

Marquise-Therese coughs theatrically.

DE BRIE
Dorine is SINGING!

Dorine, nodding vigorously, gives a rolling hand gesture, as in charades, to encourage similar suggestions; immediately she goes up on point, and starts to ballet-dance while continuing to assume grand expressions.

PRINCE (*To Du Parc.*)
                              Everybody's trying . . .

DU PARC
    WILL SOMEONE CALL A DOCTOR!?

PRINCE (*To Du Parc.*)
                                  . . . so should *you!*

DE BRIE
    She's singing and she's . . . LOOK! . . . she's *dancing,* too!

DORINE (*In a histrionic voice.*)
                                          SHOE!!

CATHERINE
    And chewing up the scenery!

PRINCE (*Guessing.*)
                    A *PLAY!?*

DE BRIE
    A *FARCE?*

CATHERINE
            An *OPERETTA?*

PRINCE
                            A *BALLET?*

MADELEINE
    She shouldn't be indulged . . .

DE BRIE
                              They *ALL* apply?

DU PARC
    IS THERE A DOCTOR IN THE HOUSE . . . !?

Dorine's vigorous nodding to Catherine's question causes everyone to look at one another.

PRINCE

O MY!

CATHERINE

O MY!

DE BRIE

O MY!

DE BRIE
Well if it's *all* those things, what could it be?

CATHERINE
A *FESTIVAL,* a . . . ?

DORINE

SHOE!!

MADELEINE

Don't look at me . . . !

PRINCE
A *GALA?*

DU PARC

Lord! I beg you . . .

CATHERINE

I don't know!

MARQUISE-THERESE (*Snapping out of her pretended stupor.*)
FOR GOD'S SAKE, CAN'T YOU SEE THE WORD IS "SHOW"!?

Dorine leaps and gives her "On the nose" signal. The door swings open. The troupe turns, gasps, screams. Blackout. Lights up quickly.

The members of the troupe are staring in disbelief at Valere, who is costumed in a bizarre, wildly garish Harlequin outfit with an immense fright wig. He crashes a pair of cymbals.

VALERE
IT'S SHOWTIME, *YES!* A MARVELOUS DEDUCTION!
(*To Dorine.*)
I thank you for that splendid introduction
(Although you might have simply said "VOILÀ";
Still, your way had a special *"je ne sais quoi . . ."!*)
But far *more* special is the gift I bear:
Breathe in, my friends, there's magic in the air!
Can you not smell that vague exotic scent
Like mystic perfume from the Orient?
'Tis but an intimation of the spell
Cast forth by this enchanting tale I tell!
MOVE BACK, YOU LOUTS! IT'S STUFFY AS A TOMB!
MAKE WAY! GET OFF THE PLATFORM! GIVE ME
   ROOM!
Go find a free *"francesca"* and stay seated
Until my presentation is completed.
No talking and no spitting, by the way:
There's nothing more disruptive to a play
Than hearing someone gab or . . .
(*Makes the ripe sound of coughing up phlegm.*)
                              . . . bring up phlegm
When you're reciting your most precious gem!
(*Suddenly aware that they are all staring at him, their jaws hanging open.*)
Good Lord! What's everybody staring at?

DU PARC
Your . . .

VALERE

    Yes? . . .

DE BRIE

      Your . . .

VALERE

          WHAT?

MADELEINE

          Your *COSTUME!*

VALERE

                O yes, *that!*
Distinctive, no? It won two *huge* awards:
"The Golden Bobbin," and "The Silver Swords."
(It took twelve peasant girls six months to make!)
No, I'm just teasing you, for heaven's sake—
I patched it up myself from odds and ends!
But this is rather off the point, my friends . . .
I've got some sheets. Take one and pass them round.

PRINCE

What is it?

VALERE

      It's the text. You see, I've found
That often the most beautiful invention
Is lost, or met with dull incomprehension
Unless the crowd can savor every word.
This lets them *read* along . . .

PRINCE

               But you've not heard!

VALERE

Heard what?

PRINCE

They're going to *join* you!

VALERE (*Tensely.*)

In what way?

ELOMIRE (*Mischievously.*)
The troupe is going to join you in your play.

VALERE (*Slow turn, suspicious.*)
To . . . *join* me?

ELOMIRE

Yes.

VALERE

You can't.

ELOMIRE

Why not?

VALERE (*He begins re-collecting the scripts.*)
NO! NO!
My lord, this is a strictly *one-man show*
Where I play every part, speak every line . . .

PRINCE
It's Elomire's idea, it isn't mine.

ELOMIRE
It should be quite revealing in that light.

VALERE (*Genuinely distressed.*)
Another time perhaps, but not tonight;
I'm feeling too much pressure as it is . . .

Elomire clears his throat and reads from his script; Valere is losing control.

ELOMIRE

The Parable of Two Boys from Cadiz.

VALERE (*Pulling the script violently from Elomire's hands.*)
JUST GIVE ME THOSE!

But Elomire is redistributing the other copies.

PRINCE (*Getting comfortable.*)
No arguments! Let's go!
I'm sitting here and waiting for the show.

MADELEINE

Will there be costumes for the troupe to wear?

VALERE

With those hips? Hardly . . .

PRINCE

Start the play, Valere!

VALERE

With *them?* But *HOW?*

ELOMIRE

You . . . handle the narration;
We'll help you to perform each situation.

*The Prince and troupe assent; Valere, grudgingly and helplessly, gives
in and turns to the Prince.*

VALERE

Then they should be advised, lord, if I may,
That it is done in verse, this hallowed play . . .

PRINCE (*To the troupe, to impress.*)
In *RHYMING* verse . . .

VALERE

Indeed, it's very odd;

It's almost like . . . a miracle of God.
Pentameter, though pleasing on the page
(*He does this line metronomically.*)
    Is SO monOTonOUS upON the STAGE . . .
    But in *my* hands the opposite is true.
    I'm not the one who says that—*others* do!
(*Hushing everyone.*)
    BUT NOW: I dedicate tonight's performance
(*Bowing to the Prince.*)
    To thy most . . . MAGNA-GRANDIFIED ENORMANCE!
    THE PARABLE OF TWO BOYS FROM CADIZ

The Parable: It may be performed in a variety of styles, from the most absurdly high to the most outrageously low—in short, anything goes. Valere must cajole, flatter, register pain and ecstasy, blow kisses as he signals various members of the troupe, like puppets, to assume assorted roles. He is the "Author/Director/Actor/Critic" using all manner of stagecraft and razzle-dazzle.

VALERE
    THE PARABLE OF TWO BOYS FROM CADIZ
    COMMENCES WITH A CHILD NAMED
        ESMEROLTA
(*Valere places a girl's wig on Bejart's head and leads him forward; Bejart endures this, slightly humiliated.*)
    THE MOST REVOLTING GIRL IN ALL OF VOLTA!
    GROWN MEN WHO GLANCED AT HER WOULD
        RUN AND HIDE
(*He directs Du Parc and De Brie to act this out.*)
    FOR WHILE THE LASS WAS BEAUTIFUL INSIDE
    WITHOUT FAIR LOOKS SHE DIDN'T STAND A
        CHANCE
    IN VOLTA'S VAIN SOCIETY . . .
(*He tiptoes up to the Prince; with a wink:*)
                                    . . . (Read FRANCE!)

ELOMIRE
　　Read France! My God! What's this? A commentary?

VALERE
　　I'm merely pointing out that there's a very
　　Illuminating parallel between
　　Contemporary France and what we've seen
　　To be the case in Volta! Why the tension?

PRINCE
　　I think it adds an interesting dimension.
　　Go on, Valere!

VALERE
　　　　　　　As lord commands, I do:
(He sneers at Elomire, then continues.)
　　CONSTRAINED TO KEEP HER VISAGE OUT OF VIEW
　　A MAIDEN AS GROTESQUE AS ESMEROLTA
　　STOOD LITTLE OPPORTUNITY IN VOLTA
　　EXCEPT TO JOIN A SIDESHOW, WHICH SHE DID.
(He hangs a frame around Bejart's head.)
　　NOW, IF THERE WAS A CROWNING TRICK AMID
　　THE SEVERAL SHE DEVELOPED, IT WAS WHEN
　　SHE'D CLAMP HER TEETH AROUND A
　　　　CLUCKING HEN
　　AND SQUEEZE THE EGGS OUT SLOWLY, ONE BY
　　　　ONE!
(He forces Bejart to do this.)
　　AND THEN, BY WAY OF ROUNDING OUT THE FUN,
　　FROM EVERY EGG SHE'D BLOW THE RAW
　　　　ALBUMEN—
(Bejart is forced to do so, and the troupe screams in disgust.)
　　AN ACT WHICH MADE HER SEEM MORE . . .
　　　　FOWL THAN HUMAN!
(Du Parc laughs, and then is quickly ashamed.)

AS ESMEROLTA'S REPUTATION GREW,
THE CROWDS OF GAWKING SPECTATORS DID,
   TOO.
(*He directs the troupe to act accordingly.*)
  BY MULTITUDES, BY LEGIONS, BY THE SCORE,
  BY BOATLOADS THEY ARRIVED FROM EVERY
   SHORE;
  BUT NONE HAD TRAVELED FARTHER NOR
   COME SOONER
  THAN TWO YOUNG FELLOWS IN A PRIVATE
   SCHOONER
(*And Valere chooses Elomire and De Brie, who step forward
resignedly.*)
  WITH "TIT-FOR-TAT" EMBLAZONED ON THE
   PROW.
  MYSTERIOUS THESE BROTHERS WERE! AND HOW!
  FRATERNAL TWINS, AND BOTH NAMED ESTEBAN!
  DESPITE THAT CURIOUS PHENOMENON
  LESS LIKELY TWINS THERE NEVER, EVER WERE:
  ONE JUGGLED,
(*Valere hands De Brie some juggling balls and De Brie begins to juggle.*)
          ONE WAS A PHILOSPHER!
(*He slips a tome into Elomire's hands.*)
  ONE WORE A CAPE, THE OTHER WORE A FROCK;
  ONE BOY WAS BIG AND SOLID AS A ROCK,
  THE OTHER LOST HIS LEG IN EARLY LIFE
  FOR PROVING WRONG A BULLY WITH A KNIFE.
(*The troupe encircles Elomire; Valere lets out a banshee cry and "cuts
off" Elomire's "leg"—a little wooden boot which he shows to the
Prince. As an aside:*)
  Unless your brain is smaller than a thimble,
  The missing leg has struck you as a symbol
  For just how very costly it can be

To fight for truth with one's philosophy!
But SOFT! We TARRY! Back to our oration:
THE JUGGLING TWIN, THOUGH SKILLED AT HIS
    VOCATION,
WAS, NONETHELESS, A WEE BIT *ORDINAIRE:*
BEYOND HIS KEEPING THREE BALLS IN THE AIR
THERE WASN'T VERY MUCH THAT HE COULD DO;
(*De Brie juggles, incompetently.*)
HIS BROTHER, THOUGH, WAS BRILLIANT
    THROUGH AND THROUGH . . .
SO BRILLIANT THAT HIS THOUGHTS WERE FAR
    TOO GREAT
FOR ORDINARY FOLK TO CONTEMPLATE!
COMPLEX AND SUBTLE THEOREMS HE'D
    EXPOUND
(*Valere slides a spool of paper into Elomire's mouth and draws it out
across the stage, the troupe bunching to read the "theorems."*)
OF WHICH THE MOST AGGRESSIVELY PROFOUND
WAS ONE THAT PROVED (AND THIS IS JUST THE
    GIST)

CATHERINE (*Reading.*)
THAT NO SUCH THING AS NOTHING CAN
    EXIST . . .

MARQUISE-THERESE (*Giggling.*)
FOR IF IT *DOES*, IT CAN'T BE NOTHING, CAN IT?

VALERE
AMAZING HOW ONE THOUGHT CAN SHAKE
    THE PLANET!
(*The whole troupe giggles; with the exception of Bejart and Elomire,
they're really beginning to enjoy themselves.*)

FOR THIS DISPROOF OF "NOTHING," SHARPLY
 PUT,
THE WORLD . . . AT LEAST CADIZ . . . WAS AT
 HIS . . .
(*He holds up the little wooden boot.*)
              . . . FOOT.
(*The troupe laughs spontaneously; they're having fun, and from this
point forward they instinctively assume appropriate roles, their pleasure
and enthusiasm building in an accelerando.*)
   IN VOLTA, THOUGH, HE COULDN'T FIND *ONE* FAN!
(*The members of the troupe act out the following characters.*)
   FROM SAGE ARISTOCRAT TO WORKING MAN,
   FROM OLDEST VILLAGE COOT TO TINY SHAVER,
   THE BROTHER WHOM THE VOLTANS SEEMED
      TO FAVOR
   WAS ESTEBAN THE SECOND-RATE MAGICIAN
(*De Brie, incompetently, pulls a magic bouquet of flowers from his
trousers.*)
   NOT ESTEBAN THE DAZZLING LOGICIAN;
   THE LATTER'S WORK THEY COULDN'T
      UNDERSTAND—
   HIS PROOF THAT NOTHING'S NOTHING WAS
      TOO GRAND,
   TOO ELOQUENT A THEORY TO ADVANCE
   IN SUCH A VAIN AND SHALLOW LAND . . .

PRINCE

                              Read FRANCE.

ELOMIRE (*Through clenched teeth.*)
   I LOVE that . . .

PRINCE

                  Shhhh!' It's almost over now.

VALERE

BUT EVEN MORE UNSETTLING WAS HOW
UNFINCHINGLY AND SWIFTLY ESMEROLTA,
HERSELF DEBASED BY PREJUDICE IN VOLTA,
GAVE PARTIAL TREATMENT TO THE JUGGLING
TWIN!
A TOTALLY UNPARDONABLE SIN,
FOR SHE,
(*Indicating Bejart.*)
                UNLIKE HER COUNTRYMEN, COULD SEE
(*Indicating Elomire.*)
THE BRILLIANCE OF THE ONE'S PHILOSOPHY
BUT LIKE *THEM*
(*And the troupe and Bejart turn towards De Brie.*)
                    CHOSE THE OTHER ANYWAY!
NOW WHY ON EARTH WOULD SHE BEHAVE
THAT WAY?
(*He draws a tiny mole on Bejart's cheek.*)
IN VOLTA, WHERE A TINY MOLE COULD MAKE
A CRUCIAL DIFFERENCE TO ONE'S SOCIAL
STANDING
(*He turns Bejart in the direction of Elomire and shakes him.*)
SHE SHUDDERED AT THE MEREST THOUGHT OF
BANDING
WITH SOMEONE SO COMMITTED TO IDEALS
HE'D SACRIFICE HIS LEG FOR WHAT HE FEELS!
SHE THEREFORE TOLD THE GENIUS TO MOVE
ON . . .
WAS WED TO
(*He pushes Bejart and De Brie together in the frame, throwing rice over their heads.*)
                    MEDIOCRE ESTEBAN . . .
SAID FOND FAREWELLS TO SIDESHOWS AND ALL
THAT,

EMBARKED FOR SPAIN ABOARD THE TIT-FOR-
   TAT
(*De Brie steers an imaginary gondola.*)
   WHICH SHE MISREAD INSTEAD AS TIT-FOR-TATRA
(*He shrugs as if to say, "Who knows why?"*)
   WAS WELCOMED TO CADIZ LIKE . . . CLEOPATRA

He winks at the Prince, to celebrate the cleverness of his rhyme.

DE BRIE
   "RUFT LAUT MEIN HERTZ!"

CATHERINE
                    BRAVA!

MARQUISE-THERESE
                         WELL, GOOD FOR HER!

VALERE
   BUT . . . WHAT OF OUR ESTEEMED PHILOSOPHER?

*It's clear at this point that there's a real rapport between Valere and
the troupe; and Valere now shoves Elomire aside, himself assuming
the role of "philosopher" for the dramatic finale, as if Elomire couldn't
possibly handle it.*

MADELEINE
   ALAS, HIS WAS A HIDEOUS DEMISE!

DU PARC
   BY HUNGER FORCED TO PLUCK OUT BOTH HIS
      EYES
(*Valere "plucks out" two gelatinous "eyes" and hurls them against
the wall, where they stick; he then staggers tragically about the stage.*)
   AND TRADE THEM FOR A SLIGHTLY TAINTED
      QUAIL

CATHERINE

HE WANDERED, BLIND AND DESTITUTE AND
    FRAIL,

DE BRIE

FROM UPPER VOLTA DOWN TO LOWER VOLTA

DU PARC

FROM LOWER VOLTA BACK TO UPPER VOLTA

MADELEINE

IN SEARCH OF SOMEONE

CATHERINE

                    ANYONE AT ALL

MADELEINE

INTELLIGENT ENOUGH TO SCALE THE WALL
OF HIS COMPLEX AND RICH PHILOSOPHY!

MARQUISE-THERESE

BUT NOTHING DOES EXIST, FOR TRAGICALLY
'TWAS NOTHING THAT WAS LEFT UPON THE
    GROUND
WEEKS LATER WHEN HIS LONELY CORPSE WAS
    FOUND

MADELEINE

EXCEPT, OF COURSE, THE PATCHES FOR HIS EYES
AND ALSO

VALERE

                    (Think what this might symbolize!)

MADELEINE

HIS WOODEN LEG!

VALERE

The wooden LEG, YOU HEAR!?

DE BRIE

THE LEG, LIKE . . .

CATHERINE

. . . TRUTH!

VALERE

Good!

DE BRIE

WOULDN'T DISAPPEAR!
IT STOOD FOR HIS CONVICTIONS, IN A WAY—

DU PARC

UNYIELDING,

MARQUISE-THERESE

HARD,

CATHERINE

IMMUNE TO ALL DECAY,

DE BRIE

A MARK OF WHAT HE'D FOUGHT FOR SINCE HIS
YOUTH:

DU PARC

ETERNAL,

MADELEINE

IF IMPENETRABLE

ALL

TRUTH!!

The troupe breaks out into spontaneous applause. Surprised delight, and mutual admiration for one another's performances. The Prince remains impassive, simply observing.

VALERE (*Shyly covering his face at the applause.*)
> You're kind! You're kind! You're really far too kind!
> O this is so embarrassing, I find.
> It's you, not I, who warrant thunderous cheers!
> Applaud yourselves! You've earned the right, my dears:
> Such talent truly takes the breath away—
> You've made the author really *hear* the play
> As though he'd never heard the play before!
> What wizardry is this that makes words . . . soar
> That on the page seemed lifeless and mundane . . .

DE BRIE
> Well, acting's very tricky to explain.
> You see, I take the character and try
> To understand not simply *how* but *WHY*
> He does the things he does, which is to say
> I get *INSIDE* the meaning of the play . . .

De Brie continues babbling as Marquise-Therese steps in front of him.

MARQUISE-THERESE
> That's nonsense. One must work from outside in:
> By putting on the costume I begin
> At once to grasp the essence of the part . . .

Marquise-Therese joins De Brie in the babble as Du Parc steps in front of them.

DU PARC
> It's ludicrous to verbalize my art,
> For truly I *BECOME* the words I say!

That chicken—when it's squeezed within your play—
I *WAS* that chicken, I *BECAME* that hen . . .

And Du Pare joins the babble; Catherine steps forward.

CATHERINE
It's really *timing:* always knowing *when*
To tilt your head or launch a comic line;
A skill which only TRAINING can refine . . .

And Catherine joins the babbles; Madeleine steps forward.

MADELEINE
Well—I'm not one who thinks or broods or whines:
I simply hit my mark and say my lines . . .

The Prince rises suddenly to speak; his words are cold and analytically unfriendly. Is he being extremely rigorous and serious about a work which he admires, or has he been so offended that he is preparing to cut off Valere's head?

PRINCE
Although the tale's essentially the same
As that which I remember having heard,
Until tonight I thought its themes referred
To Volta only, not some great expanse:
But now I see that Volta is like France . . .

VALERE (*Wary; trying to make the best of a nervous situation.*)
Well grasped, my lord!

PRINCE

                                              . . . and France like Volta is!
The Parable of Two Boys from Cadiz
Critiques, therefore, at least implicitly,
The foibles of our *own* society!

VALERE

But is my work *that* subtle and ambitious!!??

PRINCE

I consequently found it more . . . *pernicious* . . .
Than when I heard it in the public square!
For what you're really saying here, Valere,
(Unless I'm analyzing it too much)
Is that, like Volta's culture, *ours* is such
Where mediocrity is bound to thrive
While excellence must struggle to survive!

VALERE (*Really beginning to sweat.*)
Exactly as you say! It's *very* sad!

PRINCE

We punish virtue; we reward the bad;
Our age embraces dullness like a lover!
(*The members of the troupe begin to fan themselves and look
distracted, not sure which way this is going to fall. They assume a
posture that says, "We're just actors." The Prince, slowly, gravely,
creepily:*)
We've lost the taste and patience to discover
Real morals or real wisdom or real art:
We can't tell truth and travesty apart!
And those who can, as shown by Esmerolta,
Are prone in France, the way they are in Volta,
To sell their souls without a second thought
The second there's occasion to be bought!
(*Into Valere's ear, almost whispered.*)
Vain fools control the world, *that's* what you're saying!
(*Valere is stock-still, and in panic.*)
Because of them our standards are decaying!
But wiser men must bear the greater blame

Who tolerate this evil in the name
Of comfort for themselves, like Esmerolta!
Indeed, not France, but all the world, is Volta!

VALERE (*Panic.*)
Repeat that final sentence if you could!
An artist rarely feels so *understood!*
(*Closing his eyes to enjoy it as he would a haunting melody.*)
Just one more time . . .

PRINCE (*Eerily.*)
                    "Indeed, not France . . ."

VALERE (*Butting in to finish it himself.*)
                                        LET ME!
(*Saying it slowly, savoringly.*)
   "But all the world, is Volta!"
(*Gasps again.*)
                    Ecstasy!
Had thou, lord, not been born of regal stripe,
Thou would'st have been a literary type—
A critic, I'm convinced, of world renown!
(*Drawing a piece of paper out of his doublet.*)
In fact, I'd like to write that sentence down.
I mean—my God!—it really was a dandy!
Who knows when such a line might come in handy?
(*Pen poised.*)
Again please, Mister Critic? "France, not Volta . . ."

PRINCE (*Very eerily.*)
"Indeed, not France, but all the world, is Volta!"

*The members of the troupe pull away, fearful, cringing. Valere gulps,
then writes down the Prince's words, nervously speaking them in the
same eerie tone as he does so.*

126

VALERE

"Indeed, not France, but all the world, is Volta!"
(*Holding the page at a distance from his face, and reading it in a
booming voice.*)

> "INDEED, NOT FRANCE, BUT ALL THE WORLD,
> IS VOLTA!"

(*He drops the quill and paper, swallows hard, and begins to speak
frantically.*)

I'm useless as a critic. Yes, it's so!
Creative people often are, you know.
I don't know *why*, but it's a common quirk—
Especially when judging one's own work.
To do so is like . . .

(*Shielding his eyes.*)

                . . . staring at the sun . . .

But since my lord already has begun
To offer *his* impressions of my play,
For sake of balance here's the author's way
Of getting at the meaning of the tale:
Correctly, lord, you've shown how I assail
The slipping standards of our shallow culture;
How vice looms over virtue like a vulture;
How truth's devoured by mediocrity!
But what, apparently, you didn't see
(And it's essential to the story's plan)
Is my insistence that a gifted man
Should persevere no matter what the cost!
One's innovative theories may be lost
On pinheads of the drawing room elite—
In time you might be begging on the street,
Obscurely counting mishaps that befell you:
Perfection can be painful, let me tell you!
The road to Greatness is a bumpy road!

127

But better pauper prince than wealthy toad,
And if one has to beg then beg one *should!*
It's burdensome to have a leg of wood,
It's difficult to be completely pure!
But they're the heroes, those who can endure,
Excel, be true, preserve integrity:
A harder life, but . . . look, it . . . works for *me!*
(*Pause.*)
    Well, there you have *my* reading of the play!
(*Looks to the troupe for help.*)
    I'd love to hear what *you* all have to say!

But Elomire, who has been leaning against the wall, now steps forward.

ELOMIRE (*Quietly but with great authority.*)
    MY LORD: this may sound insolent, I know,
    But if *we* stay,
(*Pointing to Valere.*)
                        then *HE* will have to go!

BEJART (*Tries to preempt Elomire's ultimatum.*)
    MY LORD!

ELOMIRE
                        The troupe stands by me . . .

PRINCE (*Hushing Bejart.*)
                                        Let him finish . . . !

ELOMIRE
    . . . Bejart's afraid that frankness might diminish
    Our chances of remaining here at Court;
    He errantly presumes that you're the sort
    Who brooks no disagreement with his views,
    And would, were his beliefs contested, choose

To banish the offending opposition
Instead of reassessing his position.
How wrong he is, my lord, how *very* wrong!
And that's what I've been saying all along:
The unembroidered TRUTH is what you seek!
Since no one feels at liberty to speak,
I therefore feel compelled to speak for *them!*
In short: I unreservedly condemn
By every measure, every standard known,
A work which I believe could stand alone
Among the theatre's most profound disgraces!
Evincing neither talent nor its traces,
The Parable of Two Boys from Cadiz
Assuredly, indubitably is
As bad a stage play as I've ever seen—
It's pompous, it's insulting, it's obscene,
It should, in sum, be banned from public view . . .

VALERE
Well, that's a . . . *semi*positive review . . .

Nervous laughter from a few members of the troupe.

ELOMIRE
He says its composition is unique!
But have you ever heard a worse technique!!??
Those desperation couplets are too tragic;
Like Volta/Esmerolta

VALERE
                    That's pure *magic* . . .

ELOMIRE
And Cleopatra/tit-for-tatra! Really!
Good verse conceals its artifice ideally,

But his bends over backwards for a rhyme!
The words are warped to fit some paradigm
As though the form should legislate the meaning;
And thus, you'll find no content intervening
Where his poetic metaphors are made!

VALERE (*Tugging at Elomire's sleeve, hushing him.*)
You're giving out the secrets of the trade!

ELOMIRE
But *most* appalling is the allegory!
If I'm correct, that deeply vulgar story
Was meant to illustrate the proposition
That France is in so desperate a condition—
Its values so decayed, its brow so low—
That mediocrity is all we know!

VALERE
Exactly! Yes! Our culture is bereft
Of excellence—there's nothing *good* that's *left!*
And even *good* things aren't any good!
(*Struck by his own phrase.*)
   (Although *that* phrase was really rather *good!!*)

Guffaw.

ELOMIRE
Did you hear *that!?* Well, *that's* my main objection!
Decrying France's vulgar predilection
For cheap and undistinguished works of art,
His play, ironically, is from the start
As bad as any work that it decries!
This bleak phenomenon *itself* implies
A danger to our nation more malign
Than so-called facts of cultural decline!

It represents a far more lethal trend:
The language used by artists to defend
Against the rule of mediocrity
Has been appropriated to a "t"
By just those mediocrities who rule!
It's dangerous to be governed by a fool,
But worse when fools bemoan the sad decline
Of standards which *their* efforts undermine!
To mourn decaying values in a play
Which only reinforces the decay
Devalues the idea that it expresses!
(*Indicating Valere.*)
And so the themes he loftily addresses—
Real excellence, real wisdom, and real art—
Are each devalued, sundered, torn apart!
Devalued are the very *words* employed
Which keep ideals from being thus destroyed:
A currency, that's cheapened bit by bit
Till even *genuine* seems counterfeit!
Hence, language is, by fools, emasculated!
Because their deeds and words are unrelated,
They taint all discourse with a hollow drivel:
Words, sapped of meaning, lose their clout, and shrivel!
Convictions, truths, are merely cloaks to don,
Providing an excuse to babble on!
On words *themselves* do such false words reflect;
Indeed, instead of having an effect,
They yield more *words*—they yield *interpretations!*
His play, he says, has subtle implications
About a culture doomed to the abyss!
But since his bold and grand analysis
Is more impressive than his puny play,
It shows that what you *really* do or say

Is less important than the *commentary!*
Good art—good deeds—become . . . unnecessary:
What's crucial is *portraying* them as good!
Hard facts count less than *how* they're understood;
Pretension and the truth become confused!
The honest Word is *violently* abused;
And when the honest Word is stripped of sense,
Its *form* assumes unnatural consequence:
The *way* a thing is stated holds more weight,
Than what, if anything, one seeks to state!
"I do my play in rhyme," he says with bluff
As if refined expression were enough
To pardon an impoverishment of thought!
Yet that's the place to which we've now been brought:
A place where men, as far as *I* can see,
Aspire to saying nothing . . . endlessly!
Well: *let* them talk and talk until they're blue!
For us, the less that's said, the better . . .

DORINE

                              TRUE!

BEJART
Hush up, Dorine!

ELOMIRE

                    Valere, I *loathed* your play.
If fools control the world and its decay
It is your play itself that tells us why:
For are you not the fool that you decry!?

VALERE (*Rising.*)
Is *that a question!?* Jesus *CHRIST* it's long!!
(*Nervous laughter from a few members of the troupe.*)

132

Well! Here's a one-word answer, darling:
    WWRROOOONNG!!
(*Valere is playing to the troupe now, trying to break the tension.*)
    No, no. I'm sure you're right. I'm sure you are.
    I'm terrible. I'm quite the worst by far!
    I'm all the awful things you say I am!
    O DAMN ME!

PRINCE (*In a quiet rage, almost unheard.*)
                Silence.

VALERE
                DAMN ME! DAMN DAMN DAMN!

VALERE
    If I could get away from me I would . . .

PRINCE
    I said, be QUIET!

PRINCE (*Reeling on Valere.*)
    SHUT UP, YOU *FOOL!*
(*Valere recoils.*)
                NOW IS THAT UNDERSTOOD?!

Elomire attempts to speak, but the Prince turns on him with similar rage.

ELOMIRE
    My lord . . .

PRINCE
    AND *YOU* AS WELL: how *dare* you lecture me
    As if I lacked impartiality
    To judge this work afresh, as we agreed!
    I frankly feel insulted by your screed!
(*Deadly.*)
    Don't ever—EVER—talk to me that way!

133

(*Slight shift of mood.*)
    Still, I can hear the truth in what you say;
    You know I do. You've had my full support
    In voicing all such sentiments at Court,
    And though I recognize them and *agree*
    They've weighed upon your plays increasingly!
    Stand firm for "truth in language"—but be FAIR:
    To turn *those* arguments against Valere
    (Who has a simple talent that might be
    A happy antidote) is SOPHISTRY!
    The *truth,* of course, is that you can't allow
    That "ELOMIRE HIMSELF!" is *wrong,* somehow!
(*Indicating the troupe.*)
    "He'd ruin us," you said. You're INCORRECT.
    In fact I was delighted to detect
    A message in his play that made it more
    Intriguingly disturbing than before—
(*Indicating the troupe again.*)
    And it was met with quite a great ovation.
(*Turns to Valere; the discussion is ended, the bargain is won.*)
    Monsieur Valere: you have an invitation
    To join the troupe; to bring your talents here.

VALERE
    Who, *me!?* And share the stage with *Elomire!?*
    No, no I couldn't.
(*Very slight pause.*)
                Well, if you *insist!*
    Humility doth urge me to resist,
    But *damn* humility, I always say!
    Just show me where to sign! I'm here to stay!
    It's really too too generous of you;
    My friends, I'm speechless . . .

ELOMIRE

                                  Would that *that* were true!
But I'm convinced that that will *never* be!
My lord, I said with all sincerity
That if *we* stay then *he* will have to go:
That wasn't just an idle threat, you know . . . !

PRINCE (*Deadly serious, even belligerent.*)
Well, *he's* not going *anywhere,* all right!?
So you can pack your bags and leave tonight
(*Indicating the troupe.*)
And they can join you if they're so inclined;
And since it comes to that, I think you'll find
A precious few supporters for this action!
How sad to let a negative reaction
To someone whom you've barely even met
Irrevocably alter and upset
Your place at Court, your troupe's security!
And in the name of *what*—of *purity?*
Of strict adherence to some rigid rule?
One really has to wonder—who's the fool?
(*The question lingers. Pause. He turns to address the troupe.*)
To those who want to leave with Elomire,
I thank you for your splendid service here
And wish you well whatever you may do;
But, otherwise, as for the rest of you—
The ones without a moral cross to bear
Who might *enjoy* performing with Valere—
We have a thing or two to talk about
And therefore come . . . accompany me out!

Exit Prince and servants. Pause. Elomire turns to the troupe.

ELOMIRE
I thought . . . I hoped . . . that he would understand.

135

It's not what I . . . it isn't what I'd planned.
There simply wasn't any choice, you see?
To ask you . . .
(*He breaks off, stutters. He is silent for a moment. Emotion seizes him.*)
     . . . this is difficult for me . . .
(*Pause. He partially regains himself.*)
To ask you . . . to give up this life for one
Whose hardships we had only just begun
By mercy to forget . . .
(*And he is overwhelmed, shocked to find that he is suddenly, for the first time, inarticulate.*)
     . . . no . . . WORDS . . . will do.
(*Brief pause. Again, he finds words.*)
But know: your faith in me and mine in you
Has tided us through troubled times before
And will again. It *WILL!*
(*He breaks off again.*)
     There's nothing more . . .
(*He turns upstage to get his coat.*)
Let's get our things . . . I've nothing more to add . . .

DE BRIE (*Steps forward.*)
Excuse me, Elomire . . .
(*Clears his throat, indicates Valere; sheepishly.*)
     . . . he's not so bad.
(*Elomire turns to face De Brie, who says, with a little more confidence:*)
I mean . . . I *liked* his play . . . a tiny bit.

ELOMIRE (*Softly, from far away.*)
Don't lie.

DE BRIE
   I'm sorry. That's the truth of it.

ELOMIRE (*Softly, distant.*)
That *can't* be true . . .

CATHERINE
              Well, don't look so dejected!
He wasn't the disgrace that we expected.

VALERE (*With a hard edge.*)
Why, child. Such honeyed words. Such flattery.

ELOMIRE (*Emerging from the distance.*)
My God. This can't be happening to me.
Du Parc . . . !

DU PARC (*Genuine.*)
           I'm sorry, I agree with her.

ELOMIRE
Therese . . . ?

MARQUISE-THERESE
      Me too.

VALERE (*Quietly, enjoying this.*)
          You . . . "love me" . . . as it were!

ELOMIRE
He really took you in, this Boor of Boors?

MADELEINE
Well, dear . . . his work *is* livelier than yours.

ELOMIRE (*Shock, it's caving in.*)
It's WHAT?

MARQUISE-THERESE
    It's more accessible and fun!

CATHERINE

It frankly seems forever since we've done
A play that might have popular appeal!

DE BRIE

Were we to tour again I strongly feel
That with its showy costumes, gags, and plot
It's bound to draw great crowds . . .

MARQUISE-THERESE (*With a hint of exasperation, as if Elomire
had lost a sense of play in his work and became too didactic, too
insensitive to their needs as a troupe.*)

                              As we could not
With all the work of YOURS we've done of late.
Who really cares about the
(*As if quoting from one of Elomire's plays.*)
                              bloated state
Of language and its ethical dimension,
And other themes too ponderous to mention
Which tend to bore instead of entertain . . .

DU PARC

It's arrogance that leads you to disdain
A play which could become a great success . . .

ELOMIRE (*Deeply confused, shaken.*)
And that's what you desire?

DU PARC

                            Well . . .

ALL (*Affectionately, but firmly.*)

                              Frankly, yes.

VALERE (*Again, quietly, off to the side.*)
My dears, you're giving me a swollen head.

ELOMIRE (*Dumbfounded.*)
Are you prepared to live with what you've said?
Have you considered what this choice will mean?
Does no one understand?

DORINE (*Very quietly, almost unheard.*)
                    I do.

ELOMIRE (*Turns to her, in amazement, as in a dream.*)
                    Dorine.

BEJART (*From the other side of the stage; ambiguously, with what could be either fatalism or reproval.*)
I do as well.

ELOMIRE (*Goes to him.*)
            Then help me, please, Bejart.
Dear friend, stick with me . . .

BEJART
                        No. You've gone too far.

ELOMIRE
I have?

BEJART
        There *is* a way that's less extreme.

ELOMIRE (*Retrenching.*)
I don't believe that.

BEJART (*Crosses to the door, not looking at Elomire.*)
                    No, so it would seem.

ELOMIRE
And *you* don't either.

Bejart summons the troupe, trying to ignore Elomire; he opens the door.

BEJART

Come along, you hear?

ELOMIRE
I *KNOW* YOU DON'T.

BEJART (*Looks at Elomire; clearly.*)
I *have* to, Elomire.
(*Pause; to the troupe.*)
The Prince is waiting, everyone. Let's go.

Elomire turns to the troupe.

ELOMIRE (*Finally, beseechingly.*)
Don't leave me.
(*But the troupe exits, the door held open by Bejart. A moment passes.
To Bejart:*)

Please.

Pause.

BEJART

Then stay.

Pause.

ELOMIRE

I can't.

Pause.

BEJART

I know.

*Bejart holds up his hand to Elomire, exits. Elomire crosses up to the
closed door and leans against it. Pause. From the other side of the
stage, Valere begins to speak, with some real menace, first to the
audience, then to Elomire.*

VALERE
    WELL! Talk about a party falling flat!
    They all just . . . *disappeared!* . . . did, you see *that!?*
    A pity! We were having *lots* of fun!
    And I was so *adored* by everyone!!
    But not by Elomire, I'm sad to say
    Which casts a sort of pall across the day
    Since, after all, that's *really* why I'm here!
(*To Elomire.*)
    If only you had LIKED me, Elomire:
    We had the makings of a brilliant team!
    But now it lies there, just a shattered dream,
    And all that's left to do is say "good night."
(*Collecting himself.*)
    For me, just meeting you was a delight!
    I'm sorry that you didn't feel the same,
    But thank you, anyway. I'm glad I came.
(*He begins to exit.*)
    Our dinner here I never shall forget . . .
(*Exit Valere; then, after a beat, he sticks his head back into
the room and says:*)
    . . . Especially that DREADFUL vinaigrette . . .

Elomire winces. Exit Valere. Elomire puts his coat on and the lights
dim until he remains in a pin spot only.

ELOMIRE (*This final speech is spoken quietly, to himself.*)
    By starting on a journey once again
    (Not knowing what's to come, or where I'm bound)
    I wonder—did I stand too firmly, then,
    When this safe haven had at last been found?

    Does any way less radical exist
    To keep ideals from being trivialized?

The only way I know is to resist:
Autonomy cannot be compromised!

Elomire lifts his head to see Dorine, who has never left the stage and is standing in the shadows, listening.

With every day the peril is increased
Of yielding to this treacherous misrule,
For fools contain inside of them a beast
That triumphs when the world is made a fool!

A low murmur of voices and laughter is heard from the other room.

If LIFE—not grim survival—is the aim,
The only hope is setting out to find
A form of moral discourse to reclaim
The moral discourse fools have undermined.

Upon that road I joyfully embark!
And though it seems that joy itself's at stake,
There's joy itself in challenging the dark:
We're measured by the *choices* that we make!

An eruption of laughter from offstage. Dorine slowly crosses to Elomire, carrying his belongings to him.

Against great odds one gamely perseveres,
For nature gives advantage to a fool:
His mindless laughter ringing in your ears,
His thoughtless cruelties seeming doubly cruel;

His power stems from emptiness and scorn—
Debasing the ideals of common men;
But those debased ideals *can* be reborn . . .
By starting on the journey once again.

Laughter and noise from offstage. Elomire takes his suitcase from Dorine. Pause. He exits. From the other room, we hear Valere's voice boom.

VALERE (*Off.*)
YOU THINK ME *TOO* SELF-CRITICAL? ALACK,
TEN THOUSAND MORE HAVE LAUNCHED THE
    SAME ATTACK!

The voices dissolve and are replaced by music. Dorine, alone, blows a kiss to Elomire; her eyes welling with tears, she turns to face the audience in silence as the curtain falls.

END OF PLAY

WRONG MOUNTAIN

for

MY MOTHER *and* MY FATHER

and for

PETER CLARK

and for

RICHARD JONES

and for

MICHAEL DAVID *and* LAUREN MITCHELL

Wrong Mountain was originally produced on the Broadway stage by Dodger Theatricals, American Conservatory Theatre, Lauren Mitchell and the John F. Kennedy Center for the Performing Arts at the Eugene O'Neill Theatre on January 13, 2000. It was directed by Richard Jones; the set and costume designs were by Giles Cadle; the lighting design was by Jennifer Tipton; the sound design was by John Gromada; and the production stage manager was James Harker. The cast was as follows:

HENRY DENNETT	Ron Rifkin
CLAIRE	Beth Dixon
JESSICA	Ilana Levine
ADAM	Bruce Norris
PETER	Reg Flowers
CHEYENNE	(pre-recorded voice)
GUY HALPERIN	Michael Winters
MAURICE MONTESOR	Daniel Davis
DUNCAN	Tom Riis Farrell
SALOME	Beth Dixon
JASON	Reg Flowers
MIRANDA	Jody Gelb
ARIEL	Anne Dudek
WINNY	Mary Schmidtberger
CLIFF	Daniel Jenkins
ANNE	Mary Schmidtberger
LEIBOWITZ	Tom Riss Farrell
STEVENS	Daniel Jenkins
MIDDLE-AGED WOMAN	Jody Gelb
USHER	Jody Gelb

CHARACTERS

HENRY DENNETT, a poet
CLAIRE, his ex-wife
JESSICA, his daughter
ADAM, his son
PETER, his son-in-law
CHEYENNE, his granddaughter by Jessica and Peter

GUY, Claire's fiancé

MAURICE MONTESOR, festival director

DUCAN
SALOME
JASON   actors
MIRANDA
ARIEL

WINNY, a finalist
CLIFF, a finalist

ANNE, an aspiring poet

LEIBOWITZ, Dennett's physician
STEVENS, a bookseller
MIDDLE-AGED WOMAN
USHER

PLACE & TIME

Here and now.

The play is presented in three parts. There is one interval.

149

Note

Wrong Mountain is broken up into twenty-four scenes. Whenever possible—and particularly in the many instances when a principal character(s) in one scene is involved in the action of the next— actors should move/ pivot into subsequent scenes (or have the action of subsequent scenes overtake them) in an uninterrupted flow. While stage directions such as "Lights Fade" or "Blackout" occasionally indicate places in the text where a sense of demarcation is clearly desired, they should be adhered to literally only insofar as they contribute to the general atmosphere of streamlined boundaries between scenes—an effect that will also depend on deft physical choreography. (To make a fluid transition from the "Bookshop" (iii) to the "Motel Room" (iv) in Act One, for example, a bed might simply be slid out for Dennett to collapse upon.)

The overall visual aspect of the piece should be treated no less figuratively. However detailed some of the physical descriptions may be, they should be viewed, by and large, as blueprints. In fact, with the exception of a few images that are indispensable to the play's visual vocabulary (and these will become evident by the way in which they recur), the choice as to which scenic ideas are to be represented, and how, remains entirely discretionary. The demand for a speeding passenger train and the Himalayas onstage will, no doubt, prove for a formidable challenge to the wit and ingenuity of a designer, but the play could still function quite well if little more than a few chairs and tables were used to represent its world.

★

In this edition of *Wrong Mountain,* I have chosen to footnote variations between the original manuscript of the play and the text used for its New York premiere wherever they seem relevant and/ or illuminating.

WRONG MOUNTAIN

i. Contemptiosuarumcupiditatumfilaria

ii. Lithia Spring

iii. Wrong Mountain

VIDEO MELIORA PROBOQUE;
DETERIORA SEQUOR.
OVID

ACT ONE

Audio:
As the house lights fade, the sound of a fierce, gusting
wind spills gradually into the theatre, building
in intensity until the lights have faded
completely.

In the wind-blown darkness
the following inscription appears before the audience:

i
Contemptiosuarumcupditatumfilaria

Fade to black

153

*Audio: Over the sound of the buffeting wind comes
a strangulated, lupine howl in the dark.*

i
NIGHT

*A single light picks out what appears, at first, to be a tiny
moon suspended in the void. It is, in fact, the livid, contorted
face of Henry Dennett. The multiple pores, blemishes, and
hair follicles that stipple his sweating upper
lip seem to grow in dimension as he keens, a second time,
with the confused outrage of a wild animal caught in the
jaws of a steel trap.*

DENNETT
Aaaauuuuuuuugggggggggggghhhhhhhhh!

This harrowing expostulation carries straight over into:

ii
A DOCTOR'S OFFICE

*Dennett, a big-boned, pasty-faced man in late middle age,
is doubled over on an examination table, bellowing
preternaturally. He is observed, from a distance, by
Leibowitz, a physician in his early thirties.*

DENNETT
GgggggyyyyyyyggggggghhhhRRRAAA!

*A brief silence follows this bloodcurdling scream.
    Leibowitz continues to study Dennett with an odd, clinical
detachment.*

LEIBOWITZ
And are you experiencing any discomfort right now?

Uncoiling from the spasm, a bewildered Dennett regards Leibowitz, who suddenly explodes into jarringly inappropriate laughter.

Sorry. Lousy joke. I do that.

Just as suddenly, Leibowitz assumes the exaggerated professional sincerity of a TV doctor.

No, obviously you're in a great deal of pain.

Again, Leibowitz bursts into unseemly laughter.

Sorry.

Leiboowitz bows with a flourish of theatrical penitence, like the King of Siam.

A thousand pardons.

As Leibowitz rises from his chair to assume a more academic posture, Dennett's eyes bore into him incredulously, murderously.

(*More cocky than sincere*)
Did you know that Napoleon called Morocco "the land of menstruating men"?

DENNETT (*Sotto voce, and furious*)
Egypt, you streak of piss . . .

Leibowitz prattles on, unhearing.

LEIBOWITZ
That's because many of the locals were infected with "bilharzia," a parasite which causes blood to be released into the urine . . .

Dennett, his patience stretched to the far edge of civility, cuts Leibowitz off by raising his hand.

DENNETT

Excuse me. Are you a real doctor?

Leibowitz does not reply.

Do you understand that I'm in the process of being *garroted* by *colic*?! Do you even care?

A stony-faced Leibowitz is silent.

Is it possible to get any kind of diagnosis and treatment out of you without being subjected to some wise-ass lecture on . . .
  (*Shrieking*)
. . . Napoleon?!

Leibowitz is tight-lipped, insulted and imperious.

LEIBOWITZ

I was merely trying to indicate that the histology of . . .

As if assaulted from behind, Dennett grips his abdomen and caterwauls violently.

DENNETT

Hyyyyyyyyyyuuuaaauuuggghhhhhh!

A brief silence follows this protracted howl. When Dennett is able to recover sufficiently to fix Leibowitz again with his harrowed gaze, he finds the doctor regarding him contemptuously.

LEIBOWITZ

Are you finished?

DENNETT

Am I "finished"?

LEIBOWITZ

Are you quite done?

(*Pause*)
What I was trying to explain to you before that . . . shabbily
theatrical outburst . . . is that . . .

> *Leibowitz pulls down an anatomy chart and points to the
> gastrointestinal cavity.*

. . . you're suffering from a rare but non-life threatening
cestode which, while impossible to eliminate entirely from
the intestine, is nonetheless generally controllable by use of
appropriate medication.

DENNETT
Cestode. That's a . . .

> *Leibowitz arches his eyebrows.*

Isn't that a . . . ?

> *Leibowitz arches his eyebrows a notch higher.*

(*Queasily*)
. . . a . . . worm?

LEIBOWITZ (*With hostile indifference*)
Mmmm-hmmmm. *Big* worm.

DENNETT (*Alarmed*)
How big?

> *Leibowitz crosses behind his desk and begins to make some
> notations on a pad.*

LEIBOWITZ
Have you noticed any significant, unaccountable changes in
your body weight over, say, the past six months?

DENNETT (*With mounting anxiety*)
O my God! Yes! Astonishingly so! I've gained close to . . .
forty pounds!

LEIBOWITZ (*Nodding knowingly*)
Forty pounds.

> *Dennett's eyes widen in horror. Leibowitz tears a sheet of paper from the pad and holds it out towards Dennett, who suddenly looks down to regard his abdomen with a sense of nausea and estrangement.*

LEIBOWITZ
I'm giving you a prescription for metronidazole, an anti-filarial which effectively wipes out less aggressive trichomonads.
(*With a hint of amusement*)
It won't kill that gorgeous, highly evolved monster inside of *you*—but it should serve us well in a strategy of long-term containment.

DENNETT (*Panic*)
Long-term containment! Gorgeous monster! Christ, you're making this sound like something out of Poe! What is it?! Does it have a *name?!*

> *Leibowitz soberly relishes Dennett's panic.*

LEIBOWITZ (*Archly overarticulating*)
Contemptiosuarumcupiditatumfilaria.

DENNETT (*Severely agitated, not computing*)
O, no! O, God! What's that?

LEIBOWITZ (*Bored*)
It's a worm.

DENNETT
O, no! O, God! O, please! How did I get it? How did it get inside of me? Can't it be cut out?

> *Leibowitz crosses his arms stagily, condescendingly.*

LEIBOWITZ

I thought you weren't interested in hearing any lectures.

DENNETT (*Rage banishing panic*)

Look, you! You just tell me what I've got, you little prick!

> *Leibowitz studies Dennett. He then proceeds to make some further notations on the pad.*

LEIBOWITZ (*Snidely*)

There's a marvelous little monograph which should answer most of your questions on the subject.

> *Leibowitz, a mischievous smile curling about his lips, peels off a sheet of paper from the notepad and hands it to Dennett.*

You can find it at Libris Books. You know where Libris Books is, don't you?

> *Dennett suddenly clutches his stomach and growls.*

DENNETT

Hwwwwwwwuuugggggghhhhaaaaaaaaaa!

> *A brief silence as Dennett recovers; then:*

LEIBOWITZ (*With renewed clinical interest; scoldingly*)

Have you been eating too much corn?

> *Dennett faces Leibowitz helplessly.*

DENNETT (*Weak, yet sneeringly pedantic*)

What does that mean? "Too much corn"?

> *Leibowitz pauses. Then, with ominous authority:*

LEIBOWITZ

Don't eat too much corn.

A BOOKSHOP

Dennett is revealed with an enormous book, which he is holding open to a page that contains a lithograph, a Grandville illustration. It depicts a freakish assemblage of nineteenth-century figures reacting in horror as a serpent, seduced by a plate of steaming food, is drawn out of the mouth of an emaciated man.

Dennett nervously fingers the lips of his own mouth. He extracts from his jacket pocket a vial and swallows one of its contents, squinting momentarily at the prescription before revisiting his attention upon the book.

Stevens, the proprietor, approaches from the rear and places his hand on Dennett's shoulder, startling him.

STEVENS
Here's the young lady I wanted you to meet.

Dennett pivots to discover Anne, a fresh-faced twenty-three-year-old.

Anne, this is Mr. Dennett.
(*To Dennett*)
Henry, Anne heard you gave a reading at Bennington a few years ago when she was an undergraduate, and was, I believe . . .
(*Prompting her*)
. . . quite taken? . . .

ANNE (*Nervously*)
Very impressed.

Dennett extends his hand languidly.

DENNETT
O, well thank you.

ANNE (*Shaking Dennett's hand*)

No, thank *you*. This is . . . it's an honor.

Stevens places his arm around Anne with avuncular pride.

STEVENS

Anne's been with us for almost a year now.

ANNE (*Tremulously, emotionally*)

You said something that day which I've never forgotten.
(*Stilted*)
You said, "Every man carries with him through life a
mirror, as unique and impossible to get rid of as his shadow.
But the properties of our own particular mirror are not so
important as we sometimes think. We shall be judged, not
by the kind of mirror found on us, but by the use we have
made of it, by our *riposte* to our reflection."

STEVENS (*Proudly*)

How do you like that?

DENNETT

I'm touched.

ANNE (*Pressing a slim volume into Dennett's hands*)

Would you . . . autograph this for me?

DENNETT

Certainly.

STEVENS

Anne is quite a poet herself.

DENNETT

Are you?

ANNE (*Weirdly formal and eager*)

Mr. Dennett, whatever strides I may have taken in my life

towards becoming a true writer I feel I owe primarily to you. Does that sound foolish?

DENNETT
Not at all. I'm flattered.

ANNE
It never occurred to me until I heard you speak at Bennington that there might be a poet inside of *me*.

Dennett hands the autographed book to her.

DENNETT (*With an unsavory, telltale hint of sarcasm*)
And now you think that there *is?*

ANNE (*Slightly confused*)
Well . . . I hope so.
    (*Awkward pause*)
I mean . . . I'm not sure . . .

DENNETT (*Wickedly*)
No?

    Dennett lets this dangle awkwardly for a moment. Suddenly, his expression grows pitiless.

    (*Socratically*)
What's the chief enemy of all good writing?

    Anne opens her mouth to speak, but Dennett doesn't wait.

    (*Fiercely and impatiently overarticulating*)
What is the chief enemy of all good writing? Imprecision, right? Not ambiguity, which tends to be a virtue, but *sloppiness* . . . of thought, language, structure. Do you agree?
    (*Slight pause*)
Do you agree? Yes or no?

ANNE (*Off-balance, shaken*)
I . . . guess so.

> *Dennett observes her coldly.*

DENNETT
You *guess* so.
> (*Pause*)

What's the matter? Am I trampling on some romantic script in your mind that decrees exactly how this sort of interchange is meant to go?

STEVENS (*Alarmed*)
Henry . . .

ANNE (*Wanting simply to withdraw from the situation now*)
I don't know what to say.

DENNETT
You don't have to say anything, *dear*. I know what you're thinking. Being one of the . . . um . . . "lessers lights," as my ex-wife not so euphemistically summarizes the sub-stellar trajectory of my literary career, I suppose I'm expected to be . . .
> (*Clutching his heart*)

. . . especially moved, and grateful, at the thought that my words . . .
> (*With mock-romanticism*)

. . . "uttered in a grove of nymphdom so many moons ago . . . should have inspired a daughter of the next generation to take up the pen."

STEVENS
Henry . . . !

DENNETT (*Fiercely*)
Alas, that passage which you rather stiltedly misquoted isn't mine at all. You've obviously forgotten that I was citing a few lines from "The Well of Narcissus." Those are *Auden's* words that inspired you, not mine. Permit me to observe that down the road of that kind of misattribution lies a general sloppiness that will never stand you in good stead as a writer. Never.

> *Anne, close to tears, turns and hurries away.*

ANNE
I'm sorry . . .

> *Dennett smiles and winks at Stevens.*

DENNETT
That'll be good for her. Trust me.
(*Hoisting the medical text*)
By the way, Jerry. How much is this?

STEVENS
Get out!

> *Stevens storms off.*

DENNETT (*Genuinely perplexed*)
What did I say?

> *Dennett stares after them vacantly for a moment. He then winces and grips his stomach. Lights fade.*

iv★
A MOTEL ROOM

Drab curtains, suffused with dim winter light from outside, hang closed over a narrow length of windows. In the semi-darkness, the sound of a man and woman engaged in ludicrously noisy, carnivorous sex is heard . . .

. . . It is Dennett and Anne. He is lying supine on the tousled bedspread like a beached whale; she is straddling him, murmuring an unholy, catechismal accompaniment to his pathetic, arhythmic grunts and gyrations.

ANNE (*Variously:*)

It's an honor!
YES!
Would you . . . *autograph* this for me!
YES!
Whatever strides I've taken to becoming a true writer
YES!
I owe primarily to *you*!

Dennett continues to grunt and gyrate.

Ambiguity . . . is a virtue!
YES!
Sloppiness. . . of thought, language, *structure*!!
YES!
Until you spoke at Bennington
It never occurred to me
YES!
That there might be a poet inside of *me*. . . !

★This fantasy/nightmare sequence, after several unsatisfactory attempts to realize it, was cut in the New York production. The play proceeded directly from scene iii ("A Bookshop") to scene v ("Dennett's House").

Anne breaks off mid-sentence. She looks at Dennett and gasps. Her expression shifts suddenly from ecstasy to disbelief; then to revulsion; then to wild-eyed horror. Clutching her head as if it were about to explode, she draws a deep, silent breath before letting loose a piercing scream that is sustained virtually unabated for the rest of this scene.

Inching out of Dennett's mouth as he continues, slack-jawed and shut-eyed, to grunt and gyrate is the head of what appears to be an enormous albino snake, a blanched eel cautiously investigating the outside world, responding to Anne's stricken cries by spreading a protective, cobralike hood. It bares two lethal-looking fangs and begins to hiss and click menacingly.

Dennett, alerted to Anne's hysteria, is plunged instantly into a state of disorientation and terror at the sight of the the hideous viper rising out of his mouth. He grabs it and, choking violently, attempts to wrestle it from his throat. A protracted, vein-popping struggle ensues.

Ultimately, the creature, freeing itself, coils and lunges, fangs first, into one of Dennett's thighs, the long tube of its body stoppering his cry of agony.

Anne continues to scream as . . .

The lights fade.

v
DENNETT'S HOUSE

A living room.

Guy, a middle-aged man in an expensive sweater, is seated center stage. He is flanked by Claire, Dennett's ex-wife, a woman in early middle age; Adam, her son, a young man of about twenty-five; Jessica, Adam's sister, a young woman maybe a year or two older; Peter, Jessica's husband,

*a young black man who is wearing what appears to be a kilt;
and Cheyenne★, a small child whom Peter fusses over
neurotically.*

    *Dennett stands apart. The Family observes him with
intense anxiety.*

CLAIRE (*To Dennett*)
How do you pronounce it? Contemptio—*what?*

GUY (*To Claire*)
Contempio—stuartum—cutipitatum . . .

ADAM (*Snottily, cutting Guy off*)
Contemptiosuarumcupiditatumfilaria.

JESSICA (*To Guy, mercilessly*)
Do you know what that means?

GUY
Well, my Greek is a little rusty . . .

ADAM (*Pointedly, to Guy*)
Contempt . . . for one's own beliefs.

JESSICA (*To Guy, disdainfully*)
It's Latin.

GUY (*Sweetly*)
O. Whoops.

JESSICA (*To Guy, still disdainfully*)
It's the Latin name for the disease.

★As originally conceived, the role of Cheyenne was to be played by a flesh-
and-blood little girl. Bowing to practical considerations, the New York production ultimately represented "Cheyenne" (through the use of a concealed sound-
box) as a child's voice emanating from a perambulator. While this solution
was eminently stageworthy, I am choosing to restore, in the current text, the
original stage directions (which presuppose the presence of a living actor), if
only as a point of comparison.

167

DENNETT (*To Adam, sharply*)
Excuse me. Cicero!
ContemptiosuarumCUPIDITATUMfilaria. CUPIO!
Contempt for one's own *desires*, not *beliefs*.

> *Adam, genuinely humiliated, buries his face in his hands.*

Maybe we should take your Amherst diploma off the wall
and shape it into a dunce cap. It only cost me seventy
thousand dollars.

> *Cheyenne suddenly breaks free of Peter and toddles towards
> Guy, arms outstretched.*

CHEYENNE
Grandpa! Grandpa!

> *Peter, in a flash of disapproval, scoops up Cheyenne and faces
> Guy reproachfully.*

PETER
No, Cheyenne!
>   (*To Guy*)
Did *you* teach her to say that?
>   (*To Jessica*)
Your mother's lobotomized suitor just crossed the line again
. . .

GUY (*To Dennett*)
But it's nothing more than an intestinal parasite. Right? I
mean . . . it's not serious . . .

PETER
Were you listening in there? He just said it was a forty-
pound worm!

GUY
I know. Which is horrible. But it's not lethal, right?

JESSICA

No, not lethal. Just incurable.

ADAM

And, apparently, excruciatingly painful. Why don't you write one of your fabulously successful "Guy Halperin plays" about it?

CLAIRE

Don't speak to Guy like that!

GUY (*To Claire, preparing to leave*)

Honey, maybe I should go.

CLAIRE

Absolutely not! You're not going anywhere!

ADAM

I don't understand why he was invited in the first place.

CLAIRE (*Indicating Jessica*)

Ask your sister! It was her idea.

JESSICA (*Indicating Dennett*)

It was my idea to invite *Daddy!* So he could spend Christmas with *Cheyenne!* I didn't expect your *boyfriend* to show up!

CLAIRE

He didn't "show up." He *lives* here.

> *Astonishment from Jessica, Peter, and Adam.*

ADAM

What are you talking about?

GUY (*Diplomatically, to Adam and Jessica*)

I moved in with your mom a few weeks ago. I hope everybody's okay with that.

ADAM (*To Dennett, chagrined*)
Daddy, we had no idea . . .

DENNETT
What, do you think I *care?*

ADAM
Well, no . . . but . . . on top of the . . . contemptio . . .

DENNETT (*Impatiently dismissing the entire subject*)
O, forget about that. Look, I'm fine. I'm fine. I'm going to
be fine. Why don't we not talk about it anymore.

ADAM (*Wheeling on everyone, parroting Dennett*)
Yeah, why don't we not talk about it anymore.

Cheyenne breaks free and toddles back towards Guy.

CHEYENNE
Grandpa! Grandpa!

Peter scoops up the child indignantly.

PETER
No, Cheyenne! He's not your grandfather! Do you
understand?

*Claire, suddenly spotting a scribbled crayon drawing of
Cheyenne's, snaps it out of the child's hands and exclaims:*

CLAIRE
O, my God! This is AMAZING!

JESSICA
What is?

DENNETT
What's amazing?

Claire exhibits the drawing to the room.

CLAIRE
Look, everybody! My granddaughter's the next Baselitz!*

Adam snatches the picture from Claire and a general hub-bub of cross-talking enthusiasm ensues:

JESSICA
O, my God! It's true! I can definitely see Baselitz, but there's also a hint of middle-period De Chirico if you exclude the perimeter . . .

ADAM
Jesus! You're right! It's got a weirdly pagan sense of dislocation that seems almost intentional, "a stumbled–upon trope for human suffering," as Daddy says . . .

PETER
I'd actually noticed the similarity to Baselitz before. But you should see her watercolors. They're extremely primitive, and the interplay of flatness and depth is unmistakably Kokoschka . . .

GUY
Wow! Pablo Picasso better WATCH HIS ASS!

DENNETT (*Breaking in over the din*)
Let me have a look.

> *Dennett subjects the picture to a cursory inspection.*

> (*Thin-lipped, dropping the picture on the coffee table*)
Well, what do you know about that . . .

Dennett, annoyed at—and jealous of—the attention being lavished upon Cheyenne, intones:

I finished a new poem this week, incidentally.

---

*Changed in the New York production, for purposes of audibility and familiarity, to "the next de Kooning."

This assertion causes the room's focus to shift back to Dennett.

ADAM (*Awestruck*)
Did you, Daddy?

JESSICA
Daddy, that's fantastic!

DENNETT
It's an aubade. I read it to my first-years on Wednesday. They were dazzled. One of them thought it was a translation from *Les Fleurs du Mal*. Would you like to hear it?

As with Cheyenne, a general hubbub of enthusiasm ensues, punctuated by Guy's excited exclamation:

GUY (*Genuine, yet gauche*)
What a *treat!*

The room goes silent as all, except Claire, regard Guy scornfully.
  Dennett gathers himself with the pomp of Eliot: the aged eagle spreads his wings. He dons reading glasses and unfolds a sheet of crumpled foolscap from his breast pocket. He sighs deeply.

DENNETT (*Reading*)
"AUBADE."

"Alvaro's blunge and bucket pricked the spell
Invented by that swaying mast, its groan
Hypnotically redundant as the cry
Of tenors from a broken gramophone . . ."

Cheyenne squeals with delight at something unrelated. Dennett glances at the child fiercely. Peter hushes her. Adam hushes her a second time for good measure. A pause.
  Dennett, steaming silently at the interruption, continues:

172

"A greasy thud of turkish knots, a bell
Proceeded from his scrape of holystone
Across the clammy deck above, where I
Would scrimshaw oyster shell with amber bone . . ."

Cheyenne breaks free again, toddling towards Guy and squealing.

CHEYENNE
Grandpa! Grandpa!

Dennett wheels on the child.

DENNETT
GODDAMMIT! IS THAT KID GOING TO LISTEN
OR TALK?

JESSICA
Daddy, she's two years old!*

DENNETT
So? I had to look at her stupid painting! The least she could
do is . . .
(*Directed at Cheyenne*)
. . . SHUT UP AND LET ME FINISH!

JESSICA
Don't speak to her like that!

ADAM (*To Jessica*)
She shouldn't have interrupted!

PETER (*Scooping up Cheyenne and steering her back towards Dennett*)
No, Cheyenne! That's not your grandfather . . . !

---

*In New York, this line was changed to "Daddy, she's just a baby" to accom-
modate the perambulator conception.

DENNETT (*Sneeringly*)

What kind of preposterous, new-age name is "Cheyenne," anyway?

> *Cheyenne is thrust by Peter into Dennett's face . . .**

PETER

. . . *this* is your grandfather!

> . . . *as Dennett is struck by another violent spasm. Dennett's face contorts and he lets loose a timber-shaking howl directly into Cheyenne's face.*
>
> *Cheyenne, traumatized, bawls hysterically. Dennett continues to moan, gripping his stomach and frantically scrounging for pills. Claire berates him. Chaos erupts. Peter spirits the child away, followed by a bickering Adam and Jessica. Claire exits.*
>
> *Guy and Dennett are left alone. A moment of awkward silence between them. Then:*

GUY

Gosh.

> (*Pause*)

What a neat poem!

> *Dennett stares blankly at Guy. Pause.*
> *Guy is suddenly swept by a wave of self-rebuke.*

(*Groaning*)

Ugh! "What a neat poem!" Did that sound incredibly dumb?

(*Plaintively*)

Whenever I'm around supersmart people I turn into the village idiot! I don't know why! God, your kids! What intellects they have! And now, meeting you—I'm embarrassed to call myself a writer! You should be the

---

*In the perambulator conception, Peter thrusts Dennett towards the child in the baby carriage.

174

celebrated one, not I. You're the one who should have the shelfful of prizes and the unreasonably swollen bank account. Next to you I feel so . . . brutely inarticulate!
(*Triggered by a therapy session*)
No . . . No, that's not fair. As you can see, I have a habit of being absurdly hard on myself. It's not a question of better or worse where matters of aesthetics are concerned, right? We're just different. Different, yet paradoxically linked in a sense of purpose. It's sort of like . . .
(*Snapping his fingers—eureka!*)
Mountain climbing!

Dennett stares at him blankly.

Is that too trite a metaphor?

Dennett does not respond.

Because whether it's writing fiction or . . .
(*Indicating Dennett*)
. . . poetry or . . .
(*Indicating himself*)
. . . plays for the theatre, I think the effort required—the fearlessness, the endurance, the faith, ultimately—is tantamount to assaulting the most . . . forbidding peak.

Dennett stares at him blankly.

Does that sound too trite?

Dennett tilts his head slightly, observing Guy as if he were an insect under a microscope.

Because at the end of the day, the challenge for ALL artists is to make art more inclusive . . . to bring a whole new generation into the tent. Does that sound too saccharine?

Dennett stares at him blankly.

Because unless we reach out . . . to teenagers, women, people of color . . . theatre (and poetry) as we know them will cease to exist. I don't know. Maybe I'm talking in clichés.

Dennett's jaw drops open, but he does not respond.

vi
DENNETT'S HOUSE (CONTINUED)

The dining room: Christmas dinner.
The atmosphere bristles with tension. Dennett, Peter, Adam, and Jessica pose (and/or vie with each other to answer) questions in an extremely joyless, fiercely competitive game which appears to be familiar to everyone except Guy. Claire refuses to participate.
The following exchange is rapid-fire.★

JESSICA
Empson.

PETER
Wrong.

ADAM
Cowper.

★In the New York production, this scene began with the following exchange:

CLAIRE Couldn't we play a game where someone else has a chance of winning?

PETER And . . . go!

Preceding Jessica's exclamation of "Empson," these two lines made it immediately clear to the audience that a game was being played. In the current text, I restore the more rhythmically appealing (though potentially more disorienting) opening of the scene as it appeared in the original manuscript.

176

PETER
Uh–uh.

JESSICA
Pepys!

PETER (*Pounding the table*)
No.

ADAM
Not Pepys?

PETER (*Scowling and offended*)
No! . . . No!

ADAM
Hazlitt?

PETER (*Frustrated*)
NO!

> *Dennett groans.*

DENNETT (*Exasperated, to Adam*)
An HISTORIAN, he said!
> (*To Peter, as if it were self-evident*)
It's Camden, right?

PETER
That's correct.

DENNETT
"Betwixt the stirrup and the ground/ Mercy I asked, mercy I found." An epitaph for a man killed by being thrown from a horse. Quoted by William Camden.

PETER
You've got it. *Again.*

DENNETT (*Bitterly*)
I apologize for my children. They're the casualties of a failing university system.

GUY
I've got one! Name the longest-running Broadway show of all time!

Dennett plows ahead as if Guy had said nothing.

DENNETT
Okay. Name the only head of state in modern history whose full name qualifies as a palindrome.

ADAM (*Sure of it! Screaming it out!*)
Idi Amin!

DENNETT (*Annoyed*)
Full name, dunce.

Adam is deflated.

GUY
Palindrome . . . that's . . .

JESSICA (*Sharply*)
Lon Nol. Former president of Cambodia.

Dennett snaps his fingers. Jessica is correct.

GUY
. . . the same forwards as backwards, isn't it? . . .

DENNETT (*Smiling at Jessica*)
Niagara, O roar again!
(*Tipping an imaginary hat*)
I'm proud to call you my daughter!

GUY
. . . Or is that a spoonerism?

PETER
Didn't Cambodia change its name to Burkina Faso?

DENNETT
Burma changed its name to Burkina Faso. Cambodia is still Cambodia.

GUY
. . . Or is it a clerihew?

ADAM (*Quietly devastated*)
I was going to *say* Lon Nol.

GUY
Wait a minute. I thought it was Volta that changed its name to Burkina Faso.

The room falls silent. Guy nails it down.

Burma changed its name to *Myanmar. Volta* changed its name to Burkina Faso.

Another silence. The truth of Guy's statement, as it sinks in, causes mute embarrassment to flood the room like flop-sweat. Audio: A low rumble of thunder from outside.★

Isn't that correct?

Claire, surveying the red faces of her crestfallen family, laughs and applauds.

CLAIRE (*Surprised and delighted*)
O, my God! He's right! HE'S RIGHT!

GUY (*Good-naturedly*)
That's correct, isn't it?

★Thunder cues were eliminated in the New York production.

The others seethe and stare at their plates as Claire, a little drunk, continues to laugh, stomp, and applaud.

So does that mean that I have the honor?

CLAIRE
Baby, you got bragging rights! You got the floor!

GUY
Do I get to ask a question?

CLAIRE
You sure do. You earned it. Go ahead.

GUY
Gosh. It's a little scary with such heavy hitters . . .

Guy considers for a second as the others steam silently.

Okay. Who's the most successful playwright in Broadway history?

A general exhalation expressing boredom and disapproval from around the table.

PETER (*Shrugging and rolling his eyes*)
I don't know. You.

ADAM (*Derisively*)
How about Strindberg? Didn't he crank out a few "blockbusters" before the advent of the "megamusical"?

Jessica snorts.

GUY (*Sincerely*)
I know you're kidding about Strindberg, but he's actually a great hero of mine.

Dennett clears his throat, interlaces his fingers, and leans forward menacingly.

DENNETT (*Unfriendly*)
I'd like to know exactly what you mean by "successful."

CLAIRE
I'll *bet* you would!

> *Dennett shoots an angry glance at Claire.*

GUY (*Chiding Claire*)
No, that's fair. I think we're all guilty of making pat assumptions about the meaning of success. Especially in America. It's a national *malaise*.

DENNETT (*Sardonically*)
"A National *Malaise*"? I had no idea you were in the business of diagnosing the ills of the body politic . . .

GUY (*Backing down genially*)
Touché! I know I sometimes sound like a pompous arse straddling his soapbox! It's an occupational hazard. Loyal audiences give you an intoxicating sense that you have something of value to say about absolutely everything!

DENNETT
When in reality you may have absolutely nothing of value to say about anything whatsoever.

GUY (*Grinning and nodding with approval*)
Touché. Touché.

CLAIRE (*To Guy, but directed at Dennett*)
Although having an audience must, in itself, be a very valuable and rewarding experience for a writer.

> *Dennett shoots an enraged glance at Claire.*

ADAM (*Petulantly and defensively*)
Why? What difference should it make?

CLAIRE (*Turning to face Dennett*)
It might make a refreshing change from howling in the dark.

GUY
It *is* valuable . . . as a luxury, and a privilege. But as a measure of "value" it's obviously negligible. I have to agree with Adam.

> *Adam winces. Dennett, his face tightening into an abstract rictus of displeasure, drinks.*
> *Audio: Another, louder rumble of thunder from outside.*

I mean, who would dispute the fact that many of the greatest artists in the world have toiled in obscurity without having earned the support and recognition of an audience? In their lifetime . . . or *ever*?

> *Guy good-naturedly winks at Dennett, giving him a discreet 'thumbs-up' of support. Dennett's face flushes.*

Which brings us back, of course, to the problematic definition of success . . .

> *Dennett angrily spears a greasy chunk of turkey tail with his fork and thrusts it towards Guy.*

DENNETT
You know what we call this in Jerusalem, don't you?

> *Audio: Another, louder rumble of thunder from outside.*

(*Dripping with contempt*)
The Pope's Nose.

> *Guy looks around helplessly.*

GUY
I don't get it.

(*Confused*)
I'm sorry. Was I pontificating . . . ?

Jessica, her eyes on Dennett, says:

JESSICA (*To Guy*)
Why don't you just ask another question?

GUY
Uh . . . *me*? Another one? Uh . . . gee . . . okay.
(*With growing excitement*)
All right . . . !
(*Excitedly*)
Okay! Name . . . the largest-grossing Broadway musical of
all time!

*Dennett throws his knife and fork down on the table in
disgust. Guy doesn't notice, and continues eagerly.*

Hint: it's *not Annie!*

*Dennett, his voice quivering with resentment, bears down on
Guy.*

DENNETT
Excuse me, Mr. Broadway. What makes you think you have
the right—*any* right—to express an opinion—*any* opinion—
about art, or artists, or about ANYTHING ELSE?

CLAIRE (*Raising her glass in mock relief*)
O, Henry! Thank God! For a while there I thought you
weren't going to ruin Christmas dinner!

GUY (*To Dennett*)
Frankly, if you *must* know, I was shading my opinion to take
your personal circumstances into account.

DENNETT (*Outraged*)

You don't know the first thing about my "personal circumstances."

> (*To the others, extremely agitated*)

But apparently he feels he's entitled to an opinion about *that*, too.

> *Peter attempts to intervene . . .*

PETER

Okay, everybody! Name the subject of the most hair-raising Christmas dinner row in all of literature . . .

> *But Guy proceeds to square off against Dennett.*

GUY

Look, Henry . . .

> *Jessica attempts to override the gathering storm by offering a solution to Peter's query.*

JESSICA

Parnell, God, and Ireland . . . !

> *Dennett, severely agitated, bristles at Guy's use of his Christian name.*

DENNETT

Henry! As if we're ol' pals . . . !

> *But Guy presses forward, undaunted . . .*

GUY (*To Dennett*)

. . . given what I've been able to determine about your taste . . .

DENNETT (*Outraged*)

You don't know jack *shit* about my taste . . . !

GUY

. . . it would be foolish of me to expect that you'd necessarily find merit in what I do . . . assuming that you'd even give my work the time of day in the first place. But never mind. Isn't it qualification enough—however short, in your view, a practitioner of my capabilities might fall—to dedicate oneself, in good faith, to the pursuit of something as honorable as writing well?

DENNETT

Writing PLAYS well?
    (*Snorting*)
For the Great White Way? What honor or qualification could possibly accrue from that?

GUY (*Genuinely perplexed*)

I'm sorry?

> *Dennett rises and crosses to one of the dining room's bookshelves.*

DENNETT

A *Biblia Pauperum*. That's what the theatre is.

> *Guy is lost.*

GUY

A *Biblia* . . . ?

DENNETT (*Spitting out the words*)

PAUPERUM!: a Bible in pictures for the benefit of the illiterate!

> *Thunder. Guy absorbs Dennett's remark, then chuckles good-naturedly.*

GUY

Well, that's a pretty eccentric view of a supremely challenging form that's been practiced for centuries by some of the greatest masters of language the world has ever known.

DENNETT

Including *you*, I suppose.

> *Dennett, having extracted a book from the shelf and located a passage in it effortlessly, reads:*

"The theatre has long seemed to me a *Biblia Pauperum*, with the dramatist a lay preacher hawking contemporary ideas in popular form, popular enough for the middle classes to be able to grasp without too much effort what the minority is arguing about . . ."

> *Adam, Jessica, and Peter smirk in pedantic recognition.*

". . . It has always been a primary school for the young, semi-educated, and women, all of whom retain the humble faculty of being able to deceive themselves and let themselves be deceived—in other words, to accept the illusion, and react to the suggestion, of the author."

GUY

Well, whoever wrote that never heard of Aristophanes or Shakespeare.

DENNETT

Here.

> *Dennett flings the book rudely at Guy.*

Strindberg! Your hero.

> *Guy's face reddens.*

At least *he* wasn't vain and self-serving enough to apologize for dramatic form by leaning on the occasional poets who've managed to redeem it!

For the first time, Guy's good nature is punctured. His words are edged with anger.

GUY

Sorry, Henry. All you're telling me is what an impoverished view of theatre you have. Any fool can see there's far too much crap around. But there's far too much crap in *any* business. Yours, too!

DENNETT

I don't HAVE a business! And I prefer crap to the kind of sanctimonious kitsch that's embraced as high art by an audience of suburban morons dim-witted enough to believe that by going to a play they're having some sort of "cultural experience." As if there *were* such a thing as a "cultural experience"! As if some wheedling, "issue-for-our-time" play were less corrupt than all the crap on TV or crap at the cinema! At least outright crap is honest! At least with crap you don't feel cheap and used and invaded, as if the local vicar were wiggling his finger down the crack of your ass!

CLAIRE

O, very nice, Henry! Very "yuletide"!

DENNETT

It's pornographic, what you do! All that idiotic talk about "reaching out" and "bringing a new generation into the tent"! A new generation of WHAT? Of suburban know-nothings dumbed down to the point of expecting art to be some kind of . . .

> (*Running his hands over himself in a lubricious, "touchy-feely" motion*)
>
> . . . inclusive, fraudulently life-affirming group-grope, instead of what it is: arrogant, autocratic, potentially *monstrous* . . . !

CLAIRE (*Under her breath*)
Jawohl, mein kommandant.

DENNETT

. . . Potentially dangerous and offensive! You want to know what's going on inside the tent? I'll tell you what's going on inside the tent! A macabre peep show for third-rate minds eager to have their sympathies titillated and their sense of humanity massaged by the dime-store imaginings of *second-rate* minds. It's an orgy of therapy and mutual congratulation more pornographic than any skin-flick or fuck-mag. And the more pornographic it is—the more cajolingly earnest, unambiguous, sloganeering, UNTRUTHFUL—the greater the success! I'd sooner feast on crap all day long than be forced to choke down a single grain of hokum from that mountain of toxic kitsch! Hokum that's prized as "art" by a herd of whinnying blockheads who leap to their feet to cheer it with an enthusiasm exactly commensurate to its degree of dishonesty. At least crap is honorable! At least crap doesn't make your skin crawl! I can *live* with crap! GIVE ME *CRAP!*

> *Silence. Guy draws a breath, gathers himself, and then leans forward to speak in carefully controlled, carefully measured sentences.*

GUY

I can well understand how a man who believes that the world has turned a deaf ear to his voice, and foreclosed on his chances for success, might come to view the world as corrupt, even loveless. But it's beneath you, Henry, to let bitterness cloud your appreciation of an entire art form, and to speak in gross generalizations about a craft which is ultimately so complex.

Claire leaps to her feet and claps defiantly, sneering at Dennett.

CLAIRE
Bravo! Bra—*vo!*

GUY
Playwriting is no less difficult than any other kind of writing. Bitterness shouldn't blind you to that! You make it sound as if anybody could do it. Or that it's something you'd have to *STOOP* to do. I think you'd be surprised to discover how hard it actually is.

CLAIRE (*Applauding*)
Here, here!

DENNETT
Are you *kidding* me? To do what *you* do? *ARE YOU KIDDING ME?* It's worse than *pornography,* what you do! I could toss off a piece of pornography like that before I finished my first wank in the morning.

JESSICA
Mmmmmm. Gooooood turkey.

GUY
Again, you're letting bitterness get the best of you.

CLAIRE
Absolutely! Thank you! Thank you!

GUY

Writing is writing, Henry. And, aside from the usual agonies of composition, writing for the theatre requires respect for an audience . . .

CLAIRE

. . . which he's far too arrogant to have . . .

GUY

. . . a willingness to collaborate . . .

CLAIRE

. . . a year from *Shavuoth,* maybe . . . !

GUY

. . . and the patience to husband one's work through a grueling development process at the end of which, if you're lucky, it might get produced. Somewhere. But at a reputable theatre? Highly unlikely. And it's nothing short of a miracle, even if it's good enough, for a play ever to reach a place like Broadway. Especially *these* days.

DENNETT (*Swelling like a blowfish*)
Who do you think you're talking to? Do you realize that I was short-listed in the Yale Series of Younger Poets Competition . . .

CLAIRE

. . . about thirty-five years ago . . .

DENNETT

. . . when W. H. Auden was the judge? And that I've published at the rate of close to a volume a year ever since . . . ?

CLAIRE

. . . a literary sausage factory . . .

DENNETT

. . . not just poetry, but light verse, critical studies, translations from Virgil to Ovid . . .

CLAIRE

. . . pity the poor Oklahoma State University Press . . .

DENNETT

Do you have any idea what that means? Are you seriously suggesting that if I chose to, I couldn't do what you do? Successfully?

GUY (*Patiently*)

I think you'd be surprised.

CLAIRE (*Provocatively*)

I think you'd be *very* surprised.

> *Dennett throws his hands into the air in disgust and dismay.*

DENNETT

So! Is that what you think?

CLAIRE (*Shaking her head, sadly*)

When the heart is pierced, immodesty takes wing.

> *Dennett surveys the table . . .*

DENNETT

Is that what you ALL think?

ADAM

Daddy, of course you know I've always thought . . .

> *Dennett steamrolls over Adam, unnoticing.*

DENNETT (*Shrugging and sniggering bitterly*)

WELL! Here I've gone through my whole life blithely assuming that at least my FAMILY understood that I've put up with years of misery and neglect not because I couldn't have successfully prostituted myself, but because I *chose* not to demean my talent—especially in the service of a form as pretentious and vulgar and anodyne as what passes these days for "serious drama." I chose not to demean my talent because something higher chose me! That, Mr. Broadway, is what it means to be an artist. That's what makes it possible to endure the indignity of piddling sales, the jealous condemnation of your peers, the thinly disguised pity of your children, the malicious jibes of your ex-wife, and the condescension of pornographers like you.

GUY (*Eyeing Dennett's wineglass*)
I think maybe you should have a little something to eat.

> *Dennett angrily grabs a hunk of bread and shoves it into his mouth.*

DENNETT
You smug bastard. You sit here at *my* table, my *father's* table—in my *father's father's* house—at which I've been reduced to the status of a GUEST, because it's all been taken away from me . . . ALL OF IT! . . . by a bunch of bean-counters, none of whom, it turns out, has an inkling, not even the merest whit of an an idea, of WHO IT IS, EXACTLY, THAT I AM!

GUY
Okay. Aside from the self-pity, who are you? Exactly.

> *Dennett's eyes narrow. Then, a flicker of a smile. He bears down on Guy as if going in for the kill.*

DENNETT
Hey, pal. Has it ever occurred to you, despite all your money and all your prizes and all your success, that—to use

your shop-worn metaphor—you may have spent your entire life climbing the wrong mountain?

Guy thinks about it for a second.

GUY (*Genuinely*)
No.

    (*Sincerely, but with eyebrows arched knowingly, like a
    psychiatrist who anticipates the answer to his own question*)
Has it ever occurred to YOU?

A brutal silence and stillness between them.
*Suddenly, Dennett lunges across the table, seizing Guy by
the throat.*

DENNETT
Mother—FUCKER! (etc.)

*The entire room seems to tilt sideways as the assembled
company dives abruptly on top of Dennett, trying to prevent
him from strangling Guy. A string of Dennett's invectives
("Die, bastard! Die! Die! Die!" etc.) merges with the
hysterical pleadings of the others ("Daddy, stop! Daddy,
no!"; "My God, Henry! You're killing him!" etc.) in
operatic katzenjammer.*
    *Guy, close to asphyxiation, his face beet-red and his eyes
hard-boiled, gasps desperately for air.*
    *Adam and Peter battle to pry Dennett's hands free from
Guy's throat. Jessica holds her father in a vice-grip from
behind. Claire grabs the copy of "Strindberg's Plays" from
the table and beats Dennett over the head with it.*
    *In a single, balletic coordination of bodies, Dennett's
death-hold on Guy is loosened and he is brought crashing
down onto the table, landing on his back in the turkey platter,
his elbow sinking into the Bûche de Noël. Glasses shatter and
dishes go flying.*

Guy, curled fetally on the carpet, half-dead, struggles to swallow a lungful of air.

Dennett's expression suddenly shifts from bloodthirsty rage to horrified discomfort.

DENNETT

O, my God!

Dennett's exclamation causes the others to fall quickly silent.

O, MY GOD!

The others, exhausted and confused, are jolted into a new wave of panic and confusion. Is Dennett injured? Is he impaled on something?

Dennett's trembling hand reaches for the remainder of the bread that he's just been eating. Still on his back, he lifts the bread accusingly and says:

DENNETT

What is this?

CLAIRE (*Panicked*)

What do you mean, what is it? It's bread.

DENNETT

What KIND?! What KIND of bread?!

At first, Claire remains confused. Then, horror crosses her face.

CLAIRE (*Aghast*)

Corn bread.

Dennett explodes rabbinically.

DENNETT

No, no, no! I *told* you! The doctor said! No corn! No corn! No CORN!

Audio: A huge rumble of thunder from outside.

Mayhem erupts again as Dennett's face contorts and his body convulses. The others are torn between trying to help him up and restraining him as he begins to moan, louder and louder. Guy, gripping his collar, coughs in pathetic, staccato bursts like a cat trying to dislodge a hair-ball from its throat.

The others swarm around Dennett as his body continues to convulse and his cries become more dire. Adam wedges a fork handle between his father's teeth in an attempt to keep him from swallowing his tongue. Peter, Claire, and Jessica struggle to hold on to his arms and legs. Through it all, Dennett intersperses his moans and curses with half-audible exclamations such as:

DENNETT

You're trying to kill me! You're all against me! Murderers! Murderers! (etc.)

At a point when the commotion has become almost unbearably frantic, Dennett's body suddenly relaxes and the tumult stops. The room is filled with no other sound than that of exhausted breathing and panting. Then silence. Is he dead? Or is it the lull before a storm?

Dennett's face is now in a state of repose. Suddenly, his eyes blink open. Then, expressive of a pain more profound and splenetic than anything that has preceded it, his eyes bulge, his lips quiver, and his cheeks retract. Claire, Adam, Peter and Jessica instinctively back away in a circle. The lights fade, leaving Dennett alone in a pool of light.

Dennett's mouth opens wide. Out of it shoots the worm, now even more grotesquely evolved than before.

Dennett, spread cruciform on the dining room table, unleashes a piercing howl from the bottom of his soul as if poleaxed.

DENNETT

Aaaauuuuuuuuggggggggggghhhhhhhh!

The howl reaches its animalistic crescendo as . . . . . .

. . . Audio: Thunderclap, simultaneous with:

BLACKOUT

Audio: The sound of Dennett's unbroken howl is joined by the rushing roar of a torrential downpour of rain. Dennett's howl seamlessly transforms from human to animal; it becomes strangulated and lupine.

Lights up on a wolf, struggling to free its hind leg from the jaws of a steel trap. It howls pitifully. Rain hammers down upon it. The wolf continues to struggle, only worsening its predicament.

Across the front of the stage, a miniature passenger train suddenly goes rocketing by from left to right.

The following inscription appears before the audience:

ii
Lithia Spring

Fade to black

197

THE REHEARSAL ROOM

The lights come up on Dennett, who has just set down a suitcase.

Maurice Montesor, a soft-bellied, sagging-faced older man with a thatch of thinning hair dyed an improbable shade of red, greets Dennett and guides him around the stage grandly.

MAURICE
Herman! *Il maestro! Il maestro di color che sanno!*
(*Releasing Dennett and winking*)
"The master of those who know." Plato's description of Aristotle.

DENNETT (*Brushing himself off*)
Dante's, I think you mean.

Realizing that Dennett is right, Maurice's jaw drops open and he exclaims with comical embarrassment:

MAURICE
Zounds!
(*Striking a theatrically idiotic Harlequin pose*)
Well, spotlight on the buffoon!
(*Putting his arm around a squirming Dennett*)
I *told* them you were a genius.
(*Guiding Dennett towards the door*)
Come, my friend. Let me show you Elsinore. I hereby bequeath you my second-best bed! Not the Savoy, exactly, but no one has ever complained . . .

DENNETT
Excuse me . . . Maur-*ice*, is it . . . ?

MAURICE
MAUR-ice. It's the British pronunciation.

DENNETT

Look. Pal. I don't mean to be rude, but I was under the impression that I'd be put up in a hotel.

MAURICE

A *hotel*? Great Jupiter, no! Would that we could afford to be so grand!
  (*In character*)
"Sadly it's well beyond our means here," croaked a red-cheeked Mr. Pecksniff!
  (*Himself again*)
And anyway, Hyram, half the point is to be under the same roof with the others, breaking bread, exchanging ideas, caring and sharing . . .

DENNETT

What others?

MAURICE (*In character*)

"*What* others?" he inquires, his brow furrowed with concern.

DENNETT (*Aggravated*)

Yes. *What* others?!

MAURICE (*In character*)

"Yes! *What* others?!" he persists, grim trenches etched into his alabaster forehead . . .

DENNETT

Please!

MAURICE (*Himself again*)

The OTHERS, Harold! YOU know! The other . . .
  (*In a broad stage whisper, as if it were in bad taste to say it too loudly*)
. . . candidates.

DENNETT (*Steaming*)
Candidates for what?

Maurice crosses his arms as if to size up Dennett afresh.

MAURICE
You *are* Hyram Dennett, aren't you?

DENNETT (*Stung*)
Henry Dennett.

MAURICE
You are the *same* Hyram Dennett who sent me the remarkable *Wrong Mountain* . . .

Dennett nods wearily.

(*With great gravitas*)
. . . a play, incidentally, which, upon first reading, actually caused me to weep openly . . .

Dennett nods in faint, nauseated gratitude.

. . . and, through a blur of hot tears, turn to my housekeeper and say,
(*Punching the air*)
"Dammit, Yolanda! Here's a bloke"—and I do not use this phrase lightly—"Here's a bloke who's got potential coming out the kazoo! . . ."

DENNETT
Maurice, your letter said nothing about other "candidates," whatever *that's* supposed to mean.

MAURICE (*In character*)
Then you did not read the letter with your spectacles polished!

DENNETT (*Angry and impatient*)
Is this festival planning to stage my play? Yes or no?

MAURICE (*Himself again*)
I think there's every good chance that yours will be selected.
But it's by no means a *fait accompli* . . .

DENNETT (*In a fury*)
Where are my bags? This is ridiculous! This is outrageous!

MAURICE
Hubert! Please! Calm down! I already told you what *I* think.
But it's a competition. Didn't you understand? Others have
submitted work. I don't have the power to make life-
altering decisions unilaterally. I'm merely an actor!

DENNETT
Hang on. You led me to believe that you ran this place.
The letter was signed "Artistic Director of the Shakespeare
Festival."

MAURICE
I *am* Artistic Director of the Shakespeare Festival.

DENNETT
Didn't you just say you were an actor?

MAURICE
I *am* an actor.

> *Dennett is confused.*

And may I not be both? Was not *Shakespeare* both?
> (*Pause*)
Naturally, bureaucratic responsibilities preclude me, in large
measure, from even thinking about treading the boards
anymore, but . . .
> (*Drawing Dennett towards him "confidentially"*)

. . . it so happens that, after much arm twisting, the members of the company have coaxed me out of semi-retirement and persuaded me to take on a role that, amazingly, I've never played, but that I've always *dreamt* of playing. And I finally decided, "Dammit, Maurice! Do it *now*, this season, before you're too old!"

As if startled, Maurice halts suddenly, gasps, and points to something distant in the sky, bracing Dennett with his free arm.

MAURICE
"Two of the fairest stars in all the heaven,
Having some business, do intreat her eyes
To twinkle in their spheres till they return.

As if seized by an idea, Maurice moves a few steps ahead of Dennett, still concentrating intently on the sky.

What if her eyes were there . . .

Maurice turns to face Dennett.

. . . they in her head?

Maurice crosses his arms and smiles.

The brightness of her cheek would shame those stars,
As daylight doth . . . a lamp;

Maurice leaps.

her eyes in heaven
Would through the airy region stream so bright
That birds would sing and think it were not night.

Maurice peers behind Dennett, who half-turns to look.

See, how she leans her cheek upon her hand!
O that I were a glove upon that hand,
That I might touch that cheek!"

Pause.

> (*Like an excited boy*)
> We had our first run-through yesterday.

DENNETT

> Forgive me, Maurice, but isn't Romeo normally played by . . .
> (*Delicately*)
> . . . a *younger* man?

MAURICE (*Deeply affronted*)

> How old do you think I *am*?

DENNETT

> No, I mean . . . a *much* younger man.

Maurice's eyes well with tears.

MAURICE (*Turning away, hurt*)

> Well, I suppose we *all* could be a bit younger, couldn't we?

DENNETT

> I'm not criticizing you. I'm merely making an observation.

MAURICE

> An observation, eh? Then you'll permit *me* to make an
> observation as well, Harold!
> (*Pointing to Dennett's coiffure*)
> I was completely astonished to discover that one of the
> finalists in our New Playwrights Competition had more
> gray in his hair than I!

Maurice fluffs his Day-Glo dye job.

> But then I thought, bugger it! What matter if he's a bit
> more . . . seasoned . . . than what we're accustomed to.
> After all, hasn't he written one of the most honest, eloquent,
> most courageous first plays I've ever read? How did it
> change anything to learn that he wasn't some . . . fresh-faced

lad? The answer was: it didn't. Because I'd read your play. I already knew who you were. I knew what was *inside* you.

Dennett grips his stomach and winces.

And that's the important thing.

A group of Actors begins filtering through the door.

Great Jupiter! A band of wandering minstrels approaches from stage right! Your attention please!
(*In a stentorian, resonant voice*)
Ladies and Gentlemen . . . the Author! Harold Dennett . . . The Players!

The five Actors applaud enthusiastically.

Why don't we just go round the circle and introduce ourselves. Duncan, shall we begin with you?

DUNCAN
Certainly. My name is Duncan Hyde-Berk. I'll be reading Max.

MAURICE
Thank you, Duncan. Salome?

SALOME
Salome Blackwood. I shall have the great, great honor to read the role of The Seahag.★

Salome's eyes are misted with emotion.

DENNETT (*Nervously*)
Hi there.

★Prior to New York, the line had read, "I shall have the great, great honor to read the role of the Incubus."

MAURICE
Jason?

Jason is a surly black kid in his late twenties.

JASON
Jason Elmore. I'm playing Luc.

MAURICE (*Boasting*)
Jason is joining us from the National Tour of Disney's
Beauty and the Beast.

DENNETT (*Reflexively polite*)
O, really? Which role did you play?

JASON (*With a huge chip on his shoulder*)
Eggbeater.

DENNETT
Well, how wonderfully bold of them to go with . . . you
know . . . untraditional casting!

JASON (*Aggressive*)
So what are you saying? That eggbeaters are traditionally
white?

MAURICE (*Steering Dennett along*)
And over here we have Miranda Cortland-Sparks, who will
be reading Kim.

MIRANDA
Thank you for your anger.

MAURICE
And last but not least . . .

*Dennett's eyes light upon Ariel, a stunning, nymphlike,
astonishingly self-possessed nineteen-year-old girl. He is
mesmerized. Suddenly he is aware of a silence.*

DENNETT

I'm sorry. I didn't hear . . .

ARIEL

Lily.

Dennett is wonderstruck.

DENNETT

Lily . . . ?

ARIEL

No, I'm *playing* Lily. My name is Ariel.

DENNETT

O, I thought . . .

ARIEL

Yes, I know.

They look at each other. Dennett laughs, a little too goofily.

MAURICE

Well, there we are! You must be itching to meet your competitors!

ii
THE REHEARSAL ROOM (CONT.)

Two young playwrights, Winny and Cliff, have joined the Company. Winny is mid-story.
Dennett sets himself apart, in full antisocial rebellion.

WINNY

And so it was actually having played an aching tooth in a school play about oral hygiene. . .

She giggles and snorts hysterically, and the Actors roar.

. . . I think I was a molar, and not a very convincing one . . .

She giggles and snorts hysterically, and the Actors roar.

. . . that got me hooked on theatre!

MAURICE
What a bloody marvelous story.

Maurice notices that Dennett's eyes are closed.

Harold?! Were you listening to Winny's molar story?
You're not sleeping, are you?

DENNETT
No, no. I sometimes just close my eyes when I'm extremely
. . . interested.

MAURICE
Clifford, what about *you*? How did you come to write such
an arresting first play?

CLIFF
I'm frankly a bit of a Johnny-come-lately to the theatre, Mr.
Montesor. Fiction was my dream, originally. I wrote a lot of
bad short stories and even half a novel . . .

Winny giggles and snorts hysterically.

. . . and then, when I was seventeen, I saw a play by Guy
Halperin . . .

Dennett's eyes pop wide open.

. . . and suddenly I just *knew:* "That's what I want to do
with the rest of my life!"

MAURICE (*Waxing nostalgic*)
How extraordinary! I felt the same way when I saw Kiki on stage for the first time. I instantly knew: I *had* to be an actor!

CLIFF
Kiki?

MAURICE
Kiki, yes.

> *Pause. Cliff and Winny look bewildered.*

(*More specific*)
Olivier.
(*Pause*)
Kiki Olivier.

WINNY
You mean . . . *Laurence* Olivier?

MAURICE
Kiki.
(*Pause*)
To friends.

WINNY
You were *friends* with *Sir Laurence Olivier?*

MAURICE
Kiki.

> *Pause, as Maurice forces the others to absorb the full weight of this information.*

(*To Dennett*)
But let me put the question to *you*, Harry . . .

> *In a swift, dithyrambic chorus of overlapping voices, the actors emphatically correct Maurice . . .*

DUNCAN
  Herbert.

SALOME
  Henry.

JASON
  Harold.

MIRANDA
  Herman.

ARIEL
  Hyman.

    . . . but Maurice plows on, unhearing.

MAURICE
  I think it's safe to assume that you've been out of *alma mater*
  a wee bit longer than these two cubs here! If you don't
  mind my asking, what have you been up to in the
  meantime, and why, exactly, have you been drawn to the
  footlights at this stage in the game?

DENNETT (*Grandly offended*)
  You mean . . . how have I made a *living*?

MAURICE
  For want of a more felicitous phrase . . .

DENNETT (*Crescendoing indignation*)
  Are you serious? Is this some kind of a joke? Do you really
  not know who I am? Is literacy at such a calamitously low
  ebb in this country that poets are condemned to anonymity
  and neglect regardless of the stature they've achieved?
      (*Wheeling on the others*)
  Does my name really mean *nothing* to you? Henry Dennett,
  one of the most celebrated and revered *POETS* in the United

States of *AMERICA*, handpicked by W. H. "Kiki" Auden to
be his literary successor . . .

*Flummoxed silence for a moment. The tension causes Winny
to gurgle nervously.*

WINNY
O, goodness! Now I don't know *who* to believe!

DENNETT (*To Winny*)
Actually I write pornographic novels under the name Kiki
Von Strindberg.

Nervous, uncertain laughter all around.

(*Grim, stark*)
I'm a teacher, actually. At a women's college.

Maurice, relieved but still rattled:

MAURICE
Teaching! *Bravo!*

CLIFF
But there must have been some . . . transforming event . . .
no? . . . that led you to try your hand at playwriting . . . at
this point in your . . . life . . .

DENNETT
You know, Cliff, there was. And, strange to say,
it even involves . . . what's-his-name . . . your idol . . .
Guy . . . ?

CLIFF
Guy Halperin?

DENNETT
Yeah. Who's probably shtupping my ex-wife even as we
speak . . .

Maurice, Cliff and the Actors stare, confused. Winny snorts and gurgles very nervously.

Anyhow, last Christmas, after listening to . . . what's his name? . . .

CLIFF
Guy Halperin?

DENNETT
. . . Guy Halperin . . . rhapsodize at interminable length about the purportedly rigorous demands of writing for the theatre, I bet him that I could knock off a play and get it produced, all within six months, at a stake of one hundred thousand dollars, a figure which is equivalent to my salary for roughly . . .

Dennett doubles over suddenly as if pierced through the duodenum. Then, regaining his composure, he says:

DENNETT
That was six months ago. And this was the first place to take an interest. So here I am.

WINNY
Here you are!

Winny snorts and giggles hysterically.

DENNETT (*Somberly*)
Here I am.

WINNY
So I guess . . . the pressure's on! Tick-tick-tick-tick . . .

Winny snorts and giggles hysterically. Dennett nods grimly.

MAURICE
I liked the story about your being a famous poet better!

Maurice and Winny roar with laughter.

WINNY
O, I don't know! I think it would make a great play!

Maurice and Winny roar with laughter.

MAURICE
I think it would make an *execrable* play!

Maurice and Winny roar with laughter.

CLIFF (*To Dennett*)
You don't *really* know Guy Halperin, do you?

DENNETT (*Bitterly*)
Kiki.

iii
THE REHEARSAL ROOM (CONT.)

The Discussion of the Play.
  As the lights come up again, Miranda and Duncan are debating hotly.

MIRANDA
But isn't that the point of Luc's cross-dressing? That gender is just another . . . arbitrarily determined cultural norm?

DUNCAN
Of course not! That's why he sobs when he puts on the dirndl! That's why he makes the speech about Bosnia! Wearing a blouse doesn't change a man into a woman . . .

MIRANDA
Then how come he writes the suicide note with a styptic pencil? I think it mocks the idea that such categories, especially sexual categories, even *exist* . . .

DUNCAN

But it so obviously *celebrates* those categories! It implies that every man and woman . . . every human being . . . possesses an irreducible and unalterable essence, a *categorical* essence . . .

MAURICE

Let me interrupt you there, because I think we're beginning to touch on a desperately fascinating area. Without presuming to speak for the playwright . . .

   (*To Dennett*)

. . . though I trust he will correct me if I'm very wide of the wicket . . .

   (*Winking at Dennett*)

. . . won't you, Norbert . . . ?

   In another swift, dithyrambic chorus of overlapping voices, the Actors, even more emphatically, correct Maurice . . .

DUNCAN
Herbert.

SALOME
Henry.

JASON
Harold.

MIRANDA
Herman.

ARIEL
Hyman.

   . . . but Maurice plows on, unhearing.

MAURICE

. . . I think that what the playwright is saying, in general, is that the notion of "identity" is far more ambiguous than we normally imagine.

MIRANDA

Absolutely! And I don't think he's talking strictly about *personal* identity. I think he's talking about the identity of America itself.

MAURICE (*Electrified*)

Wonderful, Miranda! Wonderful!

MIRANDA (*Emboldened*)

I mean, what does it say about us as a people when what we *do* conflicts so dramatically with who we believe ourselves to be?

Maurice begins to jot down words.

MAURICE

Marvelous! My hand is trembling!

MIRANDA

The point is that America, as it enters a new millennium, is in the throes of this terrible identity crisis! Either we've lost sight of who we are, or we're making the gradual, painful discovery that we've been fooling ourselves all along. Hope of the world? You tell me!

MAURICE (*Jotting furiously*)

" . . . throes of an identity crisis!" Superb!

DUNCAN

Which raises an interesting question. Is it better to live according to a noble ideal of yourself, however false or misguided, or to courageously and honestly face who you actually are?

MAURICE (*Scribbling vigorously*)

Caro! Caro!

MIRANDA

I don't think there's any simple answer to that question.

MAURICE

Nor to *any* of these questions! God, how exciting! What a rich tapestry! How about it, playwright? Are we successfully teasing the threads out of the golden braid of your fervent imagination?

DENNETT (*Pause. Then, bluntly:*)

Look, why don't you just tell me what changes you want me to make and I'll make them.

> *Their faces crumbling, the Actors—especially Duncan and Miranda—look first at Dennett, then at each other, with a withering sense of disappointment. Maurice rises and crosses to Dennett, touching him lightly on the shoulder.*

MAURICE (*To Dennett*)

Hector, may I speak to you privately for a moment?

> *Leaving the Actors in the background, Maurice and Dennett engage in a whispering confab.*

Hector, this is a process. It's a "back and forth," an opportunity to exchange creative ideas in the service of producing what Yeats called, quote, "the gorgeous, green-eyed, half-naked barmaid of artistic truth . . ."

DENNETT (*Irritatedly skeptical*)

When did Yeats ever use an expression as ludicrous as "the gorgeous, green-eyed, half-naked . . ."

MAURICE (*Slightly deflated, pressing on quickly*)

. . . or something like that. Never mind. The point is, you've got to be more willing to engage with the actors in developing the marvelous raw material of your play.

DENNETT

I'll do whatever they say, whatever it takes! As long as I can win this thing and get back to Massachusetts before term begins!

Maurice pulls Dennett closer.

MAURICE

Hector . . . listen to me carefully. Though it's up to our panel of judges to decide which of the three workshopped plays will ultimately receive a full production, the reaction of the invited audience to our staged readings at the end of the fortnight is inevitably a critical determinant. Now, the energy the actors bring to those staged readings is often based on their enthusiasm for the author and the material, and unless they feel that you're as eager to enter into an artistic and personal relationship with them as you are to "win," I fear that their enthusiasm might be seriously dampened.
   (Arching his eyebrows)
Comprende, Maestro?

Maurice puts his arm around Dennett.

Herman, *Wrong Mountain* is a wonderful, rough-hewn slab of marble which, like some brilliant, latter-day . . .
   (Playfully pinching a roll of fat at Dennett's waist and winking)
. . . slightly overweight Michelangelo, you've slapped on the sculptor's wheel before us. Work with the company to draw the figure out of the stone! I know you can do it! Try! It'll be FUN!

Dennett stares straight ahead, numbly.
Duncan steps forward.

DUNCAN

Mr. Dennett? One of the things that some of us like to do in this company is to write a little poem or something that puts us in touch with our character and reflects, from an actor's point of view, what we believe you're getting at as an author. I wonder if I might read to you what I've written?

Dennett stares at Duncan blankly, not responding.
Duncan unfolds a sheet of paper from his pocket.

It's very short.

Dennett continues to stare at Duncan blankly, not responding.
Duncan, uncertain about whether or not to proceed, clears his throat and plunges in:

DUNCAN

"Soar, word-bird!
Spread your eagle-wings and soar!
Soar to the sea,
Spreading words like seeds . . ."

DENNET (*Interrupting*)
Excuse me! What are you doing?

DUNCAN (*Diffidently*)
I'm reading a poem that I . . .

DENNETT
What?

DUNCAN (*A little louder*)
I'm reading a poem that I . . .

DENNETT
No, I heard what you said. It's just . . . . Listen . . . what's your name again?

DUNCAN
Duncan.

DENNETT
Listen. Word-bird. No poems. Understand? It's a rule of mine.

Duncan, stunned, listens innocently.

(*No nonsense*)
No poems. No haikus. No sestinas or ballads or villanelles . . .

DUNCAN (*Mildly protesting*)
But this is really more of a prose meditation . . .

DENNETT
Hey! *Especially* no prose meditations. That's my *rule*. Got it? And that goes for the rest of you, too.

The Actors stare at Dennett. Maurice massages his temples. Duncan is abject.

DENNETT
Sorry, folks! No poems!

Salome raises her hand.

MAURICE
Yes, Salome! You wanted to say?

Salome gazes penetratingly into Dennett's eyes.

SALOME
I just wanted to ask Mr. Dennett how a man gets to know so much about women.

DENNETT (*Clears his throat; then:*)
Well, first he has to have screwed a lot of them . . .

The Actors stare at Dennett, stony-faced.

JASON

What did he say . . . ?

Maurice tries to gloss it over.

MAURICE

But what *I* want to know is . . . are we on the right track
with all these theories about personal and national identity
or are we just talking a lot of piffle?

DENNETT

Well, perhaps some of you are familiar with W. H. Auden's
views on the issue. "Every man carries with him through
life a mirror, as unique and impossible to get rid of as his
shadow . . ."

Maurice flips open his notepad and begins jotting.

MAURICE

Marvelous!

DENNETT

". . . But the properties of our own particular mirror are not
so important as we sometimes think. We shall be judged,
not by the kind of mirror found on us, but by the use we
have made of it, by our *response* to our reflection."

MAURICE (*Scribbling*)

O, that's sublime.

*A general hum of interest and contemplation from the Actors.
Except Ariel.*

ARIEL

"*Riposte* to our reflection."

DENNETT

I beg your pardon.

ARIEL

". . . We shall be judged, not by the kind of mirror found on us, but by the use we have made of it, by our riposte to our reflection." Riposte. Not response.

DENNETT

Well, well. A scholar.

MAURICE (*To the Company, as an aside*)

How do you like that? The genius isn't infallible after all.

DENNETT

Tell me, scholar. You've remained deafeningly silent. What do *you* think my play's about?

ARIEL

What's it *about*? To the extent that it's "about" *anything,* it's about the talent of its creator. Don't you think that's the true measure of an artist? That however significant the "issues" he raises might be, they invariably seem secondary, even incidental, to the imagination and passion with which he expresses them. What it's *about* is merely a matter of opinion. Talent, on the other hand, is a matter of fact.

DENNETT

All right, then. Let me rephrase it. Do you see evidence of talent in my play?

ARIEL

I'd rather not express my opinion.

DENNETT

But talent is a *fact*. Isn't that what you just said?

ARIEL

I know it when I see it.

DENNETT

How?

ARIEL

You tell me.

DENNETT

Well. I haven't seen it in about thirty years. At least not since Robert Lowell died. But on those rare occasions when I encounter a talent great enough to command my attention, I'm generally seized by extreme . . . nausea.

ARIEL

For me it's more of a "shiver," which is what Nabokov described as the hallmark of only the most transcendent art.

DENNETT

And my work? Does it make you shiver?

ARIEL

Why are you so interested in *my* opinion?

DENNETT

Well, I think we've got to bring a whole new generation into the tent.

ARIEL

The children of the world thank you.

DENNETT

How did you know that Auden quote?

ARIEL

Quotation. Quote is a verb.

> *Pause.*

DENNETT
Class is dismissed.

> *Dennett exits.*
> *Maurice proudly approaches Ariel and embraces her.*

MAURICE (*Beaming*)
That's . . . my . . . daughter!

iv
A MOTEL ROOM★

> *Drab curtains, suffused with brilliant spring light from outside, hang closed over a narrow length of windows.*
> *In the semidarkness, the sound of a man and woman engaged in ludicrously noisy, carnivorous sex is heard.*
> *It is Dennett and Ariel. He is lying supine on the tousled bedspread like a beached whale; she is straddling him, murmuring an unholy, catechismal accompaniment to his pathetic, arhythmic grunts and gyrations.*

ARIEL (*Variously*)
Talent is a *fact*!
YES!
I know it when I see it! It makes me *shiver*!
YES!
Which is what Nabokov described as the hallmark
Of only the most transcendent art!
YES!
Quote, not Quotation!
Quote is a verb!

★This dream/fantasy sequence, after several unsatisfactory attempts to realize it, was cut in the New York production. The play proceeded directly from scene iii ("The Rehearsal Room") to scene v ("The Lithia Fountain").

YES!

The children of the world *thank you!*

V

THE LITHIA FOUNTAIN

Lights up on a marble reflecting pool, in the center of which rises the statue of a goddess.
    Dennett enters. He observes the fountain.
    Cliff appears, reading a guidebook.

DENNETT

What in God's name is this? The Well of Narcissus?

CLIFF

It's called the Lithia Fountain. I was just reading about it. It's fed from a hot spring about a mile and a half up this mountain.

Dennett dips a cup into the water.

I wouldn't drink that if I were you.

DENNETT

Why not?

Dennett brings the cup to his nose, and recoils.

Ugh! This stuff smells like rotting monkey intestines.

CLIFF

It says here that the Indians who settled the valley believed the water possessed an extremely potent magic, both holy and evil.

DENNETT

What? Are you trying to scare me?

(*His eyes narrow*)
You don't really believe that nonsense, do you?

CLIFF

I don't know. I believe it could do some weird things.
Haven't you noticed how tall the corn grows around here?

DENNETT (*Gripping his stomach*)
You can say that again.
(*Toasting Cliff with the cup*)
My compliments!

CLIFF

For what?

DENNETT

Word is that you've written quite the *meisterstück!*

CLIFF (*Incredulous*)
I've written the *meisterstück?!*
(*As if the whole world knows*)
Yours is the play that they're all talking about!

Dennett snorts, shakes his head. Cliff continues.

No, they *are!* *Seriously!* It's *intimidating!*
(*With awe*)
Some of them seem to be . . . actually . . . *awestruck.*
Especially Mr. Montesor! I mean . . . I believe I even heard
the word "genius" escape his lips . . . I've got to tell you,
based on the bits and pieces I've heard, my curiosity's killing
me . . . !

DENNETT

It's all horseshit! *You* know that! You're smart enough to
know that!

CLIFF

Know *what? What* is?

DENNETT

Let me show you a *real* piece of writing.

> *Dennett pulls a slim volume from his pocket and hands it to Cliff. Cliff reads aloud:*

CLIFF

"SHABBAT: poems by Henry Dennett."
> (*Cliff looks at Dennett, impressed*)

My God! You really *are* a poet! I wasn't sure whether or not you were joking.

DENNETT (*Pompously*)

Composed entirely in Spenserian stanzas. Forty cantos altogether.
> (*Rabbinically*)

Something tells me that you'll be able to appreciate it.

CLIFF

This is . . . . I'm deeply . . . . Thank you very, *very* much.

> *Dennett nods solemnly.*

DENNETT

May I ask you a question?

CLIFF

Sure.

DENNETT

What's a bright kid like you doing, wasting his time in a place like this?

CLIFF

I don't think I'm wasting my time.

DENNETT (*Arching an eyebrow, 'entre-nous'*)

You don't think it's a waste of time having to put up with a bunch of nattering morons in hope that they might possibly stage your lousy play?

CLIFF

Actually, they seem like perfectly nice folks to me . . .

DENNETT (*Disgusted and impatient*)

Come on! I'm not talking about whether they're "nice" or not! Half the idiots in the world are "nice"! I mean, that Maurice! He's a pathetic, narcissistic old fraud.

CLIFF

In what way?

DENNETT

In what *way?* Take your pick. The hair, the accent, the stories about Olivier. Everything about him is either phony or self-deluded. Don't you find it draining to have to waste so much time indulging a man's fantasy of himself?

CLIFF

That's basic good manners.

DENNETT (*Scoffing*)

Playing Romeo! At his age! And to a Juliet whose youth is bound to make the relationship seem pathological! Indulging that sort of fantasy isn't good manners. It's comic exploitation of the elderly.

CLIFF

I'm sorry. I disagree. He seems like a wonderful man to me. They all seem wonderful. I mean . . . I really appreciate the hospitality around here. Don't you?

Dennett cocks his head slightly, heeding Cliff's words as if they contained some deeper, coded meaning. Suddenly: Eureka!

DENNETT
Ohhhhhhhh! So you're shagging that girl! You *are*, aren't you? You're shagging that girl!

CLIFF
What girl? What does *"shagging"* mean?

DENNETT (*Bemused*)
You're not the only one, you know, "Mr. Hospitality." Did you see the way she just came on to *me*?

CLIFF (*Nervously continuing*)
In fact, I can't remember the last time I met a group of people who were so unfailingly generous. Not only with their friendship, but with their critiques as well, which I've found to be consistently illuminating and instructive. Haven't *you*? Haven't you been learning a tremendous amount from them?

DENNETT
About *what*? About how to turn some banal and meretricious play into an even more banal and meretricious play?

CLIFF
Is your play so banal and meretricious?

Dennett leans forward.

DENNETT
Isn't *yours*?

CLIFF
I certainly hope not.

DENNETT (*Insouciantly*)

And you expect it to have a chance of winning a *playwriting* competition?

CLIFF

I . . . don't follow you . . .

> *Dennett points to the volume of his poetry in Cliff's hands.*

DENNETT

That. That's a *real* piece of writing.

CLIFF (*Perplexed, skeptical*)

So . . . what are you saying? That a play *can't* be?

DENNETT

A play is a *Biblia Pauperum:* a Bible in pictures for the benefit of the illiterate.

CLIFF (*More skeptical still*)

Well . . . for the benefit of *this* illiterate, would you mind explaining why that criticism should apply any more to a *play* than . . .

> (*Indicating Dennett's book*)

. . . to a *poem,* for example.

DENNETT

Are you *serious*?

> (*Drawing a breath*)

Young man . . .

> (*With the air of speaking to someone who desperately needs to be straightened out*)

A poem can be the uncompromised expression of a unique temperament. It doesn't have to tart itself up. It doesn't have to dumb itself down. It doesn't have to be made appealing or intelligible to a middle-class audience. And the audience for a play is inevitably, hopelessly middle-class. It was Strindberg, not I, who described the theatre as *a Biblia*

Pauperum, with the dramatist "a lay preacher hawking contemporary ideas . . .

CLIFF (*Completing the quotation*)
". . . in a form popular enough for the middle classes to be able to grasp what the minority is arguing about."

DENNETT (*Smiling, surprised and impressed*)
Bulls-eye! Now, *please.* Anyone whose education permits him to recognize a quotation like that must also recognize the fundamental dishonesty of "tailoring" his work— "developing" it, as they say around here—with the intention of making it conform to middle-class taste. No self-respecting *poet* would ever tailor his work to conform to anyone's taste but his own.

CLIFF
No. Nor would any self-respecting *playwright.*

DENNETT
But as a *playwright* you have no *choice!* You're obliged to sustain the interest of an easily bored mob that's always threatening to revolt unless it's being flattered or coddled or in some other way seduced. Forget about *honesty.* Middle-class audiences demand to be babied . . .
    (*Vehemently*)
. . . and *lied* to. They deplore truthful representations of themselves. Especially in *this* country, where Americans have been conditioned to expect art to show them not who they are, but to indulge the myth of who they believe themselves to be.

Cliff's eyes widen into question marks.

O, come on! Don't pretend you haven't noticed! Look at what *succeeds!* Look at what's hailed as "Important Art!" in America!

(*He laughs*)
It's hilarious! It's a cornball pageant of feel-good politics and pop-sociology that allows audiences to experience collective guilt as a form of collective absolution—a slam-bam catharsis on the order of "I feel your pain . . . now where we gonna eat? . . . decent, caring, humane people that we are . . ."

CLIFF
And you think we're an indecent, uncaring, inhumane people?

DENNETT
I think we're a lot more complicated than that, don't you?

Cliff studies Dennett.

CLIFF
I think that people who rail against politics in art often do so because they resent the fact that *their* politics aren't being reflected.

DENNETT
O, for heaven's sake! Kid . . . whether or not I see *my* politics reflected in a work of art is a matter of complete indifference to me. Of far greater interest to me is whether or not a work of art shows *talent* . . . whether or not it has *life*! Because if it has *life*—then right, left, center: who gives a damn what the politics are!

CLIFF
Has it ever occurred to you that maybe you don't give a damn about what the politics are because you're politically privileged enough not to?

DENNETT
Meaning what? That if I were politically *oppressed* . . . ?

CLIFF

. . . you might be more inclined to value art as an instrument for social change.

DENNETT

Well who knows whether art changes anything or not?! My point is that if it *does,* that's only one means of judging it . . . one that's been blown absurdly out of proportion here in practical, consumer-oriented America, where if it doesn't serve the public interest, it can't be good art.

CLIFF

According to whom?

DENNETT

According to an audience that would run you out of town if you actually challenged them with an honest idea instead of endorsing their way of life. Come on! You don't think people go to the theatre in this country to have their values *challenged,* do you?

CLIFF

Yes, I do. Some of them.

DENNETT

You're wrong. They go to bask in the flattering *image* of themselves as people who are *open-minded* enough to have their values challenged, which is just another way of saying that they go to the theatre to have their values *confirmed!*

CLIFF

Wow! That's incredibly . . . twisted and condescending!

DENNETT

But smack on the money, no? You have only to consider which artists the culture rewards! With nauseating consistency it's the ones who tell the most culturally affirming lies. Can you imagine the blood bath if any of them actually told the truth?! I've always said to my children that telling the truth in a work of art is like building your own coffin, and if it's solid enough and sturdy enough you can count on this truth-despising world to fall all over itself to bury you in it.

(*Pause*)

Isn't it amazing how in a country that allegedly prizes the "individual spirit" we're so relentlessly hostile to individuality in art . . . maybe because anything so potentially discordant as a genuinely original voice strikes us as too self-proclaiming and elitist.

Cliff begins to interject. He's a bit hard to read.

CLIFF

Too *undemocratic?*

DENNETT

Yes.

CLIFF

Too arrogant? Too resistant to compromise?

DENNETT

Too unwilling to seek approval from an audience, yes.

CLIFF

I see. . . . so what you're saying is that if it asserts a vision of the world that's in any way morally or politically . . . ambiguous? . . .

DENNETT

Yes!

CLIFF (*Tuning it in*)

. . . elusive in meaning? . . .

DENNETT

Exactly! . . . If it isn't all about reassuring us . . . sanctioning our taste . . .

CLIFF (*Perceiving it completely*)

. . . or consoling us with the notion that we really *are* "God's own people" . . .

DENNETT

. . . yes, exactly! . . .
>   (*As if reciting a creed*)
. . . if it isn't a voice that says with enough sensitivity training, we're infinitely redeemable. . .

CLIFF (*Echoing the creed*)

. . . committed to social improvement, climbing the right mountain . . .

DENNETT

Absolutely! That if it doesn't give us a big old hand job . . .

CLIFF (*Nodding*)

. . . gotcha . . .

DENNETT

. . . we just . . .
>   (*Deadly serious*)
. . . bury it!

CLIFF

We bury it, hunh?

DENNETT

That's right. We bury it.
>   (*Pause*)
Under a mountain.
>   (*Pause*)
Of jimmy crack corn-corn-corn.

(*Vehemently*)

And *that*! That's the *real* arrogance! Because as long as we lack the humility to look into the mirror and see ourselves for who we really are, instead of insisting that it reflect only what we *want* to see, we'll never be the Lords and Owners of our Faces, to paraphrase the sonnet . . . we'll never even *begin* to live in truth.

CLIFF

And a poet is somehow better qualified to *tell* the truth . . . ?

DENNETT (*Impatiently*)

. . . because a poet doesn't have to pander to the cornball vanity of a middle-class audience. Don't you get it, dummy?! The theatre is a *Biblia Pauperum!* Go ahead and write your little plays, but unless you want a stampede on your hands, you'd better damn well figure out what slop the livestock craves and treat curtain-up as feeding time!

Cliff winces.

And you know what Oscar Wilde said, don't you? He said that "the moment that an artist takes notice of what [the] people want, and tries to supply the demand . . .

CLIFF (*Finishing the quotation, impatiently*)

". . . he ceases to be artist, and becomes [instead] a dull or amusing craftsman, an honest or dishonest tradesman."

DENNETT (*Surprised, but less admiring this time; more nervous*)

Bulls-eye, again . . .

CLIFF (*Diffidently, but with a growing sense of self possession*)

But Wilde was a *playwright,* wasn't he? . . . as *well* as a poet. What makes you believe that he would have discriminated between a middle-class theatre audience and the audience

234

for *poetry*, which could be described in equally pejorative terms as a bunch of pimply undergraduates and the circle of bitter, unread poets and critics they hope someday to become.

Dennett winces.

(*Diffidently self-possessed*)
I mean . . . if you're going to have contempt for one audience, you might as well have contempt for them all. It's not as if readers of poetry are an especially incorruptible breed, nor that poets are any less likely than playwrights to be sycophants. Dishonest artists can be found in any field, often at the very top. Hell, if you don't think most so-called "serious" poetry isn't *cornball* . . .
(*Waving Dennett's book of poems in the air*)
. . .you can't be reading very much "serious" poetry.
(*He laughs*)
Sorry if this sounds rude, but I find it hard to imagine anything more cornball than believing that one art form is more or less cornball than another. And all your anxiety about the middle class—what the middle class thinks, and what the middle class wants, and what the middle class approves of—sounds to me suspiciously . . . well . . . *middle-class.* Or at least governed by a suspiciously middle-class idea of success.

Dennett is horrified.

And if that's what you want, then . . . yes! . . . everything you say is true . . . you'd better do your best to figure out what will please the crowd and . . . give it to them. But unless you make the demeaning assumption that an audience's taste can, or should, be ascertained by the application of some cynical calculus, nothing prevents you from expressing yourself truthfully and hoping that it's appreciated . . . and if it *is*, great! . . . and if it *isn't*, well, too bad . . . but whether it's appreciated or not can't be the *point!* It can't be the measure of success . . . !

DENNETT (*Staggered, and hurling a bitter ad hominem in defense*)
And this high-minded bullshit from someone who idolizes Guy Halperin!

CLIFF
I never said I idolized Guy Halperin.

DENNETT (*As if it were checkmate*)
You *did!* You said that seeing one of his plays made you want to be a playwright!

　　　Pause.

CLIFF (*Calmly*)
I was seventeen years old.

DENNETT (*Totally deflated*)
Oh.

CLIFF (*Shaking his head, almost comically perplexed*)
Heaven only knows what made *you* want to be a playwright!
　　　(*Bearing down, seriously*)
But this much I *do* know, Mr. Dennett: an artist is an artist regardless of the form. Talent doesn't just come and go depending on circumstances. It's as unmistakable as a fingerprint, and, like a fingerprint, it's difficult not to leave behind, even if you're unconscious of how. It always shows up somewhere—in the shadows or on the periphery—in language or architecture, or in quality of mind. I simply don't believe that any true artist is capable of mediocrity . . . in *any* form. Fiasco, maybe. And maybe brilliance, too. But never, *never* mediocrity.
　　　(*Pause*)
It's like that line by the poet John Ashbery . . .

DENNETT

Ashbery?! Ashbery's a *friend* of mine!

CLIFF

... about a wave breaking against a rock ...

DENNETT

I *know* John Ashbery!

CLIFF

... "giving up its shape in a gesture which expresses that shape" ...

DENNETT

I *know* him! Did you *hear* me?!

CLIFF

... or how a rumor whispered around a room ends up as something completely different from what it started out to be.

DENNETT

John Ashbery is a *friend* of mine, asshole!

CLIFF

Well, that's exactly what happens in art ...

DENNETT

He was invited to my son's bris ...

CLIFF

You start out *trying* to say something ...

DENNETT

Which we ended up not having, but that's another story.

CLIFF

... only to discover at the end ...

DENNETT

I just saw him at a meeting of the MLA!

CLIFF

. . . that you've omitted the very thing that you wanted to say.

DENNETT

He's recovering from root canal!

CLIFF

Because the truth of who you are always emerges *despite* yourself . . .

DENNETT

Are you listening to me?

CLIFF

. . . despite whatever it was you *thought* you were creating.

DENNETT

He's a *friend* of mine. John Ashbery is a *friend* of mine!

> *Dennett, in a blind fury, shoves Cliff to the ground.*

You don't know what the hell you're talking about. But you think you know everything, don't you? You think you've got it all figured out!

> *Dennett raises the cup.*

Here, know-it-all!

> *Dennett pivots to the Lithia goddess.*

Indian holy place my ass!

> *Dennett toasts.*

NOSTROVIA!

> *With an aggressive flourish, Dennett defiantly quaffs the Lithia water, draining the cup to its lees.*

CURTAIN

ACT TWO

i
THE REHEARSAL ROOM

The Actors, scripts in hand, have just completed a reading of Dennett's play.

MAURICE
And . . . slow curtain.

Dennett rises to his feet. He is overwhelmed.

DENNETT (*Genuinely stunned*)
My God.

The members of the Company look at one another uncertainly.

O my God!
        (*With wonder*)
Bravo! Brava! Bravissimi!

Dennett moves closer to them, cheering and clapping.

I'm dumbstruck! I'm flabbergasted!

MAURICE (*Taken aback*)
So . . . you enjoyed it . . . ?

DENNETT (*To Maurice*)
Enjoyed it?
        (*To the Company*)
Look at me! I'm beside myself! I'm in shock!
        (*Dennett wipes his tears away*)
I mean, you'll have to forgive me, but I simply had no idea!

MAURICE

No idea of what?

DENNETT

No idea that it was a good play.

DUNCAN

It's a *marvelous* play . . .

> *The Others, with the exception of a taciturn Ariel and a surly Jason, murmur in excited agreement.*

DENNETT

But I didn't *know* that. Honestly.

SALOME

Well, what did you *think,* poor baby?

DENNETT

I don't know. I suppose I thought it was . . . contemptible.

> *A collective expression of astonishment from the actors—* "CONTEMPTIBLE??"—*as if Dennett had just called* War and Peace *contemptible.*

SALOME

Darling, you couldn't write something contemptible if you tried.

DENNETT

But that's the point! That's why I'm in shock! I *did* try! I swear to God, I gave it my all.

> *Confusion from the Actors.*

What a dunce I am that this should strike me as an epiphany!

> *Excitedly, to the entire Company.*

An artist is an artist regardless of the form.

Cliff's ears prick up.

Talent shows up like a fingerprint. It's something that you inevitably leave behind, even if you're unconscious of how. It's like that Ashbery line . . .

Cliff cocks his head, bemused. Maurice begins to jot down Dennett's words . . .

. . . about a wave breaking against a rock, "giving up its shape in a gesture which expresses that shape . . ."

MAURICE (*Jotting*)
Caro bambino!

DENNETT

Well, that's what happens in art. The truth of who you are always emerges *despite* yourself, despite whatever it was you may have *thought* you were creating.

WINNY
I think that would make a great musical!

Winny and Maurice roar.

MAURICE
I think it would make an *execrable* musical!

Winny and Maurice roar.

DENNETT
And I think I may have underestimated the artistry of *you* people, as well. You have no idea what a joy it was . . . watching you all, over the last two hours . . . infusing my play with . . . life . . .

MIRANDA (*Glowingly*)
Well, that's our job . . . that's the process . . .

DENNETT
Then the process is alchemy.

The Actors variously acknowledge and protest Dennett's tribute in a chattering chorus, while Maurice's voice overrides all with:

MAURICE
The play's the thing! The play's the thing!

Dennett reaches into his breast pocket . . .

DENNETT
Actually, as I was listening, I . . .

. . . and pulls out a crumpled sheet of foolscap, exhibiting it to the Company.

. . . jotted down a little something . . .

Salome gasps.

SALOME
A poem?

DENNETT
Yes. A poem.

The members of the Company gasp and murmur in excitement.

I wonder if I might read it to you?

A collective burst of excitement from the Company. Except Jason.

JASON (*Sternly*)
I thought you said no poems.

All fall silent.
Dennett turns to face Jason.

DENNETT

Look, kid . . . what's-your-name . . . Jason . . . I guess it's clear that we're not going to be best friends. But we don't have to be, do we? We can respect each other. As artists. And in the last two hours you showed me what a superb artist you are.

Dennett offers his hand.

(*Sincerely*)
You're one hell of an actor . . .
(*Relating to him*)
. . . man.

Pause.
Jason takes Dennett's hand. They shake. The Company beams.

MAURICE (*To Dennett*)

So are you going to read that poem or not?

The Actors burble and murmur and huddle around Dennett.

DENNETT

It's written in a form called "asymptotic dactyls."

A ripple of thrilled confusion all around.

MAURICE (*Fatuously agog*)

And why not?

DENNETT

It's called, "To a Company of Actors."

Another ripple of excitement and anticipation all around.
Then, silence.
Dennett clears his throat. He reads:

(*Reading*)

> "As though awakened
> In a teeming vault
> Of legendless
> And unfamiliar stars,
> The words that faintly shone
> Like avatars
> Of secret gods
> You labored to exalt
>
> In patterns of
> Reconstellated light
> Emerge at last
> Like questions left unasked:
> Each one a face
> Hung luminously masked
> Between two distant
> Mountains in the night."

Pause.

The sound of a sharp intake of breath, followed by a wild éclat of applause and cooing and fluttering from the wide-eyed Actors as they absorb Dennett's tribute like the denizens of a startled rookery, petting and grooming each other with exclamations like: "O, my God!" and "That's amazing" and "You mean, we inspired that?" and "Asymptomatic dactyls, no less!" and "What's an avatar?"

Maurice steps forward. There are tears in his eyes.

MAURICE (*To Dennett*)

Myron, that was magnificent.

Maurice hugs Dennett.

Thank you, my friend! Thank you from all of us.

Maurice calls over his shoulder to the troupe.

Group hug, everyone!

The Actors cluster around Maurice. Dennett, uncomfortable with the idea of a "group hug," maintains a slight distance. Maurice beckons to him.

You too, author!

Dennett is drawn stiffly into the group hug.

Splendid!

(*Breaking the group hug*)
Now, then, my lovelies. On to *Romeo and Juliet*. I'm a mite concerned about the length. What was the time on that final run-through, Miranda?

MIRANDA
Seven hours and forty-one minutes.

MAURICE (*Punching the palm of his hand, mildly concerned*)
Still too long!
(*To the Actors*)
We've got a bit of tightening to do before tonight's premiere, ladies and gentlemen. But with the odd nip here and tuck there I think we're close to having something very, very special on our hands. Why don't we take a few minutes to cool down . . .
(*Inhales deeply*)
. . . catch our breaths, stretch to the ceiling . . . come on, everyone, stretch! . . . Salome, Ariel, Jason . . . let's have our playwrights, as well . . .

Winny and Cliff join in. Dennett stands off to the side . . .

. . . reaching for the stars . . . good! . . . high as you can, on tippy-toes, scraping the stratosphere . . . and now, collapsing

down, letting your body go totally limp like a rag doll . . .
wonderful! . . . and then gradually straightening up again to
become . . . your favorite jungle animal . . . what's that I
see? . . . ooooo, a boa constrictor . . . and a cockatoo . . .
good leopard, Duncan! . . .

> *Maurice notices Dennett standing off to the side.*

> (*To Dennett*)
> . . . and is that a wildebeest over there in the distance?

DENNETT
I wasn't doing anything.

MAURICE
O, I thought you were doing a wildebeest.
(*Using child psychology*)
You probably don't even know what a wildebeest is.

DENNETT
Well of course I know what a wildebeest is.

> *Maurice cocks his head, skeptically.*

It's . . . like a yak.

MAURICE (*Skeptical, à la child psychology*)
Like a yak?

DENNETT
Yes . . . like a . . . buffalo or a bison.

> *Maurice stares at him skeptically.*

You know . . . they've got thick hairy bodies and spindly
legs, and they make . . . sort of a rutting sound . . .

MAURICE (*Theatrically confounded*)
A *rutting* sound?

DENNETT (*Frustrated*)
Yes! You know! Like . . .

> *Dennett snuffles and rootles and ruts like a wildebeest.*
> *Maurice lights up.*

MAURICE (*Clapping his hands to his face*)
Maestro! That is the most convincing wildebeest I've ever
seen!

> *Dennett regains himself and withdraws.*

Do it again for the company!

DENNETT
No, I couldn't possibly . . .

MAURICE
But you're a marvelous actor! Do it again!

DENNETT
I don't even know what I was doing.

MAURICE (*Clapping his hands and chanting*)
WIL-DE-BEEST! WIL-DE-BEEST! WIL-DE-BEEST . . . !

> *Maurice prompts the Company, and they join in . . .*

ALL
WIL-DE-BEEST! WIL-DE-BEEST! WIL-DE-BEEST

> *Dennett, reluctantly, but feeling the pressure, launches into*
> *his wildebeest impersonation. The Company squeals and*
> *cheers with delight. Dennett becomes increasingly emboldened*
> *by the cheers.*
> *Duncan, still in character as a leopard, suddenly pounces*
> *on Dennett, tackling him to the ground, "mauling him."*

MAURICE (*Alarmed*)
Duncan! What are you doing?

247

DUNCAN
Sorry.
(*As if shaken from a dream*)
It was instinct.

MAURICE
Extraordinary!
(*Taking command of the situation*)
All right, everyone. Let's try to regain control of ourselves
now, relaxing our bodies, tranquilly surrendering to the
moment as if nestling into the most sensuous eiderdown . . .

*The members of the Company lie on their backs, breathing
peacefully.*
Cliff approaches Maurice.

CLIFF
Maurice, for a man whose opening night is less than three
hours away, you seem inexplicably calm. What's the secret?

MAURICE
No secret. Just a series of breathing exercises that Kiki
taught us called "Kumbalini" . . .

CLIFF (*Repeating it perfectly*)
"Kumbalini"?

MAURICE (*Correcting him slightly*)
No, "Kumbalini."

CLIFF (*Repeating it perfectly*)
"Kumbalini"?

MAURICE (*Correcting him slightly*)
No, "Kumbalini."

CLIFF (*Repeating it perfectly*)
"Kumbalini"?

MAURICE (*Correcting him slightly*)
No, "Kumbalini."

CLIFF (*Repeating it perfectly*)
"Kumbalini"?

    Pause.

MAURICE
Never mind. Anyway, Kiki taught us these breathing
exercises called "Kumbalini," of which there are thirty-
seven major variations. Unbeatable for relaxation.
    (*To the Company*)
Preparing for Kumbalini Primary Series, thank you.
    (*Checking his watch*)
I was just about to lead the company in a brief set, if it's not
a bother.

CLIFF
No, not at all.

MAURICE
You're welcome to join us.

    *Cliff shyly demurs. Winny excitedly bounds over to join the
    Actors.*
    *The Actors, and Winny, assume starting yoga postures.
    Maurice inhales deeply.*

    (*Placing hands together and chanting*)
And ... KUMBALINI DRISHTA MUHRTI

ALL (*Chanting in response*)
KUMBALINI DRISHTA MUHRTI

MAURICE
Kumbalini number twenty-seven.

Maurice and the Actors assume a downward-facing dog posture.

Dennett, having brushed himself off after the leopard attack, approaches Cliff.

DENNETT (*To Cliff*)
What's this about?

CLIFF
Maurice is leading the company through a series of breathing exercises called "Kumbalini."

MAURICE (*Upside-down, from between his legs, correcting Cliff.*)
No, "Kumbalini."

DENNETT (*To Maurice, repeating it perfectly, etc.*)
"Kumbalini"?

MAURICE
No, "Kumbalini."

DENNETT
"Kumbalini"?

MAURICE (*Sighing*)
Never mind.

Straightening up from his downward-facing dog position, hands pressed together, chanting:

POOHRI POOHRI BAHKTI PHOORI

ALL (*Rising and chanting, in response, shooting their arms out into "warrior" position on the word "HA"*)
MALAGA MALAGA MALAGA—HA.

MAURICE (*Switching postures*)
Kumbalini number six.

Maurice and Company engage in a silent breathing exercise.
Dennett raises his cup of Lithia water to Cliff in a
toast.

DENNETT
Here's to you, young man. You shook me up. You made
me think.

CLIFF (*Politely*)
You made me think, too.

Maurice begins to take note of Cliff and Dennett's
conversation.

DENNETT
No, I mean it. You helped me to understand something
fundamental about myself as an artist—and as a man.
Something that's profoundly . . . consoling.

MAURICE
Kumbalini number twenty-one.

CLIFF
I would never have guessed that you were in need of
consoling.

DENNETT (*With some poignancy*)
Well . . . you're young.

Maurice, his attention still directed at Cliff and Dennett,
breaks the meditation and dismisses the Company.

MAURICE
And . . . quietly finishing now, everyone! Off you go!
Quick like bunnies . . .

The Actors exit . . .

Into costume for the top of Act One. Jolly good!*

Winny, who lags behind the rest of the Actors, approaches Maurice.

WINNY

You know, Maurice, when I listen to you talk I think, God, you must really miss home sometimes.

MAURICE (*His eyes still on Cliff and Dennett, who are quietly conferring*)

Miss *home?* The *festival* is my home! I've been here for twenty years now . . .

WINNY

No, I mean England!
    (*Pause*)
Because . . . well . . . you *are* British . . . !
    (*Pause*)
Aren't you? Originally?

Maurice nervously clears his throat.

MAURICE

Not originally.
    (*Pause*)
Not by *birth,* no.

WINNY

But you must have *lived* there . . .

MAURICE (*Grandly*)

Ah! To live in England! Perchance to dream! That's

*In the New York production, this exchange between Maurice and Winny (beginning with "Jolly good" and ending with Winny's flummoxed exit) seemed to add too much rhythm to the scene, and was cut. I restore it here because it provides a fun (though, perhaps, self-evident) gloss on the nature of Maurice's identity.

something I would dearly love to do, and, incurable
romantic that I am, I haven't given up hope that someday I
might.

WINNY (*Confused*)
But . . . you've spent a great deal of *time* there . . . I
assume . . .

MAURICE
You know, it's very curious, but despite the intense affinity
I feel for our cousins across the pond, I've never actually had
a chance to visit Great Britain.

WINNY (*Agog*)
Then . . . where *are* you from?

Maurice, crestfallen, but with dignity:

MAURICE
How well do you know the Tampa Bay area?

Winny staggers away, perplexed.
Maurice returns his attention to Cliff and Dennett, whom
he now gleefully approaches.

Do my eyes deceive me? Or have our scribes succumbed at
last to the enchantment of these woods, meeting each other
as kinsmen, exchanging ideas, caring and sharing . . .

DENNETT
You know, Maurice, there's more value in that than I
would have ever imagined. No one's so intelligent that he
can't afford to benefit from another man's wisdom.

MAURICE
Well spoken, *maestro!*

DENNETT
In fact, I can't believe what a fool I've been!

MAURICE

But you're a genius!

DENNETT

I don't mean simply about the nature of my talent. I mean about . . . everything! Even . . . *women,* for example.

MAURICE

Ah, *women!*

DENNETT

You know that girl, Ariel? She's exactly the kind of bookish Lolita whom normally I would have had in the sack already, especially after that intellectual leg-spreading she performed for me, right there in front of you all.

Maurice's eyes widen. Cliff's jaw drops.

But watching her this afternoon, all I could think of was how beautiful she was. And I know this might sound crazy, but I was actually having . . . *feelings* . . . for her. And I wondered if she might be having feelings for me too.

MAURICE (*Irate*)

Well, how could she not? You're obviously irresistible. Why don't you write a poem about it in asymptomatic duckbills, or something . . .

Maurice storms out of the room.
Dennett turns to Cliff, who is dumbstruck.

DENNETT

What did I *say?*

THE REHEARSAL ROOM (CONT.)

The Family. Claire, Adam, Jessica, Peter and Cheyenne, flanking Guy, focus their attention with intense anxiety upon Dennett, who stands apart. A collective Gasp.

JESSICA
Daddy! What's wrong with your face?

DENNETT
There's nothing wrong with my face.

JESSICA
Is that psoriasis around your nose?

DENNETT
You're imagining things.

CLAIRE
No, it's true, Henry. Your skin has an odd pallor.

GUY
Do you think it's related in some way to the . . . contempio
-stuartum . . .

ADAM
Contemptiosuarumcupiditatumfilaria. It has nothing to do
with that.

DENNETT (*With finality*)
Look, I'm fine. I'm fine. I'm going to be fine. Why don't
we not talk about it anymore.

ADAM (*Wheeling on everyone, parroting Dennett*)
Yeah. Why don't we not talk about it anymore?

CHEYENNE (*To Guy*)
Gran—pa.

PETER

No, Cheyenne! That's not your grandfather.

Jessica, taking in the room for the first time, fixes upon a poster featuring Maurice in full Shakespearean regalia. ★

JESSICA

Who's the old man?

DENNETT

That's Maurice. He runs the place.

JESSICA

O, perfect! He looks . . . quintessentially out-of-touch.

DENNETT

I saw him on stage last night. Playing Romeo.

JESSICA (*With bloodlust*)

Daddy, no! That's too good to be true!

DENNETT

I kid you not.

JESSICA

And?

DENNETT

Well, it's very curious. Before his entrance it was pretty much Shakespeare-as-usual: the sort of snoozily tasteful, *Masterpiece Theatre* - type production that people who carry Metropolitan Opera tote bags and read restaurant reviews think is Great Art. Then, when Maurice pranced on, it was like witnessing a seventy-car pileup on an interstate. The whole play just went blissfully, chaotically awry! It was

★In the New York production, three posters were displayed in the "Lila B. Hirschhorn Rehearsal Pavilion": Maurice as a fist-clenching Henry IV, an eye-gouged Oedipus, and as Nagg in Beckett's *Endgame,* emerging from a dustbin.

hilarious and traumatizing at the same time . . . you know, the way you feel when you see an Olympic figure skater wipe out during the artistic program.

Jessica and Adam detonate into delighted laughter.
Dennett, however, suddenly shifts gears:

(*Reexperiencing it as he narrates*)
Gradually, though, an interesting thing started to happen. This older man, who admittedly had no business playing anyone younger than sixty, slowly began . . . to transform. Into another person. You honestly found yourself forgetting his age. By the end, he had you believing that he actually was . . .
(*In wonder, as though hardly believing it himself*)
. . . Romeo.
(*Pause. He turns to his flummoxed children*)
It's true.
(*Pause. To himself:*)
I wanted to tell him afterwards. Unfortunately, he's not speaking to me at the moment.

JESSICA
Daddy, I'm amazed that you can even *stand* this place! Look at it! It's a kitsch paradise. It's an Elizabethan twilight zone. It's the kind of place where they tear down an old barn and build a new barn and hang a sign on it that says, "Ye Olde Barne."

ADAM
Yes. And it's not even a barn anymore. It's a . . . scented candle emporium.

DENNETT
Well . . . the people here really have been extraordinarily nice.

JESSICA

Nice? Daddy, half the idiots in the world are nice!

DENNETT

No, I mean I appreciate their hospitality.

Pause, as Adam and Jessica register confusion.

And their talent. Yes, I know, I've always expressed a rather dim view of actors. But these people managed to elicit a quality in my work that actually made me . . . shiver . . . which is what Nabokov says is the hallmark of only the most transcendent art.

GUY (*Genially*)

Uh-oh! Sounds like I'd better cut that check right now. Hunh, Claire?

CLAIRE (*To Dennett*)

So I guess that means the Berg Collection—or whichever archive it is that involuntarily houses your *oeuvre* these days—can expect to receive a new manuscript before the end of the month.

ADAM (*Deflecting the insult*)

It's the Smith College Library. Not the Berg Collection.

JESSICA

And they do not house Daddy's *oeuvre* involuntarily. He asked them, and they agreed.

CLAIRE

O. Isn't it normally the other way around?

DENNETT

Well, I'm not Joseph Brodsky, am I?

A shocked pause.

ADAM

Brodsky's reputation is outrageously overinflated.

GUY

Can you imagine what would happen if I deposited *my* manuscripts in a library? They'd probably just smilingly dump them down an incinerator.

CLAIRE

That's not true! Anyway, you're appreciated in the here and now.
(*With her eyes on Dennett*)
Why would you need to make some lamentable attempt to inflict yourself on posterity?

DENNETT (*With his eyes on Claire*)

I agree. Feeling appreciated goes a long way. It's wonderful to be in a place where you're surrounded by people who lavish you with their affection and approval. It's really affected the way I view myself as an artist . . . and as a man.
(*To All*)
You know what they had me participating in the other day? A group hug.

Silence and shock. Then a wave of relieved laughter.

ADAM

God, you almost had me believing you for a second there!

JESSICA

A group hug! I love it!
(*Playing along, hugging herself*)
And did it make you all feel less insecure about who you are?

DENNETT (*Pointedly*)

Well, maybe if the two of you were less insecure about who *you* are, you could afford to be more generous towards people who are different from you, and to honor an aesthetic to which you might not necessarily subscribe.

> *Silence and shock. Jessica eyes Dennett's Lithia cup.*

JESSICA
What have you been drinking?

DENNETT
It's water from the local spring. Why?

JESSICA
May I see it?

> *Dennett hands her the cup.*

> (*Sniffing it, and staggered by its toxicity*)
Aughhhhhhh! What is this stuff? It smells like pig feces.

DENNETT (*Taking the cup back*)
Then don't drink it.

JESSICA
I won't.

> *Pause, as Dennett defiantly gulps another throatful of Lithia water.*

JESSICA
Daddy, are you all right?

> *Dennett crosses to Cheyenne and hands her a gift, neatly wrapped.*

DENNETT
I've never felt better in my life.

> *Cheyenne takes the gift from Dennett.*

CHEYENNE
Gran—pa.

PETER (*Ecstatic*)
   Yes, Cheyenne!

iii
THE THEATRE

*Audio: A packed house, buzzing with the Excited Voices of
an opening night crowd.*★
   *Maurice appears before the curtain. An anticipatory hush
settles over the Audience.*

MAURICE
   "O for a Muse of fire, that would ascend
   The brightest heaven of invention
   A kingdom for a stage, princes to act
   And monarchs to behold the swelling scene . . . !"

*A look of dumbstruck terror crosses Maurice's face. He glances
helplessly towards the wings.*

MIRANDA (*from offstage*)
   "Then should the warlike Harry, like himself . . ."

MAURICE
   "Then should the warlike Harry, like himself,
   Assume the port of Mars; and at his heels,
   Leash'd in like hounds, should famine, sword and fire
   Crouch for employment . . ."

Terror, again, crosses Maurice's face.

MIRANDA (*from offstage*)
   "But pardon, gentles all . . ."

★No prerecorded audience reactions were used in New York. Maurice's intro-
ductions were staged in front of the house curtain, with the real audience serving
as the "Festival Audience."

261

MAURICE

> "But pardon, gentles all,
> The flat unraised spirits that have dared
> On this unworthy scaffold to bring forth
> So great an object: can this cockpit hold
> The vasty fields of France? Or may we cram
> Within this wooden O the very casques
> That did affright the air at Agincourt?"

Maurice spreads his hands wide to the Audience.

MAURICE

Salve! Welcome, friends and family, to the Fourth annual New Playwrights . . .
> (*With a theatrical flourish*)

. . . Festival!

Audio: A burst of applause, as Maurice bows.

Our three nominated authors this year were selected from a bumper crop of fresh, exciting new voices. Their plays are truly . . .
> (*Overpronounced French*)

. . . *la crème de la crème.* Listen as each of them casts its own . . .

> *Maurice inhales deeply and flings a handful of glitter-dust into the air.*

. . . peculiar spell . . .

> *Audio: The Audience oooooos. Maurice makes balletic hand gestures.*

. . . weaves its own special kind of . . .

> *Maurice pulls a bouquet of flowers out of thin air.*

. . . magic!

Audio: The Audience aahhhhhhs. Maurice hurls the bouquet into the house.

Won't you please join me in welcoming our three talented finalists. From Judson Ridge, Miss Winifred Hill . . .

Audio: The Audience applauds warmly as . . .
. . . Winny, giggling and snorting, enters stage right.

From Redcloud, Mr. Clifford Pike.

Audio: The Audience applauds warmly as . . .
. . . Cliff enters stage right, joining Winny.
In introducing Dennett, Maurice is only partially able to conceal a profound sense of distaste.

And from Northampton, Massachusetts, Mr. Heinrich Himmler.

Audio: The Audience applauds warmly as . . .
. . . Dennett enters stage right, joining Winny and Cliff.

MAURICE
These three youngsters—dreamers all——have each, in his or her own way, had the audacity to translate into the realm of . . .
(Whispered)
. . . imagination . . .
(Grandly)
. . . the hopes, the fears, the triumphs, and, yes, even the bitter disappointments that make every one of us, as Shelley so mordantly observed, "Human. Human. All too human."

Dennett's brow furrows.

DENNETT *(Sotto voce)*
Shelley . . . ?

Maurice glares at Dennett. He then plows on.

MAURICE

For different though we sometimes are, we remain, as these three authors never fail to remind us, fundamentally . . . the same.

Audio: The Audience applauds. Maurice joins them, turning towards the Playwrights.

(*Applauding*)
I agree.

Dennett, Winny, and Cliff exit. Maurice nods to the lights booth. The "house" fades.

We begin with a remarkable *jeu d'esprit* that tells the story of the struggle for women's independence in the twentieth century through an imagined conversation between famed lyric soprano Dame Nellie Melba and American First Lady Eleanor Roosevelt.
(*Pause*)
Ellie and Nellie, by Miss Winifred Hill.

Audio: The Audience applauds. Maurice exits.

iv
THE LOBBY

The curtain flies up to reveal:
The Lobby between shows. Guy enters, program in hand, with Claire, Adam, Jessica and, ultimately, Dennett in tow.

GUY (*Wonderstruck*)
God! You arrive here in the hinterlands, you don't expect to see much of anything, and then . . . the *talent!* It's *staggering!* Not a mature talent, mind you, but one that's

almost more thrilling for the way it intuitively grasps some very tricky Aristotelian precepts. I was completely bowled over. What did *you* think, Adam?

ADAM
I thought it was like being trapped inside a body bag for two hours.

GUY
Well, that's a very facile response. What you can't deny is the quality of the writing.

ADAM (*Savoring the absurdity*)
The quality of the writing . . .

> *Adam launches into a satire of the play, using Jessica as "Nellie."*

"You, Nellie Melba, for whom no role was too treacherous, no height unscaleable! Mimi, Violetta, *Norma*! Was there not a single aria in the entire repertoire—not a phrase, not an ornament—which you did not make indelibly your own?! Princes worshiped you! Kings *died* for you! YOU, NELLIE MELBA! *LA DIVINA ASSOLUTA!*"

CLAIRE
It wasn't as silly as you're making it sound.

GUY (*Disbelieving*)
And are you seriously telling me that neither of you were the least bit moved by the makeover scene?

JESSICA (*Mimetically applying mascara and lipstick to Adam's face . . .*)
"Eleanor. You can't walk around looking like that *these* days. Times have changed. A girl can still want

world peace, but a lick o' mascara and designer pumps shouldn't be far behind on her checklist."

Jessica turns Adam's face towards an imaginary mirror.

ADAM (*Touching his face*)
"But Nellie! I'm BEAUTIFUL!"

JESSICA
"You've always *been* beautiful, Eleanor Roosevelt."

Jessica and Adam crack up. Dennett intervenes.

DENNETT
Actually, despite your satire, I thought the makeover scene expressed some reasonably intriguing notions about the nature of identity. And I was completely unaware, unless it was merely an author's conceit, of the role that ventriloquism played in Eleanor Roosevelt's life.

GUY (*Genuinely astonished*)
I was surprised by that, too.

DENNETT
You know what? I think this young woman is a far more talented writer than I expected her to be.

An Usher enters, costumed as "Annie."

USHER
Arf arf arf! Orphans and millionaires, Sandy says, "Will you please take your seats."

V
THE THEATRE

Maurice appears in front of the curtain.

MAURICE★

Citizens of Verona! Won't you kindly join me in
acknowledging our three distinguished judges.

> *A spotlight hits the front of the balcony. Maurice points:*

On the left, Dick Hirschorn. In the middle, Betty
Hirschorn. And on the right. . .
> (*Saluting the balcony*)

. . . Submarine Commander Martina Hirschorn Ablowich.
> (*Snapping the salute with patriotic respect*)

Anchors away, milady!

> *Duncan enters.*

MAURICE

What would the theatre be . . .

> *Maurice suddenly grabs Duncan from behind and points a*
> *dagger at his throat.*
> *Audio: The Audience gasps.*

. . . without *danger?*

> *Duncan struggles theatrically as Maurice digs the knife deeper*
> *into his flesh.*

Without the element of risk? Without the courage to test
the boundaries between *truth* . . .

★Maurice's introduction of the judges—Hirschorns all—made specific comic
reference to "The Lila B. Hirschorn Rehearsal Pavilion" plaque that hung on
the Rehearsal Room set in the New York production.

Maurice reaches round and bends the rubber blade of the knife with his finger.

. . . and illusion.

> *Audio: Gentle, relieved laughter from the Audience.*
> *Maurice pats Duncan on the back and dismisses him.*

Thank you, Duncan.

> *Duncan exits.*

Clifford Pike, a first-time playwright from Redcloud, goes beyond merely testing such boundaries; he challenges us to consider the nature of boundaries themselves. Navigation through his world depends on surrender to perpetual doubt, for he supplies no roadmap—no clear indication, finally, of what we are expected to think . . . or feel.
> *(Pause)*
Cerro Torre, by Clifford Pike.

vi
THE LOBBY

> *The curtain flies again to reveal the Lobby.*
> *Dennett storms on, spilling pills into his hand. The Family follows.*

CLAIRE
Henry! Why are you so agitated?

DENNETT (*Panicked*)
I'm not agitated. I'm *concerned.*

CLAIRE
Concerned about what?

DENNETT
That kid's play! It could *win*, don't you think?

GUY (*Incredulous*)
Win what? The booby prize?

JESSICA
Daddy, it was refreshingly misguided, at best.

ADAM
You can be sure it's going to seem very bush-league next to whatever you've cooked up. . .

DENNETT (*Deeply alarmed*)
No! It wasn't bush-league at all! It was *outstanding!*

GUY
What makes you think it was outstanding? I thought it was . . . smug and self-congratulatory!

JESSICA (*To Guy, impatiently*)
He means that it was *honest.*

GUY
Honest? Who gives a damn? I didn't like it.

ADAM (*Wheeling on Guy*)
He means that it was honest enough to be *itself* whether you liked it or not . . . though I suppose that to write in that fashion is as good as committing an act of high treason, especially here in the Land of Have a Nice Day.

GUY
Well, I've got news for you. High treason ain't gonna pass muster with the critics.

ADAM
So? Is it always necessary to pass muster with the critics?

GUY

It is if you want your play to run.

ADAM

Then why don't you just let the *critics* write your play?

GUY (*Exploding*)

Look, why don't you stop talking to me as if I were some bumbling idiot who's unable to measure success without the aid of a busy abacus? I know that Beckett said that to be an artist is to fail as no others dare fail, but *that* was ridiculous! Why can't you credit me with knowing a little something about theatre! I've *earned* that.

> *Dennett, sweating and gripping his stomach, pleads with Guy for reassurance.*

DENNETT

So you honestly believe this kid has no chance of winning?

GUY

Henry, it's hard to imagine that you'd have anything to worry about.

DENNETT

Then why am I feeling such extreme . . . *nausea*.

> *An Usher enters, costumed as Maria Von Trapp in* The Sound of Music.

USHER

Flibbertigibbits, will-o'-the-wisps, and clowns. Your attention, *bitte*. The *singspiel* is about to resume.

> *Dennett vomits into a handkerchief.*

Yodel-ay-*hee*-hoo.

THE THEATRE

Maurice appears from behind the curtain.
Audio: The Audience falls silent.

MAURICE

Last year, a young writer cracked open our souls with a heroic tale of how one man's talent and dexterity emboldened half the population of an occupied Polish village to laugh defiantly in the face of the Holocaust. T play—*Fingerpuppets of Hope,* by Daniel Eisenberg . . .

> *Audio: Applause from the Audience . . .*

> (*Applauding, too*)
. . . I agree . . .
> (*Continuing . . .*)
. . . not only walked away with our top prize—the coveted Lila B. Hirschorn Memorial Scepter—

> *Audio: Applause from the Audience as . . .*
> *. . . Duncan appears in a spotlight at the proscenium, displaying a sterling silver scepter on a purple velvet pillow. Maurice continues . . .*

. . . but set a standard of excellence that seemed, at the time, unmatchable. Yet if we have learned anything from our first two authors, it is that the artistic imagination, which mysteriously takes flight like some . . .
> (*Improvising expansively, and absurdly, his voice quivering with emotion*)
. . . cockamamie, madcap, semi-deranged whippoorwill . . . continually establishes a new standard of excellence, soaring to heights previously undreamed of!

> *Audio: Applause from the Audience . . .*

Our final offering is no exception. Fearlessly addressing many of the most vexing issues that touch our lives and rend our society today, a gifted poet and playwright captures the *zeitgeist* in a work that is part hallucination, part meditation, part documentary, and part prayer.

(*Pause*)

Ladies and gentlemen . . . *Wrong Mountain* . . . by Adolf Hitler.

> *Audio: Applause from the Audience.*
> *The lights fade.*

viii
THE LITHIA FOUNTAIN

Night; the celebration.

Dennett's Family stands in a cluster on one side of the stage. On the other side of the stage, Dennett stands in a cluster with Maurice, Cliff, and Winny. Upstage, Ariel is in a cluster with Duncan and Miranda.

*Dennett holds the Lila B. Hirschorn Memorial Scepter.**

MIRANDA, GUY, DUNCAN, ARIEL, CLIFF, AND WINNY (*overlapping*)
Congratulations.

DENNETT
Thanks.

They applaud.

MAURICE (*To Dennett*)
That was a magnificent speech you gave.

---

*In the New York production, the head of the scepter doubled as a bowl from which Dennett, at the scene's climax, guzzled Lithia water.

DENNETT

It was nothing.

MAURICE

No, it was rapturous. It was a bracing reminder that one should never let personal differences stand in the way of great art.

Maurice extends his hand to Dennett. Dennett takes it, gratefully.

DENNETT

I appreciate that.

MAURICE (*With a sweep of the hand, Maurice acknowledges Dennett's family.*)

Your family must be very touched.

DENNETT (*Directed towards his family*)

Well, I meant every word. How often in life do you have the opportunity to express your gratitude—publicly—to the people you love? To say to them, "Thank you for believing in me when nobody else seemed to give a damn."

MAURICE

And may I say that *my* belief in all *three* of you is *boundless*. Clifford, Winny . . . you should feel extremely proud of yourselves.

WINNY

Thanks, Maurice.

CLIFF

Thank you, Mr. Montesor. I'll try.

MAURICE

In any event, the hour is late, and Morpheus strums his lyre.
(*Calling to Ariel*)
Are you coming, dear?

ARIEL

Just a minute longer, Daddy, please?

MAURICE

Yes, very well. But no longer than a minute.
(*To the Others*)
As for the rest of you, I bid you a fond good night.

Maurice begins to exit . . .

WINNY

Yes, good night everyone.

. . . followed by Winny. Cliff turns to Dennett.

CLIFF

I should go, too. Congratulations again, Mr. Dennett.
(*He shakes Dennett's hand*)
O, by the way. Here's your book of poems. Thanks for
giving me a chance to read it.

Dennett makes no move towards the book.

DENNETT

It was a gift.

CLIFF (*Awkwardly*)

O. Thanks.
(*More awkwardly*)
Anyway . . . good night.

Cliff begins to exit . . .

DENNETT (*A growing shock of realization*)

You didn't think very much of my poems, did you?

CLIFF (*Genuinely*)

I thought your *play* was brilliant.

DENNETT (*Astonished, uncomprehending*)

But not . . . my *poems* . . .

> *Pause.*

CLIFF

Gotta go. Good night.

> *Cliff exits.*
> *Dennett crosses to Ariel.*

DENNETT

So my play . . . did it make you "shiver"?

ARIEL

Did it make me "shiver"? Hmmm. Well . . . it was a hit.
There's even a rumor going around that a critic from one of
the big-city papers was here last night and that he might
write about your play. He loved it.

DENNETT

That's not what I asked. I asked for *your* opinion.

ARIEL

What difference does *my* opinion make? *Yours* is the only
opinion that matters. You're the one who has to live with
himself.

> *Pause. Dennett takes Ariel's hand and leads her a few steps*
> *downstage.*

DENNETT

Aren't you going to congratulate me?

ARIEL (*Rather coldly*)

Congratulations.

DENNETT (*Indicating that they might go someplace*)

I meant with a kiss.

ARIEL

And what makes you think that that could possibly happen?

DENNETT

Because you're intensely beautiful to me. And because I'm not self-deluded enough simply to have *imagined* that there's an attraction between us.

> *Pause.*

ARIEL

Fair enough. I admit it.
> (*Deadpan*)

For weeks now I've been secretly pining to kiss your old man lips.

DENNETT (*As though ambushed*)

I may be a lot of things, but I'm hardly an old man.

ARIEL (*Almost compassionately*)

Hardly an old man?
> (*Pathetically*)

When's the last time you took a good look at yourself?
> (*Even more pathetically*)

Hunh . . .
> (*Sadly, with very pointed sarcasm*)

. . . Romeo?

> *Ariel exits. Miranda and Duncan go after her.*
> *Dennett touches his face. He turns to his Family.*

DENNETT (*Displaying the scepter*)

Look at this ridiculous thing.
> (*Chuckling derisively*)

I mean . . . awards!
> (*Chuckles derisively again*)

You all know my position on awards.

JESSICA (*Dispassionately, as if by rote*)

"It's hard to imagine a sight more pathetic than some talentless ninny clutching a figurine to his or her breast as if it *meant* something."

DENNETT

Exactly.
    (*Pause*)
Although . . . that being said . . .
    (*Sincerely, clutching the scepter to his breast*)
. . . this really is an amazingly beautiful scepter.

CLAIRE

Indeed, Your Majesty. 'Tis the comeliest scepter in all the realm.

DENNETT (*To Claire, philosophically*)

Well. Aren't I a bumpkin for being naïve enough to think that you might actually be happy for me!

GUY

I'm happy for you, Henry.

CLAIRE (*To Guy*)

No you're not! How can you possibly be happy for someone who's just held you up, in front of a sniggering audience, as an object of derision?

JESSICA

He probably didn't realize that that oafish, bombastic character was based on *him*.

GUY

I didn't think the character was oafish.

JESSICA

I guess people see what they want to see.

DENNETT (*To Jessica*)

Listen to you! You're assuming a direct correspondence between a real-life human being and a character in a work of fiction! That's a fallacy that only an ignoramus would embrace.

GUY

In fact, I thought I came off pretty good.

JESSICA

So I guess that would make me an ignoramus twice over, hunh?

DENNETT

What are you talking about?

> *Jessica takes Peter's hand and faces Dennett, her voice quivering.*

JESSICA

An interracial couple with an infant daughter? A black man who studies Sufi philosophy and just happens, occasionally, to cross-dress?

DENNETT

Darling, I'm sure your husband isn't the *only* student of Sufi philosophy on the *planet* who has a little . . . problem with cross-dressing.

JESSICA

His cross-dressing is not "a problem"!

PETER

It's not "a problem."

JESSICA

It has never *been* "a problem."

PETER

Never been "a problem."

JESSICA

Not until *now*. Now that the whole *world* knows about it. Thank you, Daddy. Thank you very, very much.

DENNETT

Look, if I choose to expose my life in a work of art, that's *my* business, not *yours*.

JESSICA

But you didn't expose *your* life. You exposed *our* lives. *Our* lives are not yours to *expose*.

CLAIRE

Absolutely! But then I expect that's been the plan from the start, hasn't it? To humiliate *everybody*!

CHEYENNE

Gran-pa! Gran-pa!

DENNETT

What's that she's got in her hands? I hope that's not what I think it is.

JESSICA

You gave it to her, Daddy.

> *Dennett snatches a sheaf of mangled pages out of Cheyenne's hands.*

DENNETT

Look at this! It's covered in crayon! She's torn it to pieces, for Christ's sake!

CLAIRE

Well, now you know what happens when you give a present like *that* to an eighteen-month-old child.

DENNETT

Most children would be thrilled to get a present like that!

CLAIRE

Most children would be thrilled to get a copy of your *play?*

DENNETT

That play is going to be her *legacy!* She's going to get to *know* me through that play . . . when I'm gone!

JESSICA (*Beyond despair*)

Daddy, why does it always have to be about getting to know *you?* Why have you never taken the trouble of getting to know *her?*

CLAIRE

Or Jessica!

JESSICA

Or Adam!

CLAIRE (*With finality*)

Or ME!
    (*Pause*)
Or anybody else . . . !

DENNETT

God, you're behaving like a bunch of lunatics!
    (*Looking overhead*)
Is there a full moon tonight, or something?

CLAIRE

You really are something, Henry! You can't even step outside yourself long enough to appreciate how *insulting* all of this is . . .

DENNETT

And none of you can step outside *yourselves* long enough to appreciate my play as a Work of Art rather than a personal attack on *you,* which is nothing but your own hysterical, narcissistic fantasy. Now if you'll excuse me . . .

> *Dennett begins to stride away . . .*

GUY (*Quietly*)
Henry. Wait.

> *Dennett keeps walking.*

> (*More forcefully*)
Henry! Wait!

> *Dennett keeps walking.*

> (*Shouting thunderously*)
WAIT, I SAID!

> *Dennett, stunned, stops and turns.*
> *Guy reaches into his pocket and pulls out a check.*

Aren't you interested in collecting your winnings?

> *Guy dangles the check in the air teasingly.*
> *Dennett considers for a moment. He then gathers himself and, warily, strides up to Guy.*
> *Pause.*
> *Dennett reaches for the check. Guy jerks the check away . . .*

Crap!

> *. . . and begins to walk in tight circles around Dennett, as though cornered.*

Remember what you said about *crap?* Crap required a level of competence that I could only aspire to. And I thought . . . okay. So this poor devil needs to knock me down a few pegs, right? Fine. My ego can handle it.

And why? Because writing, for me, has never been *about* being regarded as an "eminence in my field." It's an act of *love* . . . one that's propelled me up increasingly higher peaks, to heights I would never have dreamed myself capable of attaining. *Love,* Henry . . . not ego . . . is what has inspired me to strive towards as ideal of theatre that should be inclusive and life-affirming and democratic and all those other things you find so *dumb* and *disgusting.*

> (*Pause*)

So that to have to sit there tonight, knowing that the . . .

> (*In horrified awe*)

. . . masterpiece . . . before me was written by someone who doesn't even care, someone who *abominates* theatre, someone for whom it's all one big fat
joke . . .

> *Guy begins to shake and cry.*

Goddamn you! That's the play I've always wanted to write. You're the playwright I've spent my whole life trying to be.

> (*Pause*)

Maybe you're right. Maybe I *should* aspire to writing crap. Maybe crap is too good for me after all.

> *Guy faces Dennett directly.*

> (*Bitterly*)

Congratulations, Henry. You didn't just win. You *flattened* me.

> *Guy jams the check into the bowl of Dennett's scepter.*

> (*With revulsion*)

Here! Here's the *money!*

> (*Over his shoulder, exiting*)

I was going to give it to you anyway.

Guy exits. Silence.

CLAIRE (*Applauding*)
Well done, Henry.

Claire exits, going after Guy.

JESSICA (*Quietly, sadly*)
Congratulations, Daddy.

Jessica exits, with Peter and Cheyenne following.
Dennett turns to Adam, who, unmoving and unspeaking, has been a silent but powerful presence throughout this entire sequence.

DENNETT
Well, what are you looking at?

ADAM
Nothing.

DENNETT (*Indicating the others*)
What's the matter? Don't you want to join the ranks of the aggrieved, wailing jeremiads about how inexcusably I've mistreated you all?

No answer.

Don't tell me there's a member of my family who's managed to escape the evening feeling less than unalterably offended!

ADAM (*Quietly*)
I'm not offended.

DENNETT
What then?

ADAM

I was just thinking . . . how sobering it must have been to hear your work praised by a cretin like him.

DENNETT

O, he's not so bad.

ADAM

Not so bad? Since when? Since he lionized you for having written such an embarrassing piece of kitsch?

DENNETT

I don't think it's fair to call it "an embarrassing piece of kitsch."

ADAM

What would *you* call it, then?

DENNETT

Well, it's obviously no . . .
(*Imitating Guy*)
. . . "masterpiece" . . . if that's what you think I'm fooling myself to believe.
(*Very reasonably*)
But it's certainly no disgrace, either. I mean, at least you see the unmistakable hand of an artist at work.

No answer.

(*The truth suddenly sinking in, distastefully*)
O, you didn't think so.

ADAM

Uh-oh. Don't tell me *you're* feeling unalterably offended.

DENNETT

On the contrary. I applaud your courage. Speaking your mind to the old man. It makes me feel almost semi-unashamed of you for once!

284

ADAM

You can never have been as ashamed of me as I was of you tonight.

DENNETT

Are you sure?

ADAM

What surprises me is that you're not more ashamed of yourself.

DENNETT

Ashamed for what? Were you sitting in the same theatre with everyone else? Did you happen to notice how deeply moved the audience was? Were you present for the standing ovation?

ADAM

Boy, you've really scrambled up those well-worn stairs into the Fool's Tower, haven't you? You've really swallowed the corncob whole.

DENNETT

Why? Because I'm not the kind of knee-jerk snob who automatically assumes that if ordinary folks like something, it can't be any good?

ADAM

I never said that.

DENNETT

Christ! I'm sorry I invited you! You and the rest of the Art Police, for whom nothing can ever be worthy unless it's obscure! Maybe if you were capable of achieving a tiny bit of recognition yourself, you'd be less nervous about it.

ADAM

Are you not made even a tiny bit nervous at the idea of achieving recognition for being somebody you're not?

DENNETT

And who am I, exactly? In *your* opinion.

ADAM

Well, when I saw you up there on the stage tonight, clutching that scepter and sobbing as though you'd just won the Miss America Pageant, I guess I realized that you can't be the same person who's spent a lifetime denouncing the idiotic desire for middle-class success. Or *can* you be? Because if you are, you couldn't have chosen a more perverse means of finding satisfaction in life than writing poetry.

DENNETT

I didn't choose to write poetry.

ADAM

Sorry. Of course. Writing poetry chose you.

DENNETT

Yeah. In the same way that being a shit-heel tax attorney chose you.

ADAM

At least I'm not a slave to the values I purportedly despise.

DENNETT

Okay, fine. I get the picture. You thought my play was a piece of crap. So it's a piece of crap.

ADAM

I wish it *had* been crap! But it was even worse than that *woman's* play—*Minnie the Pinny* or whatever it was called. And that was written at about the level of an in-flight magazine.

DENNETT

Don't you remember what I set out to prove? That the more banal and meretricious the play, the more likely it is to succeed . . . ?

ADAM

But that's *not* what you proved! You proved how convincingly *you* were able to write a banal and meretricious play! *Too* convincingly, if you ask me. Mr. Broadway was right. It was the real thing . . . the sort of thing that could have been written by anybody . . . or nobody . . . yet in some eerie way was more distinctively your own than any poem you've ever written in your life . . . !

DENNETT (*Disgusted*)

O, for fuck's sake . . .

ADAM (*Hammering at Dennett*)

No, it *was!* I was bowled over at how skillfully you managed to refashion all those warmed over pieties into allegedly subversive declarations of principle, or how you "courageously" took stands on social and political issues that only a Nazi or a nutcase could possibly disagree with! Remember what you said? It's not crap when you use politics as just another form of titillation—it's *pornography!* It's like having a hand thrust down the seat of your pants!

DENNETT

Okay, then! *Fine!* Whatever makes you happy! I wrote a piece of *pornography,* all right?! *Happy?!* BIG . . . FUCKING . . . DEAL!

ADAM

Who in God's name have I been defending all these years?!

DENNETT

I don't know. Who?

Pause.

ADAM

You said that an artist's true voice emerges despite himself,
regardless of the form. Well . . . your true voice emerged,
all right. It just wasn't the voice of an artist.
  (*Calmly, matter-of-factly*)
It was the voice of a pornographer.
  (*With finality*)
And you either *are* that, or you're not.

  Dennett viciously slaps Adam across the face.

DENNETT (*Livid*)

Who are *you* to tell *me* what my "true" voice is? You're
nobody. You're just some shit-heel tax attorney who's never
done anything with his life! You've never succeeded at
anything. You've never gotten married, you've never had
kids. You've never brought me anything but embarrassment!
You're completely stunted! What makes you think I give a
shit about *your* opinion?!

ADAM (*Discovering the truth of these statements even as he
speaks them*)

Because my opinion *is* your opinion. When have
I ever been allowed an opinion of my own? There is
no me! I'm you! You might as well be staring into a
mirror . . .

  *Dennett wheels as if struck by a blow, shaking his head in
  disgust and sniggering bitterly.*
    *Avoiding eye contact with Adam, he storms explosively
  around the stage . . .*

DENNETT

Boy, o boy! You can't *stand* it, can you? You make a great
show of aesthetic indignation, but what *really* burns you up

is the acclaim! Right?! Because that's the one thing the Art Police will never forgive you for. The minute you get any kind of public acknowledgment from *actual people* you're immediately disqualified as an artist, because art can only be appreciated by the select few—which usually means eight or nine of your closest friends who are forced to *schlep* to some dilapidated warehouse and sit through an abomination that they then have to pretend was good! And it's only "good" so long as no one's ever heard of it, because the one thing the Art Police will never forgive you for is *success*! They can't *stand* it! Success is too vulgar! Success is in bad taste! Success is the ultimate betrayal!

> *Adam, in silent shock, slowly begins to exit.*
> *Dennett, tracking him aggressively, hectors him from behind.*

So what kind of *mea culpa* will satisfy the Holy See?! What sort of confession do you want to hear me make, high up there in your *own* little Fool's Tower—atop the Magnificent Cathedral of Art?! How about . . . how about . . . what Ovid said: "VIDEO MELIORA PROBOQUE; DETERIORA SEQUOR!": "I see and value the good; I follow the bad!" *HA!*

> *Adam exits.*
> *Dennett thunders after him:*

Is *that* what you want to hear me say?! Well if it's true of me, it's true of you, too!
> (*Swinging madly towards the audience . . .*)
Is there really one among you who can say any different? Hunh, you silly snobs?!
> (*. . . into the rafters, and beyond*)
Wipe the shock off your faces, you snobs—you *losers!* You can't *stand* it! You can't stand the fact that for once in my

goddamn life *I'm on top of the FUCKIN'*
WOORRRRRLLLLD!!

> *Dennett swoops the scepter into the water of the Lithia*
> *Fountain, filling its bowl to the brim. He hoists it in a toast.*

Here's to ME! Here's to the end of howling in the dark to a
world that's not listening! Here's to the end of the snubs and
the slights and of no one ever getting your name right!
Here's to *respect*! Here's to being *somebody* . . . somebody
who matters . . . and not just some *nobody*.
> (*Raising the scepter*)
Here's to SUCCESS!

> *He drinks, pivots, raises the scepter.*

SUCCESS!

> *He drinks, pivots, raises the scepter.*

SUCCESS!

> *He drinks, pivots, raises the scepter.*

SUCCESS!

> *He drinks, pivots, raises the scepter.*

SUCCESS!

> *He drinks, pivots, raises the scepter.*

SUCCESS!

> *Accompanied by the sound of a Roaring Mob that might greet*
> *a gladiator's victory in the Coliseum, Dennett, taking a final,*
> *mammoth swig of Lithia water, collapses in an intoxicated*
> *swoon.*
> *The sound of the Roaring Mob dissolves instantly into,*
> *and becomes indistinguishable from . . .*

THE HIMALAYAS*

. . . the deafening sound of harsh, buffeting winds, which combines with the image of blinding snow blown furiously across a whited-out terrain.

A man, lying on his back, gradually becomes discernible as the fierce, driving snow abates.

It is Dennett who, exhausted and panting, sits up, discovering himself at the apex of a majectic Himlalyan peak. Pure, golden light floods his figure as the snow abates further and the sky clears.

Like a colt being born onto shaky legs, Dennett struggles to his feet. A deep breath. He surveys the scene around him.

Dennett is on top of the world. From where he stands, the entire planet curves away below. Vast topographies are reduced to doll-size proportions.

As Dennett, with an air of mastery, continues to survey the spectacular scene, he is suddenly seized by a crippling abdominal spasm.

Audio: The sound of an earthquake.

Gripping his stomach, Dennett, with a howl that is identical to the one heard at the opening of the play, appears to lose his balance and plunges, in slow motion, from the lofty summit into a dark abyss.

---

*In New York, scene ix ("The Himalayas") was represented as follows: as Dennett raised his scepter in the toast to "Success," a cloth with a mountain painted on it was flown in from behind. The cloth proceeded to roll at its base, giving the impression of Dennett ascending. The dream became nightmare when, at mountain's peak, Dennett, taking a final swig of Lithia water, was struck by a spasm of abdominal pain. Howling, he appeared to plunge into a dark abyss as the mountain cloth rolled rapidly in reverse.

x
NIGHT*

The middle of the night. A full moon hangs like a bright coin overhead.

Dennett awakens—or seems to—in a bed whose sheets are stained with blood.

DENNETT (*Delirious, reacting to the blood soaked sheets*)
What, am I *menstruating* now . . .?

Scepter in hand and wrapped in a bloody sheet, Dennett staggers out of bed and across the stage. He is unaware at first, and then horrified to discover, that dragging behind him is a long, thick umbilicus-like object that is apparently dead or dying. Dennett's mouth twists open in a silent scream.

The lights fade.

xi
THE LITHIA FOUNTAIN

The following morning. Dawn.

Dennett is standing downstage, facing the audience. A suitcase is by his side. His expression is one of after-shock: intense, alert, somewhat frightened. He is clearly in distress.

Maurice enters, startling Dennett.

MAURICE (*Seeing the suitcase*)
Maestro! We're not losing you today, as well, are we?

---

*After several unsatisfactory attempts to represent the "Worm Evacuation" (as it came to be known) in the New York production, it was cut entirely. The play proceeded directly from scene ix ("The Himalayas") to scene xi ("The Lithia Fountain").

DENNETT (*Agitatedly preoccupied*)
I'm afraid I'm already overdue for my fall term classes,
Maurice.

MAURICE
O, what a shame! It's true, what Kiki used to say. You meet
these wonderful people . . . you begin to know them, to
care about them . . . you go through so much together,
laughing, crying, even having the occasional . . .
    (*Arching his eyebrows knowingly at Dennett*)
. . . *contretemps* . . . and then to have to part so abruptly! It's
cruel!

> *Dennett turns suddenly to Maurice, appealing to him
> urgently.*

DENNETT
Maurice! I need . . . !
    (*Pause*)
I need you to tell me the truth.

MAURICE
About what?

DENNETT (*Casting about, not even knowing where to begin*)
About . . . well . . .

MAURICE
I don't understand.

> *Dennett settles on what could be the first of a million
> questions.*

DENNETT
For one thing . . .
    (*Pause*)
You didn't *really* know Laurence Olivier, did you?

Maurice smiles slyly. From his pocket he unfolds a foxed scrap of paper that is threadbare from folding and unfolding.

MAURICE

Have I never shown you this?

Maurice hands the scrap of paper to Dennett.

Read it. Go on.

DENNETT

Dear Boy,

Hail and farewell! Your great good cheer
and high dedication over the past few months,
whether it was sweeping up backstage or
pressing costumes for the matinee, have made my
task that much easier. Permit me to say that I foresee,
for you, a grand future in the theatre.

Much love,

Laurence Olivier

(Stunned, moved)

My God. You really did know him.

MAURICE

Yes . . .

(Philosophically)

. . . if by "knowing" someone you mean . . . occasionally
combing out his wig.

DENNETT *(Appalled at himself, now prepared to hear ANYTHING)*

And?

MAURICE

O, he was a gorgeous person! He was a genius, very much
like you! In fact, he exuded the same kind of commanding
presence when he entered a room—an indescribable aura of
talent and *noblesse oblige* that you simply wanted to be close

to, to warm your hands by. Yet he made everyone feel important . . .
>	(*Indicating himself*)
. . . everyone, right down to the lowliest stagehand.
>	(*Indicating the letter*)
He actually thought that I'd amount to something.
>	(*Taking the letter back, with genial self-rebuke*)
Imagine how disappointed he'd be.

DENNETT

Disappointed? I should think he would have been very proud.

MAURICE

Henry, please. Look at my life! I mean, don't get me wrong. I've been extraordinarily lucky. This festival has proved an ideal place to raise a daughter, which, as any widower will tell you, is an issue of paramount importance, and I've managed to build a reasonably fulfilling career in a field that I believe in deeply. But look at my life!
>	(*With no regret; triumphantly, in a peculiar way*)
It didn't work out!

>	*Dennett tries to object, but Maurice insists.*

It *didn't*. And it doesn't bother me really! All I'm saying is that . . . you don't always end up becoming the person you thought you were going to be. Can't you understand that?

>	*Dennett turns away from Maurice, troubled.*

Now, then. Henry.
>	(*Gently*)
Tell *me* the truth. You didn't *really* know W. H. Auden, did you?

>	*Pause.*

DENNETT
I . . .

> (*A shamed, rather painful admission, to himself*)
. . . occasionally combed out his wig.

> *Maurice places his hand on Dennett's shoulder from behind.*

MAURICE (*Softly*)
Farewell, Alcibiades.

> "The eternal snows appear already past,
> And the first clouds and mountains seem the last:
> But those attained, we tremble to survey
> The growing labours of the lengthened way;
> The increasing prospect tires our wandering eyes,
> Hills peep o'er hills, and Alps on Alps arise!"

> *Maurice pats Dennett's shoulder and starts to exit, adding as he goes:*

Alfred Lord Tennyson.

DENNETT (*Reflexively, as if from a great distance*)
It's Alexander Pope, actually . . .

> *Maurice stops in his tracks and smacks his forehead. He turns and sighs.*

MAURICE
I told you.

> (*Striking an absurd Harlequin pose*)
I'm a complete buffoon.

> *Maurice lifts his hand in affectionate farewell to Dennett, and exits. Dennett stares after him for a moment, in wonder and bewilderment. The lights shift.*
> *Dennett touches his face. He turns to the Lithia Fountain and gazes into its water, observing his reflection.*

Dennett's face reflected in the Lithia water: it bobs and floats like a ghostly, foreign apparition, fractured now by ripples and then reconstituting itself, alternating between the familiar and the unrecognizable. It is Dennett's face, but it is also not Dennett's face.

Audio: The sound of a train.

FADE TO BLACK

A miniature passenger train goes rocketing across the stage from right to left.

Fade in inscription:

iii
Wrong Mountain

Fade to black

i
A BOOKSHOP*

Stepping to the rear of Libris Books, Dennett, a newspaper folded in his hand, approaches Anne. The smile vanishes from Anne's face as she turns to see him.

DENNETT
Anne?

Anne does not reply.

I'm Henry Dennett.

Anne does not reply.

You might remember me. We met a year ago.

Anne does not reply.

I fear that I may have been extremely rude to you at the time.

Anne does not reply.

Which I regret.

Anne does not reply.

(*Brandishing the newspaper*)
I just read that you were named this year's winner of the Yale Series of Younger Poets Competition. A prize for

---

*This is a restored scene that, after several unsatisfactory attempts to realize it, was cut in the New York production. Though it runs the risk, in the playing, of adding too much rhythm to the finale, it is, I believe, an important scene that offers three considerable advantages: it establishes, after his sojourn at the Shakespeare Festival, a kind of return-to-earth for Dennett; it creates, and then defies, expectations of a conventional "wisdom gained–redemption received" denouement; and it provides, when Dennett is recognized as a poet, an appealing irony in the context of his identity crisis.

which I myself was short-listed, incidentally, but did not win, back when W. H. Auden was the judge.

>   (*Pause*)

Wasn't it a quotation of Auden's that you mistakenly attributed to me?

ANNE (*Impassively*)

"Every man carries with him through life a mirror, as unique and impossible to get rid of as his shadow . . ."

DENNETT

Yes, well.

>   (*Drawing a breath*)

I suppose that what I wanted to say to you, by way of apology, is that I never really understood what those words meant until very recently.

>   Pause.
>
>   *In one smooth, relaxed motion, Anne leans forward and spits, hard, directly into Dennett's face. Dennett's jaw goes slack.*
>
>   *Anne walks away calmly. She turns to face Dennett, and says, almost as an afterthought, more with amazement than anger:*

ANNE

Who . . . do . . . you . . . think . . . you . . . are?

>   *Anne exits.*
>
>   *Dennett, stunned, mops his face with a handkerchief. A middle-aged woman approaches him. Dennett, in a fog, tries to push past her.*

MIDDLE-AGED WOMAN

Excuse me. Aren't you . . .

>   (*Clutching at Dennett's jacket*)

. . . I can't believe that I've forgotten your name . . . aren't you . . . the poet? Aren't you the wonderful poet who comes from around here? You *are*, aren't you?

Dennett turns to face her, still dazed.

MIDDLE-AGED WOMAN (*Breathlessly*)
Because . . . I'm sure you hear this all the time, but . . . . When my mother was dying, she kept a volume of your poems by her bed. "Roaming the Shallows," I think it was. And the lines about finding grace in

> "The cold rock seawall,
> Beaten dumb by the grey slap of neap-tide
> Into an obdurate reticence
> That makes eloquent
> All the love that life denies . . ."

Those lines meant so much to her! Their sense of faith. Their stoicism and longing . . .
(*Emphatically, emotionally*)
They really meant so *much* to her! I wrote a letter to tell you . . .
(*Suddenly remembering*)
Henry *Dennett*, right?! Isn't that who you are?! *Henry Dennett? The poet?*

The question hangs in the air. Dennett opens his mouth to speak, but says nothing.

ii
A DOCTOR'S OFFICE

Flicking a switch to backlight an X-ray of Dennett's abdominal cavity, Leibowitz examines the chart in disbelief, shaking his head.

LEIBOWITZ

It's incredible! It's truly uncanny! I've never heard of a case where the entire parasite simply vanished without a trace! And you're sure, aside from eating as little corn as possible, that you've made no other significant changes in your diet?

Dennett stares determinedly into the distance.

DENNETT (*Concentrating deeply*)

Have you ever heard of a naturally occurring compound called Lithia water?

LEIBOWITZ

Lithia water?

    (*Considers*)

No. I don't think so. Why?

DENNETT (*Waving it away, his mind racing ahead*)

Never mind.

    . . . but Leibowitz considers it further . . .

LEIBOWITZ

Lithia . . .

    (*Pause*)

Isn't "Lithia" the Goddess of Success in the mythology of Ancient Greece?

    Dennett is hardly listening. His mind is elsewhere.

Or is it Ancient Rome?

    (*Screwing up his face*)

Or is it Egypt?

    (*Pause; then, as if it's news:*)

Did you know that Napoleon called Egypt "the land of menstruating men"?

Dennett looks quizically at Leibowitz, then gradually drifts back to his own thoughts. Leibowitz continues.

Actually, spontaneous cures were viewed by the ancient Greeks as the physical manifestation of Delphic good fortune.

Leibowitz snaps off the X-ray and turns to Dennett.

I understand that you've recently had quite a healthy dose of good fortune yourself! I mean, speaking of the Goddess of Success . . .

DENNETT (*Deflecting the remark, his attention focused elsewhere*)
O, yes. That.

LEIBOWITZ (*Incredulous*)
"O, yes. That"? Come on! If I were in your shoes I'd be on top of the world! It must be exhilarating to be getting so much attention all of a sudden. So much . . . recognition! Especially—if you don't mind my saying so—after a lifetime of . . . relative . . .
        (*A clumsy attempt at treading gingerly*)
. . . obscurity?

DENNETT
Yes. It's a peculiar fate.

LEIBOWITZ
Fate? You're too modest. I believe that the defining events of our lives are a product of character, not fate.

DENNETT (*Weighing the words solemnly*)
A man's character is his fate.

LEIBOWITZ
Oooooo. Great line.

DENNETT (*Reflexively, as though from a great distance*)
It's Heraclitus . . .

LEIBOWITZ (*Not even paying attention*)
Well . . . I certainly wouldn't have the character to be so blasé about having written a play that's about to be produced on Broadway! On Broadway, for God's sake! And not just some piece of junk, I gather, but the rare drama that's courageous enough to examine who we are as a nation, and where we're destined to go. Christ, if I'd written something like that I'd be the biggest bore in the world. Every patient who came into this office would be forced to sit in that chair and listen to me sing "I'm a Broadway Baby . . .

> *Dennett, his mind urgently focused elsewhere, begins to launch sporadic objections over the nauseating vaudeville of Leibowitz's singing.*

DENNETT (*Firmly*)
Stop it.

LEIBOWITZ
". . . Walkin' off my tired feet . . .

DENNETT (*More firmly*)
Stop it. Seriously.

LEIBOWITZ
". . . Poundin' Forty-second Street . . .

DENNETT (*Even more firmly*)
Seriously! Stop it!

LEIBOWITZ
". . . To be in a show!

DENNETT (*Glaring at Leibowitz*)
Would you stop it, please?

LEIBOWITZ (*Crowing*)
". . . OOOOOOOOOOOOO . . .

DENNETT (*Pounding his fist on the examination table*)
Christ!

LEIBOWITZ
". . . Someday, maybe . . .

DENNETT (*Frantically*)
Are you a *real* doctor?

LEIBOWITZ
". . . If I stick it long enough . . .

> *Dennett slides off the examination table.*

DENNETT (*Panic*)
I don't know who the hell anybody is anymore!

LEIBOWITZ
". . . I may get to strut my stuff . . .

DENNETT (*Beseechingly*)
Would you stop it, please?

LEIBOWITZ (*Big finish*)
". . . In a GREAT . . .

DENNETT
Christ!

LEIBOWITZ
". . . BIG . . .

DENNETT
Please!

LEIBOWITZ
". . . BROAD . . .

DENNETT
Stop!

LEIBOWITZ
". . . WAY . . .

DENNETT
Help!

LEIBOWITZ
". . . SHOW-OW-OW!"

Dennett begins to stride offstage. Leibowitz wheels.

LEIBOWITZ
Where are you going? Don't you want to know the results of the dermatological test?

Dennett turns, touches his face.

DENNETT
I thought you said that I had nothing to worry about.

LEIBOWITZ
It's more of a good news/ bad news situation, I'm afraid.

DENNETT (*Nervously*)
What's the bad news?

LEIBOWITZ
The bad news is that it's not, as I originally thought, a simple mutation of psoriasis, but a far more esoteric skin disorder whose symptoms might be described at their most extreme as . . . uh . . . biblically severe.

DENNETT (*Alarmed*)
What are you telling me? That I have leprosy?

LEIBOWITZ
We don't like to use the word "leprosy" because it frightens people.

Dennett claps his hands to his face.

(*Waving it away*)
And, anyway, it's not leprosy.
(*Drawing a breath . . .*)
It's . . .

Leibowitz fishes for the mot juste. Dennett cuts in . . .

DENNETT
Worse? Worse than leprosy?

Leibowitz holds up his hand to calm Dennett.

LEIBOWITZ
It's called Lunafibramitosis. "Luna" because in its advanced stages it's been known to cause the extremities to atrophy— the nose, the ears, et cetera—so that certain patients have come to resemble a sort of . . . featureless moonscape.

DENNETT (*In shock*)
What's the good news?

LEIBOWITZ
The good news is . . . it only affects the face.

Leibowitz bursts out laughing.

And, cards on the table, were you really so much to look at to begin with?

Leibowitz laughs some more; regains himself.

Sorry. Lousy joke. I do that.

DENNETT (*In shock*)
How did I get it?

LEIBOWITZ

I don't know. Maybe you've been drinking too much of that . . . what's it called? . . . Lithia water?

Leibowitz arches his eyebrows enigmatically.

Hey, come on! Cheer up! It won't kill you, you know.
(*Pause*)
You'll still be the same person.

DENNETT (*In shock*)
What if a man achieved the greatest triumph of his life for something that he viewed with absolute contempt?

LEIBOWITZ

Hunh?

DENNETT

Could he still be the same person?

LEIBOWITZ

Could *who* still be the same person?

DENNETT (*As though piecing something together*)
I knew a man once . . .
(*Slowly*)
He was a poet. But he became a pornographer.
(*With a grim, existential nod*)
He became . . . nobody.
(*To Leibowitz*)
He became who he truly was.

LEIBOWITZ

Well, that would depend, wouldn't it?

Dennett looks at Leibowitz intently.

On whether you ever really knew who he was to begin with.
(*Pause*)
I mean, forgive the cliché, but you know the saying: "One
man's pornography . . . is another man's . . .

Leibowitz startles Dennett by bursting into song again—
ghoulishly, brassily.

. . . GREAT . . . BIG . . . BROAD . . . WAY . . . SHOW-
OW-OW!"

Dennett buries his face in his hands.
Leibowitz assumes the exaggerated professional sincerity of
a TV doctor.

Sorry.

Leibowitz bows with a flourish of theatrical penitence, like the
King of Siam.

A thousand pardons.

Audio: The sound of the wind, in whispering gusts.

So . . . good luck with your play! What's it called again?

DENNETT
It's called *Wrong Mountain.*

LEIBOWITZ
What does that mean, Wrong Mountain?

DENNETT
I suppose it means that we never know, any of us, whether
or not we've spent our entire lives climbing the wrong
mountain.

Leibowitz considers. Then:

LEIBOWITZ

Maybe there's no such thing as a wrong mountain.
(*Pause*)
Then again, maybe they're all the wrong mountain.

> *Dennett looks at Leibowitz intently.*
> *Audio: The sound of the wind, gusting more forcefully.*

Which way are you headed?

DENNETT

I'm not sure.

LEIBOWITZ

Well . . . that's a start.

> *Leibowitz smiles enigmatically. Dennett nods slowly in return.*
> *Dennett begins to walk away. After a few paces he stops, turning to the audience as if he were catching his "reflection" in a mirror.*
> *Darkness falls around him, leaving him alone in a pool of light.*
> *Dennett brings his hands to his face and says, very softly, almost inaudibly:*

DENNETT

"Betwixt the stirrup and the ground
Mercy I asked . . ."

> *In the darkness behind him, the Voice of Leibowitz interrupts . . .*

LEIBOWITZ

. . . and are you experiencing any discomfort right now?

> *The light narrows on Dennett's face. He does not respond.*
> *The light continues to narrow until, as Dennett continues to stare at his "reflection," his face gradually dissolves into . . .*

iii
A VAST, STARLIT PLAIN

. . . the face of the moon. It hangs like a giant, unblinking eye . . .
. . . between the stark silhouettes of two distant mountains. Audio: The sound of a fierce, howling wind.
Across the face of the moon, wisps of clouds are blown like cannon smoke.

*Upon this image—the moon, the mountains, the starlit plain—are now superimposed the following words:**

As though awakened
In a teeming vault
Of legendless
And unfamiliar stars,
The words that faintly shone
Like avatars
Of secret gods
You labored to exalt

In patterns of
Reconstellated light
Emerge at last
Like questions left unasked:
Each one a face

---

*In the New York production, Dennett recited the poem ("searchingly, as if for the first time" according to revised stage directions). The play ended as he spoke his name: Henry Dennett.

When the house lights came up, the text of the poem was legible on a painted cloth that appeared in lieu of a final curtain, to be read by members of the audience as they filtered out of the theatre.

The moment is restored here as it was conceived in the original manuscript.

Hung luminously masked
Between two distant
Mountains in the night.

—HENRY DENNETT

*As the clouds continue to blow past the moon and the
mountains, and the wind continues to howl . . .*

Slowly,

THE CURTAIN FALLS